1966

THE STUDENT TEACHING PROCESS
IN ELEMENTARY SCHOOLS

MERRILL'S
INTERNATIONAL EDUCATION SERIES

Under the Editorship of

KIMBALL WILES

Dean of the College of Education

University of Florida

THE STUDENT TEACHING PROCESS

IN ELEMENTARY SCHOOLS

Pose Lamb
Purdue University

Charles E. Merrill Books, Inc., Columbus, Ohio

PREFACE

Faculties of many teacher education institutions are currently examining and re-examining the professional laboratory experiences of their students, with emphasis upon the most important of these—student teaching. Changes in facilities for student teaching and in plans for supervision of student teaching are taking place at a very rapid rate. For example, institution *A*, a teacher's college with university aspirations, is now placing student teachers in public schools. There are simply too many student teachers to place in the campus laboratory school. In institution *B*, a medium-sized liberal arts college with a rapidly growing enrollment in teacher education, the trend is toward supervision by carefully selected graduate students; senior staff members are seldom involved in supervision. In institution *C*, a large state university located in a relatively small town, student teachers are now being placed in large metropolitan centers throughout the state. Supervision is the assigned task of the personnel resident in the center, and there is, at best, only minimal coordination with programs on the main campus.

Too often, significant changes such as those just described are made with inadequate concern for their implications. The press of large numbers of students, the "population explosion" which has resulted in severe teacher shortages in some communities, and overburdened teacher education faculties at colleges and universities have been paramount in causing changes in student teaching facilities and patterns of supervision. Important as these concerns are, they are *not* proper responses to the following significant questions: What kinds of laboratory experiences contribute to superior teaching? What types of cooperating teacher–student teacher–college supervisor relationships are most desirable? How important is the level of supervision from the college or university?

Although major portions of this book are directed to the student who has not had a student teaching experience, portions of each chapter are designed to help student teachers on the job. Consideration is also given to the roles of the college supervisor and the cooperating teacher, for these professionals perform vital functions in the student teaching process, and each participant in the process will benefit from increased understanding of the role and functions of the other.

The suggestions at the conclusion of each chapter are included to help generate discussions and exchanges of ideas about student teaching and to help the student teacher grow toward effective membership in his chosen profession. It is not intended that these be considered the only logical questions, report topics, or activities that could arise in connection with the text. Other material in each chapter will, it is hoped, raise questions for discussion in classes, seminars, and meetings relating to student teaching.

Student teaching provides one of the most significant experiences encountered by a student preparing to teach. The quality of the experiences he has and the level of guidance and help he receives will do much to influence the kind of teacher he will become. This book maintains that this important task, or process, involves at least three major participants and that each of these must perform his task honestly, sincerely, and with a high level of competence if we are to prepare the kinds of teachers our elementary schools need so desperately. It is hoped that this text will aid and enhance the work of these three major participants in the student teaching process—the student teacher, the college supervisor, and the cooperating teacher.

Bibliographies at the conclusion of each chapter are of value primarily to the student teacher. The works included in the following list are of special interest to the college supervisor and the cooperating teacher and may be used to supplement the various chapter references.

Cottrell, Donald P. (ed.). *Teacher Education for a Free People.* Oneonta, New York: The American Association of Colleges of Teacher Education, 1956.

Edwards, Helen E. *Building Good Relationships, a Major Role of the College Supervisor.* Iowa Falls, Iowa: The Association for Student Teaching, 1961.

Sarason, Seymour B. Davidson, Kenneth S. and Black, Burton. *The Preparation of Teachers.* New York: John Wiley and Sons, Inc., 1962.

Smith, Elmer R. (ed.). *Teacher Education, A Reappraisal.* New York: Harper & Row, Publishers, 1962.

Pose Lamb
Purdue University

TABLE OF CONTENTS

THE STUDENT TEACHING PROCESS
IN ELEMENTARY SCHOOLS

1

Process and Participants

In an era when most aspects of the education of a prospective elementary teacher are under constant scrutiny, if not attack, student teaching, although variously regarded as a "capstone" and a "millstone," is nevertheless held to be an essential part of this education. James Bryant Conant, a critic of what he calls the professional education establishment, advocates fewer methods courses and fewer professors of methods courses; but he notes "Interestingly enough, amid all the conflict over teacher education, I have found only two points on which all are agreed: first, before being entrusted with complete control of a public school classroom, a teacher should have had opportunities under close guidance and supervision actually to teach—whether such opportunities are labeled 'practice teaching,' 'student teaching,' 'apprenticeship,' 'internship,' or something else; and second the ultimate question the state should ask is 'can this person teach adequately?' "[1] Conant makes several rather specific recommenda-

---

[1] James B. Conant, *The Education of American Teachers* (New York: McGraw-Hill Book Co., Inc., 1963), p. 59.

1

tions about student teaching, including suggestions about the length
of time devoted to it. This will be referred to later. My purpose here
is to underscore the central position of this part of the preparation of
an elementary teacher and to do this through the words of one of
education's friendly critics.

As Stratemeyer and Lindsey have written,

> Future generations of America's children will be guided in their
> school experiences by college students currently preparing to teach.
> The quality of the educational opportunity available to these children
> will depend to a large degree upon the kind of teachers our colleges
> prepare now. While many factors contribute to the development of
> skillful and artistic teachers, few are more important than the first-
> hand contacts with children and youth in school and community situ-
> ations which are provided by teacher education programs.[2]

It hardly needs to be suggested that student teaching is among the
most important of these "firsthand contacts."

Definition of Terms

Student teaching may be defined as a period of guided or supervised teaching during which the college student takes increasing
responsibility for a given group of learners over a period of several
weeks.[3] Even though the central purpose of student teaching is the
increased professional competence of the student teacher, the experience can and should result in the professional growth of each of
the major participants in the student teaching process, as they are
identified in Figure 1.

This diagram represents the student teaching experience; and its
three interrelated parts represent the three persons most intimately
concerned with this professional venture, since their roles are basi-
cally interrelated.

---

[2] Florence B. Stratemeyer and Margaret Lindsey, *Working with Student
Teachers* (New York: Bureau of Publications, Teachers College, Columbia University, 1958), p. v.

[3] This is the definition accepted by the Association for Student Teaching,
Cedar Falls, Iowa.

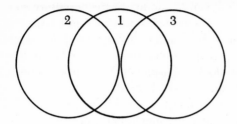

1. The Student Teacher
2. The Cooperating Teacher
3. The University Supervisor

FIGURE 1

The Student Teacher

A college or university student assigned to observe, participate, and teach in a cooperating classroom is called a student teacher. The emphasis in this book is on the role of the student teacher in the elementary school, usually the kindergarten through the sixth grade. Two concepts of this role are brought sharply into focus by Haines. She writes:

> If student teaching is viewed as an apprenticeship, for example, the emphasis is apt to be placed upon encouraging the student to imitate the master teacher and to become competent in the established routing and ways of functioning found to be effective by the teacher.
>
> In contrast, if student teaching is viewed as an internship in teacher education, stress will be placed upon creative application of fundamental principles, abstraction of sound generalizations from immediate involvements, and continual explorations of varied possibilities for implementation.[4]

It is the concept of the student teacher as an *active, purposeful* and *creative* intern—not as a flattering imitator—which I seek to further.

Cases

Ann, an example of the kind of student teacher we're discussing, is in the second semester of her senior year at State University. Be-

---

[4] Aleyne C. Haines, *Guiding the Student Teaching Process* (Chicago: Rand McNally & Co., 1960), pp. 13–14.

cause the university is located in a large metropolitan area, Ann can do student teaching locally and continue to live at the dormitory and retain some campus contacts.[5] About three-fifths of Ann's program has consisted of general education including history, English, chemistry, and a modern foreign language; Ann's doubts now relate to her teaching competence—"How do I teach phonics? I've had 'modern math'—will they like that in this school? How do you start a social studies unit—or do they teach geography and history separately?" She wishes her professors had given her much more specific and detailed information about planning, about disciplinary approaches; yet she knows more than she thinks she does. Her grades have been good and she has been carefully screened on the basis of her speech, vision, hearing, and general physical and emotional health. Ann's personality is warm, outgoing, and friendly; people instinctively like her. She has filled many leadership roles, both in high school and at the university. She has taught Sunday school, supervised arts and crafts at a summer day camp, and held Saturday-morning swimming classes at the "Y." Although there are no teachers in Ann's immediate family, she can recall no other vocational objective. Ann has always asked questions, even when this was not the most tactful thing to do; she will not be the "flattering imitator" type of student teacher. She has been placed, fortunately, with a teacher who won't feel threatened by Ann's questions and who welcomes the fresh viewpoint and new ideas a competent student teacher brings with her. The student teaching supervisor knows Ann's tendency to be outspoken and Mrs. Brown's ability to handle this beginner's enthusiasm and concern. There will be frequent visits to the classroom, several group and individual conferences, meetings of all the student teachers and all the cooperating teachers—the lines of communication are open and the

---

[5] This is a point of some controversy; many authorities feel that full-time, off-campus student teaching forces a clean break, a clearly marked transition from student to teacher. They also feel there is value in living in the community where the pupils live and being accepted as an adult in that community. After observing a number of student teachers under both types of programs, however, I tend to favor an easier, smoother transition. There is some question concerning how many new experiences one ought to expect the student teacher to adjust to, and there is even more question regarding the amount of identification with and involvement in the life of a community which can occur during the few weeks of student teaching, particularly when the student teacher is confined to a furnished room or shares a furnished apartment with other student teachers from his campus.

three principals in our cast of characters will see that they remain open, that this student teaching situation becomes an internship in the truest sense.

Not all student teachers are Anns, and few student teaching situations contain the ingredients for excellence described above. Another student teacher, Susan, is married, and her husband is also in school. There is a baby on the way, but Susan must complete her academic work and teacher certification program so she can teach in the fall while her husband pursues his degree. She would rather stay at home, be with her husband, and take care of her baby. Her parents both teach, and Susan was never encouraged to plan for anything but teaching. Outlook: not very bright—for Susan, her family, or the professionals who will work with her in student teaching. Bill, also a student teacher, is a shy, retiring, thoughtful young man who has never been at ease with groups of people. Although various instructors have expressed doubts about his ability and his eventual happiness in the profession, the consensus has been, "Give him a chance— maybe we're wrong." Bill is attracted to teaching apparently because so many people have questioned his vocational goals that he's determined to succeed, just to "show them." Outlook: doubtful.

Susan may well try the flattering-imitator approach, and a cooperating teacher who is less than alert may well be trapped into requiring little or nothing of Susan. Thus Susan may, with help, cheat herself out of one of the most valuable experiences in her professional preparation. Bill's instructors may have done him a disservice rather than a favor by letting him get as far as he has. A student who discovers early (or who is *helped* to discover) that teaching is *not* for him should consider himself lucky. Both Susan and Bill will require a great deal of skillful guidance. Their college supervisors and cooperating teachers will have to devote a great deal of time and energy to helping these prospective teachers.

Most students will expect a great deal from the student teaching experience. Some expectations are quite specific and are limited to the few weeks of student teaching, as the following comments—condensed from papers written by student teachers—show.

1. I expect and hope to be able to relate theories to practice. I hope to be able to apply what we have learned in class and to discover its effectiveness and mine.

2. I expect to learn more about the role of the teacher in her relationships with others—students, parents, the principal, other teachers, etc.
3. I hope to discover how to conduct a classroom in which the children have self-discipline and there is a happy medium somewhere between chaos and a rigid, strict discipline.
4. I want to see how well I can "get through" to the children.
5. I expect to learn how to manage the classroom.
6. I expect to learn to plan, direct, and evaluate learning.
7. I hope that I can learn to be sensitive to the children's needs and feelings.
8. I expect to become familiar with school policies.
9. I expect to learn how to create an environment for learning.
10. I expect to learn from my critic teacher, other teachers, and the children
    —To strive toward security as the teacher of a group of children.
    —To become familiar with and use a variety of materials.

Some students, however, look beyond student teaching and relate this series of experiences to those they will encounter as fully qualified professionals. The expectations of one such student are these.

I expect from student teaching:

1. To increase my appreciation for other people.
2. To become even more aware of other people's feelings, thoughts, and opinions and to appreciate them simply because they are other people's.
3. To become even more aware of individual differences in people.
4. To increase my ability to interpret and perceive situations with tact and good judgment.
5. To become more confident in classroom management techniques.
6. To appreciate and enjoy children.
7. To become a bigger and better person from the experience.
8. To become even more aware of the role conflicts a teacher must deal with in our society and try to cope with these conflicts.
9. To become more objective in my thoughts and actions.

10. To gain an even deeper appreciation for our democratic way to life.
11. To learn just as much as the children and more.
12. To work hard and enjoy it.
13. To pass through the metamorphic stage of a student to an adult and teacher, ready to assume greater responsibilities.

Each student teacher approaches this new situation with some doubts; each brings to student teaching a different set of qualifications, strengths, and competencies. It is the task of the cooperating teacher and the university supervisor to build upon these strengths and to help the prospective teacher make a successful venture of student teaching.

The Cooperating Teacher

A cooperating-school faculty member in whose classroom one does his student teaching is called a cooperating teacher. Other terms used to refer to this person are *supervising teacher* and, less frequently, *critic teacher*. Stratemeyer and Lindsey write:

> Cooperating teachers hold a significant and enviable position among teacher educators. Studies of beginning teachers, follow up studies of graduates from teacher educational programs, and students' evaluation of their college preparation, reveal that student teaching and other kinds of laboratory experiences have a profound influence in determining the kind of teacher a student becomes. Tomorrow's teachers will tend to teach by principles they observe and use during their student teaching; they will tend to behave in ways they see their advisers and teachers behaving today; they will tend to operate on the values and to hold the attitudes they perceive as they observe, participate and take responsibility in classrooms as student teachers today. So, in a very real sense, a cooperating teacher holds more of the future of the world in his hand than any single classroom teacher holds, for each day he works with college students he is making a vital contribution to their future teaching, which will in turn greatly influence the lives of hundreds of children and youth.[6]

---

[6] Stratemeyer and Lindsey, op. cit., p. 4.

Conant recommends that school systems designate as cooperating teachers:

. . . only those persons in whose competence as teacher, leaders, and evaluators administrative and supervisory personnel have complete confidence. To implement this recommendation, it would be necessary for the school board to formalize its relation with the institutions that send student teachers into its school. If no contract now exists, one should be prepared and signed.

More important, the school board should adopt a policy that would show recognition of the continuing value of its responsibility. The board should direct the superintendent to have his principals see that the best teachers become cooperating teachers. The board should also require the superintendent to report from time to time on the way arrangements for practice teaching are functioning.[7]

These authorities only note what anyone seriously involved in teacher education knows: that a high-quality, effective student teaching situation depends in large measure on a high-quality, effective cooperating teacher. Who are those who fill this important position? If we think first in terms of requirements—job specifications, if you will—Conant is not much help; in fact, his requirements are so general they seem to describe no real individual. Master's degrees are becoming increasingly common. In a few states (Indiana is one), almost every teacher graduated in 1964 must, within five years of receiving his provisional certificate, complete work on a master's degree. Advanced certification is withheld until the degree is earned. Thus, it doesn't seem unreasonable to expect that every cooperating teacher will have completed work beyond the bachelor's degree; and most, it is hoped, will possess the master's degree. One should *quickly* add that there are, undoubtedly, highly competent cooperating teachers who do not possess even the bachelor's degree. Nor is the possession of a master's degree a guarantee of success as a cooperating teacher. A cooperating teacher who holds a master's degree may not be particularly effective. For example, her behavior may be characterized by constant interference with the student teachers' work and by frequent interruptions while the student is teaching. She may never permit the student teachers to use their best judgment or to make important decisions. Nonetheless, a master's degree or its equiv-

---

[7] Conant, op. cit., p. 63.

alent would seem a minimal standard to set for one bearing so much responsibility. Unfortunately, too few graduate programs are designed specifically for the preparation of supervisory personnel, including cooperating teachers. It would be desirable if, in the master's program, some work might be directed toward better preparation for the guidance of student teachers. For the most part, only in the larger institutions and in those with highly developed departments of education are courses or workshops of this nature offered regularly and successfully.

Various other kinds of help are often made available to cooperating teachers, however. Handbooks are often distributed, detailing the procedures to be followed (How much time should John spend observing? What kinds of records should I keep? Who assigns the final grade?). One large university gives each cooperating teacher a copy of a well known book about student teaching. Many institutions invite the cooperating teacher to campus for meetings, seminars, and so on. At such meetings the common goal is learning to work with the student teacher more effectively. College supervisor and cooperating teacher alike profit from a mutual sharing of ideas and concerns. Working effectively with student teachers is not necessarily a natural outgrowth of excellent classroom teaching. Most persons concerned with the laboratory phase of teacher education profit from specific help in this area; and, increasingly, colleges and universities are providing this help.

Three qualifications for cooperating teachers have been suggested thus far. Excellent classroom teaching is a basic requirement; successful graduate work is increasingly accepted as a criterion; and courses or workshops dealing with the supervision of student teachers are more and more common. There are personal characteristics which are even more significant, however. The cooperating teacher must be a person who is personally and professionally secure enough to handle questions without considering them to be attacks. He must be willing to let the student teacher *try*, to let the student teacher be more than an imitator and work with the children in his own unique way. Of course the cooperating teacher will provide guidance, direction, encouragement and support; however, it has been my experience that too many cooperating teachers interfere too soon, say too much, and offer advice which isn't requested. Admittedly, it is unpleasant to see a class out of control, a favorite topic of instruction handled ineptly

and amateurishly; but the mature and secure cooperating teacher will
let the beginner make mistakes, because he knows the resilience of
children and is aware that most mistakes can be corrected and that
permanent damage is unlikely. In fact, the cooperating teacher must,
on occasion, put his role as teacher educator first and his role as classroom teacher second.

Who selects the cooperating teacher? Who decides that a given
teacher does or doesn't possess the teaching ability, the intellectual
competence, and the maturity of personality to work successfully with
neophyte teachers? One hopes this will be a joint effort, involving
both public school personnel and college or university representatives; but it is somewhat naive to expect that the prospective cooperating teacher will be visited by someone from the teacher education
institution and that there will be a careful matching of personalities
to ensure a successful student teaching experience. In the first place,
it should be recognized that there are too many student teachers, in
most situations, to make this method practical. Can a coordinator or
director of student teaching take enough time to make the necessary
inspections? How long can he visit each teacher—can the desirable
matching of personalities really take place after one brief visit and a
hurried conference with the principal? If the public school administrator operates with a list of criteria for cooperating teachers which
approximates that used by the college or university, and if the lines
of communication between the college and the school system operate
as they should, such inspections are less important, and the decisions
connected with placing student teachers can be made efficiently and
with no more mistakes than occur when the more time-consuming
method is used. This is not to say that the teacher education institution should abdicate its role or deny its responsibility of maintaining
acceptable standards for student teacher placements; it is simply to
state realistically what must happen in these times of heavy enrollments and overworked college faculties. The lines of communication
must operate effectively, and both parties must be speaking the same
language when desirable situations are discussed. This is far more
important than the hallowed and time-honored preliminary visit to
see if Miss Y is "good enough to have one of our student teachers."
A report by L. O. Andrews, of The Ohio State University, underscores
the problem of selecting effective cooperating teachers. He notes that
very few colleges or universities have enough good schools and com-

munity agencies nearby to provide laboratories for comprehensive, well planned student teaching programs. Andrews points to the dilemma faced by one director of student teaching who must use every certified teacher within a 120-mile radius of the campus in order to secure placement for 600 student teachers.[8] In this situation, obviously, selectivity is impossible.

Isn't the situation, then, to move out into the state? This seems especially logical, in view of the increasing number of programs requiring full-time student teaching. Any director of student teaching will tell you that moving out into the state immediately involves one in a competitive placement struggle with other teacher education institutions. Some, and not a few, school administrators have been forced to limit the number of student teachers accepted by their school systems and have requested that cooperating teachers accept not two or three but only one student teacher a year. It seems clear that although we have recognized the vital role played by the cooperating teacher, we are reaching the point where it is difficult if not impossible to choose the type of person we would like to fill this important position.

The cooperating teacher has a difficult and challenging role. He is under scrutiny by the student teacher and the college supervisor. He is envied by his "less fortunate" colleagues because of the "free time" he has now. Besides attending committee meetings, faculty meetings, and parent conferences, he must find time for planning with the student teacher and for evaluation conferences with the college supervisor. The cooperating teacher's dilemma is illustrated by the following incident: It's Friday afternoon, and Mrs. Jones, cooperating teacher, would like to leave school before five o'clock, for the first time this week. As the last child leaves, the student teacher, Susan Smith, asks sweetly, "I wonder if we could talk about my social studies unit—I'd like to start making definite plans this weekend." So, thoughts of the hairdresser, of marketing before the supermarket is crowded, or of having the car serviced are all put aside; and Mrs. Jones replies in her best professional manner, "Of course—let's have a cup of coffee and we'll see what needs to be done."

On the credit side, most student teachers are sincerely grateful for

---

[8] L. O. Andrews, "State and Federal Aid for Student Teaching—Now?" *Journal of Teacher Education*, V (June, 1964), pp. 165–75.

the help and guidance of the cooperating teacher. Many, many teachers would name their cooperating teachers first on the list of those who have contributed most to their professional preparation. The fact that colleges and universities still try to be selective about student teaching placement is a sincere tribute to the significant role these people play in teacher education.

Usually cooperating teachers receive for their efforts something more than the gratitude of their student teachers. The results of a survey conducted by the American Association of School Administrators indicate that only 7 per cent of the systems involved in the study offer no remuneration at all to the cooperating teacher. In the great majority of school systems surveyed, cooperating teachers are offered money ($50 to $60 for a semester's or quarter's work with a student teacher seems typical) or tuition-free courses at the cooperating college or university. A few school systems receive money from the teacher education institution involved in the student teaching process but do not directly reimburse the cooperating teacher. Whatever the monetary compensation, direct or indirect, for the great majority of cooperating teachers the real reward consists of watching a student teacher grow, progress, and mature and of the gratitude shown to the cooperating teacher by the student teacher, the teacher education institution, and teachers in the school system who are cognizant of the contribution made by an effective, dedicated cooperating teacher.[9]

One cooperating teacher expresses in the following way her attitude toward working with a student teacher:

> The first time I was asked to be a cooperating teacher, I felt extremely apprehensive. Was I too set in my ways to allow the student teacher to experiment with new methods and new approaches? Would I be able to take a back seat and release the children to an inexperienced teacher without interrupting? Might I feel pangs of jealousy when the children turned to the student teacher for help or showed confidence in her guidance? Would I have a tendency to "mother" the student teacher? These and other doubts flashed through my mind; however, I believed it my professional responsibility to accept the

---

[9] *Cooperation in Student Teaching* (Educational Research Service Circular, No. 4 [Washington, D.C.: American Association of School Administrators, National Education Association, 1964]), pp. 5–6.

challenge, and in so doing I have been richly rewarded. In fact, the very doubts I had at first were reversed into the reasons I enjoy working with student teachers.

When I am asked to work with a student teacher, I no longer hesitate. No longer do I believe it to be my professional responsibility, but rather I believe that I am making an important contribution to my profession. We supervising teachers are holding in the palms of our hands the experiences which will have a profound influence in determining the kind of teacher the student will become. I know how the diamond cutter must feel when he takes a rough stone and under his skillful hands sees the stone turn into a glittering gem. Yes, and sometimes just as the diamond cutter may miscalculate and may see the stone fall into many pieces, we supervising teachers may miscalculate. Unlike the diamond cutter, however, we may pick up the pieces, put them back into shape, evaluate our miscalculations, and correct them. In so doing we may add to the profession a young teacher who as a result of our patience, understanding, and guidance will in turn greatly influence the lives of hundreds of children. This is our reward!

To the reader it may appear that there are no problems involved, that all student teachers are ready to teach. This would be a false assumption. Just as all children are unique persons with individual problems, so are all student teachers. It must be acknowledged that there are certain personal characteristics which are pertinent if the student is to become an effective teacher. Most college students in teacher education are receiving excellent training, but there are many who possess what might be called the undefinable "it" or the "feel" for teaching. Many students exhibit personal qualities which will be immediately recognized as characteristic of excellent teachers. There are four which seem to be imperative.

1. A genuine love for children and a natural instinct for guiding their development
2. A sense of humor
3. The ability to teach creatively
4. Initiative

There are many more which are important; but if a student teacher possesses these qualities, then it is a challenge for the supervising teacher to accept the responsibility of guiding this future teacher in his professional development.

The University Supervisor

The university supervisor is the person on the university staff who visits the student teacher at the student's assigned location and works with the cooperating teacher in guiding and evaluating the student's progress.[10] This person's role has been somewhat neglected in the professional literature. His is a "hidden power," or so it would seem. As he makes his first visit, the classroom teacher shudders, takes a deep breath and says, "Boys and girls, I'd like you to meet Dr. Jones. Say 'good morning' to Dr. Jones." She then beats a hasty retreat because "you certainly didn't come to see *me* teach." The student teacher squares his shoulders, takes a firm grasp on his textbook (*with* annotated teacher's guide) and begins speaking to the children in a somewhat shrill and tense voice, mentally noting, "Here goes my *A*." The cooperating teacher and the student teacher almost invariably form a coalition which makes the college supervisor an outsider, even an enemy, by virtue of the grading power he wields and the cooperating teacher's unspoken recognition of the knowledge that he, as well as the student teacher, is being evaluated. Every college supervisor knows the student teacher who has defended the poor practices of the cooperating teacher—"but she's kind to the children, and she *has* been so good to me"—and the cooperating teacher who states, "I know Ann has a lot to learn as a student teacher. She's a sweet girl though, and I hope . . ."

In those rare situations in which a mutually enriching student teaching situation exists, the college supervisor has used remarkable tact, sound professional judgment, and a considerable amount of personal charm and magnetism. Of course, these qualities must be *exhibited* to produce the hoped for beneficial results, but in student teaching situations all over the country, the college or university supervisor is "the man who isn't there." One visit a semester, seldom more than two, is becoming an altogether too common pattern. In "State and Federal Aid for Student Teaching—Now?" Andrews

---

[10] Adapted from the "Guide to Student Teaching in the Elementary School," developed by the faculty in elementary education at Purdue University (Rev. ed.; mimeographed, 1963).

quotes the superintendent of schools in a large city (there were 23,000 pupils enrolled in the school system surveyed) as stating that, on the average, each student teacher has only *one* fifteen-minute conference with his supervisor during the semester. With the pressures of rapidly increasing enrollments and decreasing funds allocated for teacher education, it would appear that the supervisor problem is not likely to be solved in the immediate future. Many college or university supervisors are responsible for thirty to forty-five student teachers. Twenty-five student teachers is a "normal" supervisory load at a number of institutions. Yet, the supervisor is expected to know each student teacher well enough to provide a discerning and knowledgeable evaluative statement and/or assign a letter grade, and he is expected to know each student teaching situation well enough to work with the director of student teaching in arranging future placements.

Another contradiction within the supervisory role relates to the status of the supervisor. On campus, he is often a "second-class citizen," seldom really involved in faculty decisions because of his frequent absences from campus and/or because of his temporary faculty status. Reference has been made to the complexity of the supervisory problem. Many institutions have solved this problem by assigning the supervision of student teaching to graduate students who are employed at the instructor rank and who are not expected to remain at the institution after their degree objectives are achieved. Providing continuity in the student teaching program and in the in-service work which should evolve from student teaching is a difficult process under existing conditions. At the larger institutions, at least there is "senior staff," whose members are almost completely divorced from the student teaching program, and there are instructors, who assume the heavy burden of operating this important aspect of the professional preparation of a teacher. An associate professor of education at a state university enrolling more than a thousand undergraduates majoring in elementary education admitted knowing little or nothing about the opportunities provided in student teaching for dramatization, choral speaking, or even reading to children, although his teaching area is children's literature. This very competent teacher did not know where student teachers from his institution were placed or, more to the point, whether these situations included adequate library resources and other opportunities for students to utilize the knowledge and understanding gained from the children's literature course he taught.

In contrast to the low-status, ambiguous position of the supervisor on campus, we find the situation referred to in the opening paragraphs of this section—the undue deference, bordering on fear, with which public school personnel regard the supervisor. The supervisor appears to be an outsider in each aspect of his role. He never quite belongs; and he works against tremendous obstacles to effect change, in methods classes as well as in public school situations. He finds much which convinces him of the value and significance of his contribution to teacher education; but he may also question the need for even the minimal number of visits his crowded schedule and heavy load permit, since he often appears to accomplish so very little.

The college supervisor is in an excellent position to inject strong elements of practicality and realism into methods courses and into the entire professional sequence. He is also in an excellent position to communicate to public school personnel (subtly and upon request) the findings of educational research and to recommend changes in educational practice which should result from the newly acquired knowledge. To assign a role with such tremendous responsibilities and opportunities to a graduate student, who is primarily concerned with getting a degree, seems somewhat unwise. It also seems unwise to give the supervisor so many student teachers to oversee, in so many widely separated public schools, that he finds it physically taxing merely to appear in the appropriate classrooms on schedule.

There is much evidence relating to the impact of the student teaching experience upon future teaching effectiveness. It is difficult to understand, therefore, why supervision of this phase of the teacher education program is treated so casually and why the most vital portions of this process are being handled, by default, by the cooperating teacher. If we can assume that the cooperating teacher possesses all the requisite skills, competencies, and understanding for student teaching supervision, then, surely, we should admit that the college supervisor is superfluous, and this role should be eliminated. For the following reasons, it seems justifiable to take the position that the college supervisor is *not* superfluous and, further, that the trend toward minimizing the position of the supervisor should be reversed.

1. The college supervisor has, one hopes, been involved in the

other two major roles identified in the student teaching experience. If the supervisor has not been a student teacher and cooperating teacher, one would certainly hope that his other qualifications would more than compensate for those major deficiencies. Assuming he has had this breadth of experience and has, perhaps, been an administrator and/or a college teacher as well, he can do much to keep the student teaching experience from becoming narrow and parochial. He knows, and can help to avoid, the pitfalls inherent in thinking there is only one way of maintaining cumulative records, writing lesson plans, or reporting to parents. Both of the other participants can benefit immeasurably from the rich and varied background of experiences which a carefully selected college supervisor can bring to the student teaching experience.

2. Experience has suggested that it is a bit optimistic to suggest almost total reliance upon state authorities and the local boards of education to insure a high-quality laboratory experience in student teaching. State departments of education are usually understaffed, and boards of education tend to be preoccupied with new buildings and the management of problems created by exploding enrollments. In one suburban school system, enrollments are increasing so rapidly that an additional elementary classroom is needed *each week*, if class sizes are to be kept near previous limits of thirty-five pupils. To expect administrators and school board members faced with problems of this nature to serve as effective watchdogs over the types of experiences provided for college seniors who are in their schools on a temporary basis is somewhat unrealistic. The public schools are gradually taking a more active part in the provision of laboratory experiences for prospective teachers, as the college-controlled laboratory schools discard this role (reluctantly) for a more active role in educational research. The assumption of a new function is always difficult; and the public school did not seek this role, any more than the laboratory school is giving it up of its own volition. There are simply too many prospective teachers for the personnel of the laboratory school to help effectively; the public schools *have* to be involved, and administrators are slowly recognizing this. We are, however, far from the position where recognition of the need for providing places for student teachers and properly certified classroom teachers to work with them leads to clearly adequate safeguards for the quality of the student teaching experience. Because many public schools are not

yet supplying these safeguards, the colleges must do so—and this "must" will be an imperative for some time to come. The college supervisor is one person, under present conditions at least, who can see to it that the student teacher has experiences in many curricular areas, is permitted the freedom to try his own ideas, works with many materials and media, studies children, and so on. Haines notes:

> The trend toward off-campus student teaching has shifted the challenge of teacher preparation from the delegation of total responsibility to colleges and universities. It has now become a cooperative enterprise involving public schools and teacher education institutions in the provision of adequate laboratory experiences. It should not be a matter of the use of public schools by the colleges in extending their programs, nor should public school personnel train the prospective teacher for one term of his college program. Rather, student teaching in the public schools should be a cooperative endeavor. Public school personnel offer guidance to the teacher in daily involvement in the wider school program, and teacher education personnel assist with the guidance and strengthen the student's preparation through encouraging his analysis and re-formulation of sound educational principles. Thus, theory and practice should proceed in concurrent development with each person making his unique contribution to the student teaching process.[11]

3. The college supervisor is in a unique position to help the student teacher turn theory into practice. It cannot be overemphasized here that the transition from *elementary education major*—sitting in methods classes, reading books on educational psychology—to *teacher*—attempting to *utilize* the good practices one has read about and discussed—is a very difficult transition indeed. The transition is not aided by the cooperating teacher who says, "Forget all that theory you've learned! It *just* doesn't work!" The college supervisor can guide the student teacher toward techniques and materials which will make the application of theory both practical and worthwhile.

4. The final justification for giving the college supervisor a major role in the student teaching experience relates to the benefits which accrue to the supervisor as an instructor of college methods classes or as a consultant to teachers or administrators interested in improving instruction in a curricular area. It is so easy to retreat to a world of

---

[11] Haines, op. cit., pp. 4–5.

"should be" and forget educational realities—such as crowded classes, a wide range of abilities among pupils, and limited facilities and materials. In one sense, the instructor's students are the real beneficiaries of the practical approach suggested here. It is not intended that we abandon dreaming, for progress depends upon dreams. It is suggested that the educator who never visits a classroom soon loses touch with schools, teachers, and the real everyday problems faced by teachers and children. Many beginning teachers have retreated to the protection of textbook teaching and rigid scheduling because their teacher education programs suggested no practical solution to problems which arise in teaching situations which are less than ideal. Methods instructors who have had a background of successful classroom teaching and who also visit classrooms with some regularity are likely to provide a more practical and realistic foundation for teaching.

The Director of Student Teaching

There is a fourth person whose role is significant in the student teaching process, and although he is not included in Figure 1, some reference should be made to the position of the *Director of Student Teaching*. He is responsible for the details of student teacher placement and for maintaining a constructive relationship with public school administrators. His position is, in some respects, as unenviable as that of the college supervisor. When difficulties develop in the student teaching situation, it is usually the director who first hears of the problems, from the student teacher, the college supervisor, the cooperating teacher, or all three! The importance of good lines of communication between the college or university and the public school system cannot be overemphasized, and the director bears much of the burden of maintaining this essential rapport.

FACILITIES FOR STUDENT TEACHING

Although at one time most student teaching took place in a campus laboratory school almost wholly controlled by the college or university, public schools, rather than laboratory schools, are providing the facilities in an increasing number of student teaching situations. This trend is of relatively recent origin and appears to be gaining momentum. It is both a response to the increasing numbers of student teachers and a result of the tendency to regard laboratory schools as atypical and the concern to provide student teaching situations which are more similar to the typical teaching situations the prospective teachers will encounter after graduation.

When, in 1959–60, I conducted a study of the functions of laboratory schools, I found that student teaching occupied first place on the lists of functions submitted by questionnaire respondents. In fact, 94 per cent of the respondents to the questionnaire indicated that laboratory functions were predominant. These functions included participation and observation as well as student teaching. It is of interest to note that these respondents indicated concern for providing adequate facilities for student teaching and that a majority of administrators who completed the questionnaires returned suggested that laboratory school personnel ought to be more actively involved in educational research than they are at the present time.[12] Another study, conducted by Charles R. Blackmon in 1962, had as its purpose determining the extent to which the research function has been accepted by laboratory school personnel. Blackmon wrote:

> The data revealed important changes in the functions of the laboratory schools studied. . . . Research and experimentation are receiving more emphasis, with a slight trend toward becoming a co-equal or primary function. Laboratory experiences were offered at earlier levels in undergraduate teacher education programs. A trend toward increased participation of graduate students in laboratory school research studies was perceptible. Student teaching has declined somewhat in importance as a function in the selected schools studied.[13]

These two studies are cited as evidence of the trend toward moving student teaching out of the laboratory school and into the public school.

The problems which have been created by the movement of the center of operations in student teaching from the laboratory school to the public school have been delineated rather specifically through-

---

[12] Pose Lamb, "An Investigation of Educational Research in Selected Laboratory Schools" (Doctoral dissertation, The Ohio State University, 1960).

[13] Charles R. Blackmon, "The Research Function in College Controlled Laboratory Schools" (Doctoral dissertation, University of Florida, 1962), p. 3.

out this chapter and need not be repeated here. They are essentially human relations problems resulting from the involvement of more educators in the preparation of teachers. These problems may now seem unsurmountable, or nearly so; but they will be solved, and their solution will undoubtedly result in the improvement of not only teacher education but the education of children enrolled in our public schools as well.

TIME DEVOTED TO STUDENT TEACHING

A second trend should be identified at this point, for it is equally as significant as the relocation of facilities. Student teaching is occupying a longer period of time than in previous years. Haines points out:

> In some places, students observe and participate in classrooms for one or more hours a day for a portion of a semester. In some programs, one half of each day or of certain days each week is spent in student teaching situations. Other institutions offer student teachers a full day of participation in schools on alternate days. These and similar situations, are valuable in providing actual teaching experience in public schools, but the limitations are apparent in furnishing means for students to gain insight into a total school program and to have contact with many of the responsibilities of teaching. When several students are placed in a selected classroom for part-time participation, their teaching experience is, of necessity, restricted by the needs of other students, and by the time available. Student teachers who are in the school for only a portion of the day or for specified days do not have an opportunity to become involved in the continuous development of a school program.
>
> The most promising trend noted in recent years has been in the direction of full-time student teaching every day for a full quarter, or the major portion of a semester or for a full semester. In this procedure it is possible for a student teacher to have continuous intensive and prolonged pre-service experience in public schools.[14]

Conant's recommendations in this area are quite specific. He wants all elementary education majors to have at least eight weeks of practice teaching, to spend during this time a minimum of three hours a

---

[14] Haines, op. cit., p. 8.

day in the classroom, and to have at least three weeks of complete responsibility for the classroom under the guidance of a cooperating teacher and a university supervisor.[15]

A major point of controversy in any discussion of facilities for student teaching relates to the desirability of "typicalness" in student teaching situations. In Stratemeyer's and Lindsey's words:

> . . . concurrently with program revisions calling for a wider range and greater number of professional laboratory experiences for children, there developed a belief among professional educators that future teachers should have at least some experience in representative schools. By representative is meant those schools in which population, materials and equipment, community setting and working conditions approximate the kinds of schools to which most graduates will go as teachers. This belief prompted those responsible for teacher education to seek the services of such schools to work with college students in programs of professional laboratory experiences.[16]

I agree that the community setting and the pupil population should be representative if the student teaching experience is to be of maximum value; however, if the student teacher sees and uses only representative materials and equipment, how will his sights be raised toward the superior equipment and materials which ought to be provided? Is student teaching an internship or an apprenticeship, a period of growth or a period of adjustment? The cooperating teacher should not be *typical* but should possess *unusual* skills in human relations, unusual teaching competence and knowledge of teaching resources, and unusual knowledge of and ability to apply the findings of recent educational research. At least, it should be our goal to place a student with this type of cooperating teacher.

Obviously, in these times of a genuine shortage of desirable student teaching situations, we are not going to be able to find nearly enough cooperating teachers who meet the standards sketched in this chapter; but we can and *must*, for the protection of the student teacher, insist on something more than mediocrity. Not every classroom teacher can be a capable guide to student teachers, nor can every professor of education successfully meet the requirements of the college super-

---

15 Conant, op. cit., p. 162.
16 Stratemeyer and Lindsey, op. cit., p. 5.

visor's role. Quality has a higher priority than representativeness in this important phase of the preparation of teachers.

It is somewhat unrealistic to hope for any adjustment to individual differences in the amount of time spent in student teaching. It seems logical to note that one student can gain, probably, as much in nine weeks as another can in twelve and that for some students two short (six- or seven-week) student teaching experiences would be more beneficial than one extended period. The latter arrangement would especially benefit the person who comes to student teaching with a background of less than adequate experiences working with children and who may well be undecided about the age level or levels with which he prefers to work. There is also something to be said for the "second chance" aspect of the two experiences. For some students these advantages would far outweigh the advantage of depth and breadth in one longer experience. For other students, they would not. Flexibility, more flexibility than presently exists in most highly structured programs, is a real need, and a need unlikely to be met in this age of automated course registration procedures and student teachers numbered in the hundreds; however, beyond the adjustment of time spent in the various phases of student teaching observation, participation, and full teaching responsibility, time allotments remain relatively rigid. A beginning is made, of course, when the student teacher is treated as an individual with needs and competencies unique to him. That this recognition should be extended to include the time differential does not seem impossible—only difficult—under present conditions.

Summary

It has been emphasized that the major purpose of this book is to point up areas, within the student teaching experience, where the college supervisor, the cooperating teacher, and the student teacher can coordinate their efforts, with resulting enhancement of the professional growth of each. Although attention has been focused on the work of the student teacher, the roles of the other major participants are considered more fully than in similar books. If the goals of each participant are achieved, the educational experiences of the youngsters in the classroom which is the center of operations will also be enriched. My view of the student teaching experience as one that can and should further the professional growth of all who take part in it is the direct result of what I have observed in myself and in others during my involvement in each of these facets of student teaching.

Assumptions and Principles upon Which This Book Is Based

The student teaching experience provides an opportunity for the prospective teacher to try the ideas, the techniques, and methods, to which he has been exposed throughout his teacher education program.

The student teaching experience should be a testing ground for the student's educational philosophy and for his understanding of child growth and development and the nature of learning.

The student teaching experience should not be typical if *typical* is synonymous with *mediocre*. The cooperating teacher, the elementary school, and the school system selected for these initiating experiences should be chosen with great care and should exemplify that which is good, if not ideal. This position is not accepted by everyone. Many would say that if the student teaching situation is rich in materials and equipment, if the building is representative of a community's concern for the health and well-being of its children, if class size is reasonable, if consultant and supervisory help are adequate and easily available, and if teaching competence is obvious, we do not prepare prospective teachers for the harsh realities of life in a "typical" teaching situation. This is the basic argument used when student teaching is moved from a campus laboratory school into the surrounding community's public schools. If, however, the student teaching situation is ordinary, it seems inevitable that from student teaching will come ordinary teachers who will perpetuate some of the practices condemned by nearly everyone in education.

The student teaching experience benefits the cooperating teacher in that it causes him to examine candidly and objectively his practices and procedures. Student teachers, fresh from exposure to research, literature, and classroom discussions of good pedagogy, ask some very searching and perceptive questions. Very few cooperating teachers leave the student teaching experience unchanged. Some administrators, in fact, request student teachers and ask that they be placed not in the best situations but in situations most in need of change. In view of the plea for atypical teachers, creative teachers, and rich student teaching situations, this practice can hardly be supported; but it does indicate that these administrators are aware of the growth which can accrue to the cooperating teacher during student teaching.

Although it is true that the cooperating teacher accepts a responsibility when he agrees to work with a student teacher, the responsibility should not be considered a burden. In a very real sense, the cooperating teacher is repaying a professional debt by guiding a prospective teacher, much as he himself was guided at one time.

The professional induction of a prospective teacher is a shared responsibility. Children, their parents, the other university faculty members (including the director of student teaching), and the public school administrators all play an important part in this aspect of the making of a teacher.

The college supervisor grows through making regular contacts with public school personnel, real children, and real teachers facing real problems. This is especially important if the supervisor is also a teacher of professional courses. The teacher of a methods course who visits classrooms regularly is not likely to suggest procedures which don't work or methods which are impractical.

These beliefs form the rationale from which this book has evolved. The points of view are not universally accepted, but surely there is room for individual differences here as in other areas of the educational enterprise.

Suggested Activities for Student Teachers

The following activities and projects are designed to aid the student teacher, the cooperating teacher, and the college supervisor as each prepares to engage in the student teaching process.

1. Prepare a brief statement, perhaps entitled "What I Expect from Student Teaching," written from *your* point of view. It might be useful to compare your statement with those prepared by other student teachers.

2. Interview a student who has recently completed student teaching. Prepare a report relating:
   a) How this former student teacher's views on teaching changed during student teaching.
   b) The aspects of this person's preparation for teaching, professional and general, which he in retrospect considers most beneficial.

c) This former student teacher's views on his relationship with the cooperating teacher and the college supervisor.

The emphasis here should be on the student teacher's role in these relationships and on the development of constructive lines of communication throughout the student teaching process.

3. Using the statement of certification requirements for your state[*] and Conant's recommendations about the length of time spent in student teaching, prepare to discuss the following questions.

a) Is the length of time I'll be doing student teaching typical? How does it compare with that suggested by Conant?

b) How many states have reciprocal agreements with the state in which I'll be certified? Will I have to take additional course work to be certified in neighboring states?

c) What are the basic requirements for being a cooperating teacher in the state for which I'll be certified? (It may be interesting to invite several experienced cooperating teachers to address your group of student teachers to express their attitudes toward student teaching and to discuss what they believe is important in qualifying them to work with prospective teachers.)

4. Ask the college supervisor to detail his philosophy of student teaching, including his expectations and his concept of his role, the cooperating teacher's role, and your role. Ask that he specifically discuss the number and purposes of his visits, and the functions of your meetings and conferences.

SELECTED REFERENCES

Andrews, L. O. "State and Federal Aid for Student Teaching—Now?" *Journal of Teacher Education*, V (June, 1964), pp. 165–75.

Blackmon, Charles Robert. "The Research Function in Selected College Controlled Laboratory Schools." (Mimeographed.) Extended abstract of doctoral dissertation, Gainesville: University of Florida, 1963.

Conant, James B. *The Education of American Teachers*. New York: McGraw-Hill Book Co., Inc., 1963.

Concern for the Individual in Student Teaching. (Sixty-fourth Yearbook.) Cedar Falls, Iowa: The Association for Student Teaching, 1963.

Cooperation in Student Teaching. (Educational Research Circular, No. 4.) Washington, D.C.: American Association of School Administration, National Education Association, 1964.

---

[*] Available from your state department of education or from the placement office on your campus.

Haines, Aleyne. *Guiding the Student Teaching Process in Elementary Education*. Chicago: Rand McNally & Co., 1960.

Hunter, Elizabeth, and Amidon, Edmund. *Student Teaching—Cases and Comments*. New York: Holt, Rinehart & Winston, Inc., 1964.

Lamb, Pose. "An Investigation of Educational Research in Selected Laboratory Schools." Doctoral dissertation, Ohio State University, 1960.

Smith, E. Brooks, and Johnson, Paluck (eds.). *School-College Relationships in Teacher Education: Report of a National Survey of Cooperative Ventures*. Washington, D.C.: American Association of Colleges for Teacher Education, 1964.

Stratemeyer, Florence, and Lindsey, Margaret. *Working with Student Teachers*. New York: Bureau of Publications, Teachers College, Columbia University, 1958.

2

Getting Started

Before the student teacher first visits the classroom, much can be done which will promote a successful student teaching experience. A few general comments in the preceding chapter suggested the importance of placing the student teacher in a classroom where he would be welcomed, helped, guided, and treated as a colleague, not as an assistant teacher and not as another pupil. The administrative officials of the public school system, the director of student teaching, and the college supervisor who is somewhat familiar with a school, its faculty, and administrators will work together to place a student teacher in a situation which will be both pleasant and professionally rewarding for all the personnel involved.

Before the Student Teacher Comes to the Classroom

The first of the procedures leading to student teaching would appear to be the determination of a student teaching situation for the student—a classroom in which student teaching may take place. The following steps are appropriate parts of the placement procedure.

1. The prospective student teacher files an application for place-ment. The application form will include requests for such information as the student's name, address, age, sex, marital status, and perhaps his home town and his parents' occupations. It is also very helpful if a brief autobiography in which the student tells something of his inter-ests, hopes, ambitions, and personal background is included along with the vital statistics listed above. In some states, information re-garding religious preference and race may not be required, and photographs are not included on applications because they may give clues to race or religious background. It seems clearly unfair, how-ever, to place a student teacher in a situation where his race or re-ligion will be detrimental to his chances of success. I recall, unhappily, the problems which accrued when Linda, a Jewish student teacher, was placed in a strongly fundamentalist Protestant community. At Christmas time, Linda was asked to discuss Hanukah, the Jewish holiday which also occurs in December, with the children in several classrooms. These brief, informational discussions were followed by telephone calls from disturbed parents who asked the school super-intendent why Mrs. A was trying to convert their children to Judaism. The superintendent complained to the director of student teaching, who asked the supervisor what had happened. The situation was very unpleasant for everyone concerned. One's personal convictions not-withstanding, it seems obvious that student teaching is not the very best time to test the racial or religious bias of a community. The situ-ation described above could have and should have been prevented by not placing Linda in a community where her religious preferences would be suspect. Whether such information can legally be requested on an application is of less importance than is the placement of a stu-dent teacher in a community and in a school where his race and religion will not be considered a liability.

The application might also include a checklist of skills. Can the student type, play a musical instrument, operate a film projector? Such a checklist is helpful to the student in assessing his readiness for student teaching and helpful to the cooperating teacher as he plans to build upon the student's strengths and correct, or compensate for, evident weaknesses. A typical student teaching application ap-pears as an appendix to this book.

2. The application is processed by clerical personnel in the student teaching office; and data about the applicant's health, physical and

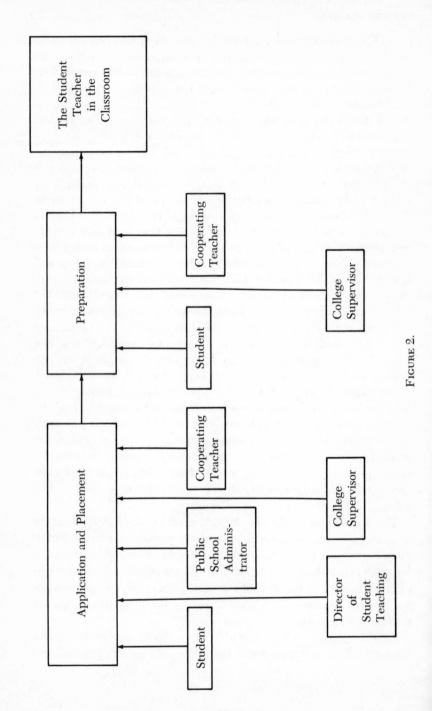

FIGURE 2.

emotional, are added. Whether or not the student's course grades should be included is a controversial issue. In some situations, the knowledge that a student is weak in certain academic areas (math, science, foreign language would alert the cooperating teacher, and the student teacher could begin teaching in areas where he felt strongest. In a few situations, however, a poor academic record would cause prejudgment of the student's competence, and the student would have some difficulty convincing the principal and the cooperating teacher that he did have *some* areas of strength.

The problem of interpreting student teachers' grades is discussed in a recent yearbook of the Association for Student Teaching:

> Even in institutions where goals of intellectual competency are stated in beautiful phrases, marks are still the means of expressing success or failure. There is a tendency to consider marks as concrete evidence. A counselor can point to marks and say, "See, you do not meet our standards." The hard truth is that there is not yet a reliable system for assigning and interpreting marks. There doesn't seem to be a predictable and useful correlation between marks and effectiveness in teaching. Although it can be said that intellectual competence is essential, it is not certain that the student who is in the top decile of a class will become a better teacher than the one who is in the next decile. Even an intelligence test does not give a measure of how apt and disciplined the student is in using his intelligence.
>
> For years to come, marks will probably be used in many places as the final criteria in questions of intellectual development because institutions have fallen into the habit of making basic judgments in this manner. But the fact that there is no completely satisfactory way of determining readiness is no excuse for not seeking within each faculty new ways of examining students' readiness to assume responsibility for guiding intellectual development.[1]

It is probably wisest not to include grades but, rather, to attempt to consider the student as a whole person with academic and nonacademic competencies and deficiencies.

It does not seem unreasonable to request a health clearance before a student begins an experience which is usually exhausting, physically

---

[1] *Concern for the Individual in Student Teaching* (Forty-second Yearbook, Aleyne C. Haines, general ed. [Cedar Falls, Iowa: The Association for Student Teaching, 1963]), p. 100.

and emotionally. Applications for certification in many states require a physician's signature, and often these applications are filed soon after student teaching is concluded. Possibly, then, one thorough physical examination could serve both purposes. At any rate, it is most important that the student possess the physical stamina to endure the long periods of standing, the hurried lunches, playground duty, and the other physical demands of teaching. If a student has had periods of emotional disturbance and there is a chance that student teaching may cause a recurrence of the difficulty, it hardly seems fair to conceal from the cooperating teacher or the college supervisor, or both, that this possibility exists. Surely people with the background requisite for holding such responsible positions would consider such information highly confidential and would not expect a collapse each time a discipline problem arises with a child or a difficult parent challenges the student teacher's authority.

3. Public school personnel, the director of student teaching, and the college supervisor who normally work with the particular school where placements are being planned confer and agree upon a desirable placement. This procedure sounds simple; it is not. It is complicated by principals who are anxious to reward "good" teachers and are fearful of staff relationships if the same teachers are used too frequently and by teachers who have had an unhappy experience with a student teacher in the past and "*won't* have another one from X Teachers College." It is complicated by mistakes which have occurred and damaged the relationships which should exist between supervisor and teacher; and, finally, it is complicated by the numerical imbalance which exists between the number of places needed and the number of desirable situations available. Nonetheless, after compromises and much discussion, decisions are finally made, and a professional "home" is found for each student teacher.

4. The application is forwarded to the cooperating teacher, and it is to be hoped that this is received eagerly or at least willingly. It is sad indeed when a student teacher isn't welcome, when a principal or a superintendent tells a teacher he is going to have a college student in his classroom and the cooperating teacher feels imposed upon and forced into a position in which he doubts his ability to succeed. Most of the readers of this book have known, second-hand at least, of student teaching experiences that began with statements like these from the cooperating teachers:

"So you're Jane Jones! Let me tell you *right* away that my methods *aren't* modern. I *know* why Mr. Andrews assigned you to me. I'm happy teaching as I do, and the children and their parents seem to be satisfied. *Don't* expect to change me with your new ideas and methods. We'll get along all right if we decide right away that you're here to learn from me, not I from you."

"I haven't been very well. I know someone as young and healthy as you are will be a *big* help. The art paper we ordered weeks ago just arrived. Would you mind going to the office, loading it on one of the little library trucks, bringing it back to the room, and storing it in those high cupboards? Don't forget to sign the receipt for the paper—in triplicate."

"I *hope* you're more energetic (or a better disciplinarian, or a better writer, or a more meticulous room housekeeper) than Betty, the last student teacher State sent me! I really *wasn't* very eager to have another student teacher after my last one!—she was really terrible. Let me tell you about the afternoon she ..."

Remarks simliar to those recounted above are not nearly so uncommon as they should be, and they are not at all amusing to the student teacher who is already somewhat frightened, apprehensive, and eager to succeed. It seems difficult to imagine anyone's beginning an interpersonal relationship of any kind with such ill-conceived remarks; but it does happen, as those with experience as school administrators, college supervisors, or cooperating teachers know very, very well. The positive approach is the healthy one, however; and we'll assume that the placement we are discussing is one in which the student teacher is welcomed and in which his strengths, competencies, and values will be respected and fostered.

The Student Teacher Prepares

Whether he gets word of the placement in the mail, through a telephone call, or in a personal conference with someone from the student teaching office, it's an exciting day indeed when the student teacher learns where he is to do student teaching. His application form probably includes a place for recording his grade level preferences; and this, rather than the teacher who will be his "critic," will probably be his first concern. This is natural, since lesson plans, committee assign-

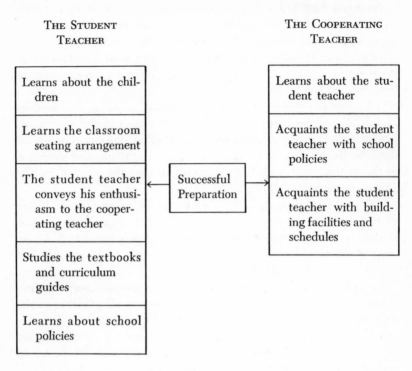

THE STUDENT
TEACHER

THE COOPERATING
TEACHER

Learns about the children	Learns about the student teacher
Learns the classroom seating arrangement	Acquaints the student teacher with school policies
The student teacher conveys his enthusiasm to the cooperating teacher	Acquaints the student teacher with building facilities and schedules
Studies the textbooks and curriculum guides	
Learns about school policies	

Successful
Preparation

FIGURE 3

ments, even term papers in so many of his methods courses have been geared to a specific grade level, or at least to a general concern for children at the primary or intermediate levels. This is not the proper place for a discussion of the characteristics which seem to contribute to successful primary grade teaching as contrasted with those more important for successful intermediate grade teaching, but it is a fact that most student teachers are very specific about wanting a first grade ("There're so *cute* at that age, with their lisps, and they think the teacher is so wonderful") or a sixth grade ("I want to *teach* them something. No shoe tying and mitten hunting for me!"). The competence and concern of the cooperating teacher may be of far more significance in a successful student teaching experience than the specific grade level. There are children in every third grade who exhibit characteristics similar to those expected in first grade, and there are childen who are like third-graders in every sixth grade. There is such a range—physically, emotionally, socially, and academically—in every elementary classroom that it is unwise and unnecessary for the student teacher to feel disappointment if he's assigned to a second grade instead of a first or to a sixth grade instead of a fifth.

The Initial Visit

Soon after the assignment is made, the student teacher will get in touch with the cooperating teacher with whom he'll work and will request an appointment to talk with him about the children, the teacher's program, and student teaching. The initial visit is very important; and it is best if the student teacher can visit while class is in session, to see the children and the classroom equipment and to watch the cooperating teacher at work. Sometimes such a visit is not convenient, and a conference after school, perhaps on campus, must substitute. Specific concerns to be discussed in this conference or visit will relate to class size, the seating arrangement and names of the children, and the establishment of the foundations from which a truly productive relationship can emerge. The student teacher is careful to look for *positive* aspects of the situation—an attractive and neat classroom, a very effective math lesson, a variety of instructional materials and media. From this crucial first meeting a friendly and mutually rewarding series of experiences can develop; or the opposite can occur, and this student teaching situation may be doomed before it really begins. The prudent student teacher does *not* remark that she would have preferred another grade or that she won't have much time for student teaching because of family responsibilities or campus activities. The student teacher who is engaged and indicates, "I really doubt that I'll ever teach" is not likely to be accepted with much enthusiasm. Such a remark is tactless, at least.

The student teacher who is mature, has had another career, and has decided upon teaching as a profession for reasons of financial security or an immediate need for additional income ("With both girls in college now, Bob's salary just isn't enough") presents a rather different set of problems. In some cases, such a student teacher is more mature by a number of years than the cooperating teacher. It will be the cooperating teacher's professional competence, rather

THE STUDENT TEACHER CHECKS TO SEE WHAT HELP CAN BE
PROVIDED ON THE FIRST DAY OF STUDENT TEACHING

than his years of experience, which will earn the respect of the student
teacher in situations of this nature. It goes without saying that this
student teacher's family will not receive the attention from mother,

or father, which they may have come to expect. Decisions regarding such "neglect" of one's family need to be made before student teaching begins. Actually, a mature person who comes to teaching without fully understanding the demands of the profession shows a lack of judgment which probably should not be present in one who is well beyond his teens. Observation of the career teacher at work, for even a short period of time, should quickly disabuse anyone who thinks of teaching as an eight-to-three job, with vacations at Christmas time, in the spring, and all summer long. At any rate, if family schedules are disarranged, if the children must perform more household chores so mother can be free to read and plan in the evening while she's student teaching, so be it. This is not the primary concern of the cooperating teacher nor the college supervisor. They may be sympathetic to the problems of trying to achieve success in a career while raising a family; indeed, they may well be struggling to solve such problems themselves, but student teaching is important enough to justify some sacrifices without expecting pats on the back or allowances which would not be made for the more typical college-age student teacher.

These concerns are detailed here because they will be items for discussion during the initial conference visit, and the student teacher will certainly desire to present a desirable professional image, as well as an attractive and wholesome personal image. The student teacher will also, during the period preceding actual student teaching, make an effort to acquire at least the following information. This may be gathered during the initial visit or at some other mutually convenient time.

1. The name of each child in the group and enough background information to prevent embarrassing and unnecessary mistakes during the initial period of student teaching. The student teacher should know, for example, which children have a hearing loss or which ones come from homes where there has been a divorce.

2. A chart depicting the usual seating arrangement, to aid in the rapid learning of each child's name. If the student teacher isn't provided with a seating chart by the cooperating teacher, he should make one as soon as possible.

3. Copies of the textbooks used and the curriculum guide for the school system, if there is one. Teachers' editions of the textbooks should be furnished the student teacher if at all possible; and if there

is to be only one visit before student teaching actually begins, some planning about to "where we'll be in the text by then" should occur. I am, of course, hopeful that the teaching will not be completely textbook-centered; but experience suggests that the textbook occupies a very prominent position in most elementary school classrooms. The curriculum guide should be surveyed to see, for example, whether the social studies–science unit the student teacher plans is considered appropriate. These matters are only touched upon here; the whole area of planning is dealt with more thoroughly in the next chapter.

The initial visit should include a tour of the building. (Children make excellent guides, and the student teacher will thus become fairly well acquainted with at least *one* child in the group.) The student teacher will need to know where to put his belongings when he arrives, where the library is, where audio-visual aids are stored, where the principal's office is, where the custodian's headquarters are, and where to go during a fire drill. These are minimum essentials, and the student teacher will feel much more comfortable if he has this type of information before he assumes his duties.

It cannot be assumed that the student teacher knows when he is to arrive each morning, what luncheon facilities (if any) are available, and when his professional day (the portion spent at school, that is) ends unless someone tells him! Such knowledge is commonplace to the cooperating teacher; and, unfortunately, the student teacher sometimes finds out that he's arriving late, leaving early, or not bringing a sandwich for lunch when everyone else does. It is a courtesy to the student teacher to help him feel at ease in every possible way, and sharing important information about school routines will help to accomplish this goal.

Soon after student teaching begins, if not during the initial visit, a conference should be arranged with the principal. Topics covered during this conference might include grouping and promoting practices, professional meetings which the student teacher will be expected to attend, and scheduled duties for teachers (playground, cafeteria, or hall duty, etc.). An alert elementary teacher is always searching for prospective teachers (in these days of a teacher shortage, especially); and even if the student teacher is not viewed as a candidate for a teaching position, a constructive professional relationship between the principal and the student teacher is important for the welfare of the children in the student teacher's classroom. One student teacher related with much amusement the number of errands the building principal was "forced" to run, past and into the student teacher's classroom, on the day the cooperating teacher visited in another school system and the student teacher was on her own. A good building principal knows his student teachers almost as well as his teachers, and the wise student teacher works to maintain a cooperative and healthy professional relationship with the principal.

If the student teacher is remaining in the dormitory, in the sorority or fraternity house, or staying at his parents' home, living arrangements are not a problem, but transportation may be. After learning when arrival at school is expected and departure acceptable, the student teacher needs to check bus schedules or arrange for transportation of some kind. This appears to be a mundane matter, hardly worth mention in a textbook; but student teachers have had such serious transportation problems that effective classroom work was impaired. For example, one student teacher arrived late every morning because of bus transfer problems. This was most annoying to his cooperating teacher, and the relationship between the two suffered accordingly. In another instance, a college supervisor arrived at a school in mid-afternoon, expecting to visit a student teacher and to confer with her after the children had been dismissed. The student teacher's husband, in order to help his wife, was in the habit of calling for her precisely at 4:00, the earliest possible moment when teachers could leave. This left no time for a conference. I have no desire to prolong this discussion, but it is important to point out that getting to and from school is the student teacher's responsibility, and such matters should be arranged with proper concern for conscientious performance of one's professional duties as well as for convenience.

Finding a Place to Live

The student teacher who is placed in an off-campus center which is not near his home, has the additional concern of finding suitable housing. Many property owners will only reluctantly, if at all, rent to a tenant who plans to stay for no more than three months. Student teachers who look forward to sharing an apartment with friends are occasionally very disappointed to find they are lucky to obtain a room! A drive around the area adjacent to the school will help the student teacher decide whether or not this is the neighborhood in which he wishes to reside. It is of doubtful value to the student teacher to recommend housing near the school (for purposes of convenience) if the neighborhood is neither safe nor clean. Student teaching presents enough possible pitfalls—personal danger need not be among them.

The superintendent's office often keeps an up-to-date list of available apartments and rooms, since teachers are ordinarily desirable tenants. The cooperating teacher may know of vacancies. The local newspaper may be consulted, if someone has helpfully indicated which areas are close to the school and which neighborhoods are safe and might offer desirable housing. Problems related to housing differ in kind and intensity in almost every student teaching situation; the matter can receive only the most general treatment here. The objective, clearly, seems to be finding living quarters which will enhance, not impede, the chances for successful student teaching.

Behavior in the Community

Once housing has been secured, the off-campus student teacher begins the job of acclimating himself to his new surroundings. As a young newcomer to the community, the student teacher may expect to be observed rather closely. Most communities no longer expect the level of behavior once expected of teachers, but formerly many teaching contracts stated something to the effect that the teacher must spend at least three week ends a month in the community and would be expeced to teach a Sunday school class. Behavior which can most politely be described as nonconformist is not going to reflect positively on the student teacher, his college or university, or the school system in which he's been placed. Briefly, financial irresponsibility, loud, late parties, and excessive drinking are not qualities which one associates with the personal or professional behavior of ladies and gentlemen. Student teachers are human, and recreation is a very human need; but the need can be satisfied in ways which will not result in harm to themselves or the residents of the community in which they are temporarily residing. It has been my experience that most student teachers are so involved in their work and so tired at the end of a teaching day that unacceptable behavior is out of the question. Unfortunately, however, there are exceptions; and it is because of these exceptions that this brief sermon has been included. The student teacher can now look back on at least three years of preparation. His general knowledge and his professional competence have been judged to be adequate. He has at least a superficial acquaintance with the situation in which he'll be working and more than a superficial acquaintance with his supervisor and his "critic." His personal life has been so adjusted that nothing extraneous to the student teaching situation itself will cause him to fail. He is ready (although he may not think so) for the almost overwhelming cluster of impressions, feeling, attitudes, and experiences which is called student teaching.

The College Supervisor Makes Plans

The college supervisor's role in the placement procedure varies tremendously from institution to institution. Much depends upon the size of the institution. In smaller institutions (or in larger institutions in which teacher education occupies a minor role) the cooperating teacher may make the placements personally, and the task of processing applications is almost entirely a clerical task. At the other end of the continuum, in some very large universities, the cooperating teacher may have so little information that he is merely handed, a few days before student teaching begins, a list of names and a stack of folders representing the student teachers assigned him. If the cooperating teacher operates in a situation similar to the first one described, knowledge of the student and of the situation in which he's placed can be presupposed. Making plans in this case involves expanding and deepening the knowledge already possessed. Holding a conference with the student teacher, helping with plans for the initial visit, forwarding significant information to the cooperating teacher—the supervisor's planning will involve these activities at least. The college supervisor will probably proceed through the following steps to prepare for an effective and productive student teaching experience.

1. He may carefully note all the data in student personnel folders. This should give nearly complete information about each student teacher assigned to him. A copy of the application form, the autobiography (suggested in the preceding section), the student's aca-

demic record, his health record, and the pertinent vital statistics to which reference has already been made should be available to the supervisor.

2. The supervisor may visit the school where each student teacher is to be placed, if he is not already familiar with the situation. Time spent getting acquainted with the principal, the staff, and most important, the cooperating teacher or teachers is time well spent. For one thing, if the situation is undesirable, it is better to make a last-minute change than to cause the student teacher to stagnate or diminish in a professionally sterile atmosphere. Hopefully, however, this will be a rewarding get-acquainted period, in which information is exchanged and viewpoints are shared. Tentative plans may also be made at this time. These plans may include scheduling conferences, dates and times for visits, etc. It is helpful if some information about

THE UNIVERSITY SUPERVISOR MEETS WITH THE STUDENT TEACHERS
ASSIGNED TO HIM BEFORE STUDENT TEACHING BEGINS

the student can be shared: "Jane's rather shy, but I've noticed that she seems to lose herself completely when she's with a group of children—then she almost glows with the delight she feels." Sometimes, though, the student is a stranger to both these professionals, and this kind of preparation must be delayed.

3. A group meeting with all the student teachers assigned to him will possibly be arranged. If the number of students is twenty or thirty as it is in some situations, the meeting may consist of general announcements and statements relating to requirements, followed by smaller group sessions in which the students assigned to a particular school meet together to share their concerns and hopes and to make plans.

4. If this is not completely impractical (and in some situations it is) a great deal can be gained from individual conferences with each prospective student teacher. It is here one can discover some of those problems, personal characteristics, and concerns which even a frankly written autobiography won't reveal. This conference can help establish the kind of relationship—friendly, honest, and full of mutual respect—from which a good student teaching experience can grow. The supervisor's role as "outsider," the one who can be fooled into thinking that things are better than they really are in the classroom, has already been mentioned. A truly productive conference, before student teaching begins, in which both participants honestly share their expectations may minimize the need for such deception.

5. After gaining necessary background information about the student, the teacher, and the student teaching situation, thoughtful and careful planning should begin. How can I help ease the way for Sue's social studies unit? It's obvious Mrs. Elliot doesn't use the unit approach. How can I tell Bill, tactfully but firmly, that loud shirts and an unshaven look aren't appropriate for a teacher? Others have tried, and failed. Questions like these will have to be considered as the supervisor makes plans. From this planning should evolve a method of operation, a way of working with each student teacher and each cooperating teacher, which will help achieve a productive, effective student teaching situation.

The student teacher is not alone in accepting responsibility for maintaining healthy, professional relationships. The student teacher is, understandably, not vitally concerned with the supervisor's heavy course load, his languishing dissertation, the distance he must travel to supervise, the unequal distribution of student teachers, and other such problems he faces. There may be good reasons for making fewer visits than the student teacher has a right to expect, and there may be adequate reasons for arriving at the end of a lesson the student teacher has especially prepared for the supervisor's observation and criticism. These reasons should not sink to the level of excuses, however; sympathy is probably the one emotion the supervisor should not expect to arouse in either the student teacher or the cooperating teacher. Fortunately, few supervisors want or expect to generate such feelings, much preferring an attitude of friendly respect.

After the preparation outlined above, secure in the knowledge he has about each student teaching situation, viewing his task objectively and with a sense of humor, the college supervisor, too, is ready.

The Cooperating Teacher's Preparations

Since there has been a rather thorough discussion of placement procedures, this discussion will focus on the work of the classroom teacher after he has been notified that a student teacher has been assigned to his classroom. It is to be hoped that this news meets with his full approval and that, in fact, he and the principal looked at the student's folder together and agreed that the chances for a successful experience for the student, the teacher, and the children are excellent. The following case illustrates the kinds of things the cooperating teacher must do to prepare for the arrival of the student teacher.

Mr. Brown has had student teachers before—good ones, fair ones, a few poor ones; but most of them have been very successful, and his relationships with State University and with members of the education faculty have been good. Now, as he surveys his classroom, he wonders what the new supervisor will be like and how he'll react to the supervisor's visit tomorrow. His class is large, and there are a number of children he feels he hasn't yet reached. He dusts a bit, straightens the things on his desk, and notices that the bulletin boards are even less stimulating and attractive than usual. Then, he decides to take another look at the student's folder, so his questions tomorrow will be somewhat more intelligent than they were when he met the previous supervisor. He notices that Ed, the student teacher, plays the piano, and can operate all of the types of audio-visual equipment the school owns. Mr. Brown frowns, as he also notices that Ed is actively campaigning for an important campus office and is involved in several of the major campus organizations. How much time will he devote to student teaching? Mr. Brown is convinced that his fifth-graders deserve something very special in teaching—he doesn't want short-cuts, poorly planned lessons, or that part of Ed's energies which remain after his campus responsibilities are met. He makes a note to ask Mrs. Ames, the university supervisor, about this tomorrow. He scans Ed's health record, notices that Ed is engaged to be married, and glances at his autobiography. A sense of commitment to children and teaching underlies everything Ed has written, and Mr. Brown is no longer quite so worried about Ed being "half" a teacher. He makes a note to have a new seating chart ready when Ed visits on Friday and to ask for class volunteers to escort Ed around the building. Extra teachers' editions for all the textbooks have been located, and so have copies of the faculty handbook and the school system's curriculum guide.

Mr. Brown wonders what to do about a desk for Ed; will he want one of his own, or could they share the desk already in the room? Mr. Brown spends very little time behind his desk—especially during the day when the children are around. If he were to clear two or three drawers for Ed. . . . He finally decides to wait until Ed comes and then ask him about this.

The class's study of the American westward movement is nearly finished. The children are presenting a program Friday, for their parents and for Ed, which will conclude the unit. When Mr. Brown and Ed talked on the phone, Ed suggested a unit he called "Modern Pioneers," having to do with the contributions of contemporary scientists, physicians, and statesmen. It sounded interesting, but Mr. Brown wondered about the time gap. Would the children be confused? They could discuss this on Friday. Something could be done to make a smooth and logical transition.

The last student teacher had come from a teachers college in the northern part of the state, and there had been a housing problem which had persisted throughout student teaching—there was an overly curious landlady, as Mr. Brown recalled; but Ed would be living in the dormitory. Might there be a transportation problem this time? Does Ed have a car? Would he be riding with other student teachers? Another note, another item for Friday's agenda. Mr. Brown almost vocalized the hope that Ed wouldn't have to rush away, that they would have time to talk, to get to know each other.

Was Friday the best day for Ed to come? With the program and the parents, it wouldn't be a typical day. Mr. Brown was glad that Ed would meet the parents, and he hoped the parents would like Ed. The children were very eager to present their program; perhaps Ed could find time to visit again, when things were more normal.

A final check—oh, he must remember to see the principal so some time could be cleared for a meeting on Friday—lunch perhaps? Tucking in his briefcase the student teaching guidebook sent him by the university, Mr. Brown closed the door of his classroom; he was ready to meet his new student teacher.

Summary

In this chapter there has been an effort to discuss in some detail the earliest stages of the student teaching process, from application through placement and up to the point where the student teacher is more teacher than student.

It has been pointed out that the application filed by the student teacher should include adequate information concerning his physical, emotional, and academic preparation for teaching. The information requested from the student teacher will be treated confidentially and will be used to help him in student teaching, not as a weapon or collection of evidence to be used in case of failure.

Placement of a student teacher is a cooperative affair, involving public school officials, the director of student teaching, and the student teaching supervisor from the college or university. With the tremendous increase in the number of student teachers and the problem of finding enough competent cooperating teachers, it is likely that the colleges and universities will have to depend increasingly upon the recommendations of the public school personnel and forego the luxury of inspection visits to each prospective cooperating teacher. The cooperative development of standards for student teaching situations is recommended.

Before the three major participants in the student teaching process begin to work together, a series of conferences serves to introduce them to one another and to establish open and effective lines of communication. Both the student teacher and the college supervisor should try to visit the school where student teaching will take place; and the student teacher will attempt to learn as much as possible about the children, their program, and the materials they'll use, in order to be as well prepared as possible for student teaching. The cooperating teacher also will try to inform himself about the student teacher, about his strengths and abilities as well as his weaknesses. The college supervisor facilitates the interactions outlined above. The foundations of honesty, respect, and understanding upon which a successful student teaching experience depends are laid long before the student teacher presents his first lesson, and each participant plays a major role in establishing this foundation.

Suggested Activities for Student Teachers

1. Discuss the major categories included on the application form you completed, or the categories on the composite application form appended to this book. Why are previous experiences with children important? Why is evidence regarding your health requested? Are grades in college courses important? Why or why not?

2. Discuss, or prepare a written report dealing with the reasons behind the grade placement you requested. Why do you feel you are better equipped for the grade level (primary or intermediate) you chose?

3. In what way will your socio-economic background influence your success in student teaching? On the basis of your knowledge of the community in which you'll be doing student teaching, do you anticipate major or minimal adjustment problems? (Again, this could be a topic for a panel discussion, buzz sessions, or individual reports.)

4. Arrange for the initial visit referred to in this chapter. If this isn't possible, correspond with your cooperating teacher and gather the information suggested—location of the school, community background, class size, information about the curriculum. Ask whether a guide is available. What textbooks are used? Is the teacher's guide relied upon heavily? At what point in the textbooks will the children be working when student teaching begins?

5. Write to the principal of the building in which you'll be doing student teaching or arrange a personal interview if possible to inquire about daily schedules, luncheon arrangements, professional meetings, etc. It will be interesting to compare notes on these matters with other student teachers, since there is a great deal of variation from school system to school system, even from school to school.

SELECTED REFERENCES

Burr, James B., Harding, Lowry W., and Jacobs, Leland B. *Student Teaching in the Elementary School*. New York: Appleton-Century-Crofts, 1958, Chapter 1, "Beginning Your Student Teaching."

Concern for the Individual in Student Teaching. (Forty-second Yearbook.) Cedar Falls, Iowa: The Association for Student Teaching, 1963.

Haines, Alleyne C. *Guiding the Student Teaching Process*. Chicago: Rand McNally & Co., 1960, Chapter 6, "Guiding Beginning Teaching."

Michaelis, John U., and Grim, Paul R. *The Student Teacher in the Elementary School*. New York: Prentice-Hall, Inc., 1953, Chapter 1, "Responsibilities in Student Teaching," and Chapter 2, "Preparation for Student Teaching."

3

Observation and Participation

Let us now consider Mary, a student teacher who has planned carefully. Her initial visit was a complete success. She knows the children's names, she's surveyed their cumulative records, and she feels extremely lucky to be working with such wonderful children and with her cooperating teacher, Miss Williams, who has been very helpful so far. Mary feels she's dressed appropriately— low heels, nylons, and her newest sweater and skirt. She's careful not to overdo the make-up, and her hair style is more conservative than it is when she attends classes. Mary and Miss Williams are having lunch at a restaurant near school today, but usually they'll eat in the school cafeteria. It's still early, but Mary is excited; she doesn't want to risk being even a little late on the first real day of student teaching. Mary meets another student teacher, Joan—she's early too! The two girls have decided to ride together, Joan driving one week, Mary the next. They're not sure of traffic, and neither girl wants to get a ticket for speeding.

Isn't it somewhat incongruous that these two eager young women will arrive at school, ready to embark upon the professional tasks for which they've been preparing for three and a half years or more, and *sit*? And, if typical procedures prevail, they'll sit *tomorrow* and the next day, too. Directed observation undoubtedly has value, but at this point it seems that sitting and *watching* when one wants to be *doing* only serves to dampen the enthusiasm of the student teacher and to result in impatience and boredom. Whether or not one agrees that the student teacher is usually impatient, eager to get started and to try the ideas he has heard about, it seems obvious that a protracted period of observation is not the best beginning for him. Rather, a combination of directed observation and participation is probably the best plan. The dialogue might be somewhat as follows:

Miss WILLIAMS: Mary, as you noticed when you looked at my plans, I'm trying something a little different with Joe's (a pupil's) reading group today. They've finished their basal materials and the librarian has helped me select fifteen or twenty books from which each may choose the one he wants to read. I've read about individualized reading and I'm eager to try it. I'll be interested in your reaction.

MARY: We talked about individualized reading in my language-arts methods class. I think it sounds wonderful! That group is so capable; I'm sure they're ready for this approach. Mike (a pupil) has seemed quite interested in astronomy—I think he'll like a book dealing with that much better than the basal text.

Now, Mary will be watching for two things—the reaction of the group, in general and of Mike, specifically, to a particular teaching technique, the introduction of self-selection in reading materials. Assuming this phase of the lesson has been successfully completed, Mary might follow up with any one of several activities:

1. Knowing Mike's interest in astronomy, she might locate several other books in this field.
2. Sensing that the book Bill has selected is too difficult (or too easy) for him, she might ask him to read aloud to her "a funny part," "a mysterious part," etc., and report her findings to Miss Williams who along with Mike will decide whether his choice was a wise one.
3. She may notice certain specific kinds of problems, as the children read in their individually selected books. As a result of her diagnosis, she may develop or select some drills, exercises, or games which will give necessary help.

Mary is learning to observe not only for general aspects of teaching methods but for specific techniques and the response of the children to these methods and techniques. She is also learning that some action typically occurs as a result of observation, that observation is not an end in itself but the means to an end—the improvement of the quality of education for a group of children or a particular child. The point is that Mary is not told simply to "watch the children—see what you can learn about them." With college students as with children, the highest quality of learning is active and purposive, and the greatest benefits are derived when the learner is physically and intellectually involved. The student teacher has spent approximately three and a half years absorbing ideas about teaching and learning and, one hopes, expects in student teaching an opportunity to put these ideas into practice. The wise cooperating teacher will not delay this participation in the learning process too long.

Of course, there are certain prerequisites to moving from directed observation, and the student teacher must satisfy these. He must know each child's name. He should be familiar with the cooperating teacher's program and with the materials and facilities with which he may work. These are routine matters; and the bright, alert student teacher will have each of them under control by the end of the first or second day of teaching, particularly if there has been an introductory visit and if the cooperating teacher has given him a curriculum guide, teacher's editions of the textbooks, and other such materials.

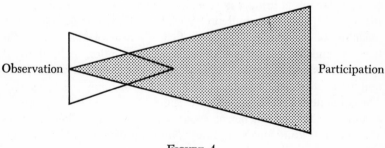

FIGURE 4

As Figure 4 shows, even during the student teacher's first day, there can be some involvement. The student teacher can bring a record to play, read or tell a story to the children, teach a game during the supervised play period or recess. He can help out during the independent work period (being careful not to do for children that which they can and should do for themselves). In situations where there is a firm commitment to the one-week observation period, it seems best to concentrate on observing specific children or small groups of children, specific kinds of lessons or areas of the curriculum. Taking notes, to be discussed later with the cooperating teacher, will help to focus the observation and help the cooperating teacher correct false impressions and/or add to the student's store of information about a child.

The following suggestions may be helpful to the student teacher as he begins the observation and participation phases of student teaching.

1. The student teacher should make sure the cooperating teacher knows he's eager to work, to try, to become a real part of the group as soon as possible. He should see what needs to be done and ask about doing it. Do the phonograph records need to be rearranged? Does the aquarium need to be cleaned? Is there some mimeograph work to be prepared? Does the "Room Helpers" chart need to be changed or a new one prepared? These are simple, routine tasks; but they are part of the elementary teacher's work, and they'll give the student teacher an opportunity to help and to learn more about teaching while he is getting to know more about the children and the cooperating teacher's methods of working with them.

2. The student teacher should come to student teaching prepared to work. He might bring a story he has selected to read or tell or some pictures to be used on a bulletin board. Even if the first day of student teaching is the student teacher's first glimpse of the school, the teacher, and the children, a telephone conversation or brief correspondence should give him some ideas for appropriate activities or materials which will help him make a place for himself in the group. The student teachers' appearance should also suggest a desire to assume the role of teacher as soon as possible—spike-heeled shoes and delicate, white angora sweaters (for example) do not convey this message very well, nor do short, tight skirts.

3. Note taking has already been suggested; however, the student teacher should be certain the cooperating teacher knows what is being written and why. The questions asked during a discussion of the notes should be phrased tactfully and without a trace of challenge;

for these first few days of student teaching are absolutely crucial in terms of establishing a friendly, relaxed relationship between the student teacher and the cooperating teacher. "Bobby seems to have trouble managing his time, doesn't he?" will evoke a more positive response than "Bobby played for the entire work period, and I noticed you didn't stop him; why?"

4. Although they are not the student teacher's only concern, almost inevitably the first children to be noticed are those at the academic, physical, or emotional extremes: the brightest, the heaviest, the angriest. Individual help for those needing help or challenge academically will usually be welcomed by the cooperating teacher. So will efforts at involving the withdrawn, shy child in the discussion of a book, or in a flash card drill, or in the preparation of a report for presentation to the group. Such activities provide an excellent opportunity to act on what has been learned in courses in child development and educational psychology. It should be noted that one doesn't make assumptions regarding the cause of a specific type of behavior on the second day of student teaching and on the basis of three anecdotal records. Cooperating teachers smile indulgently at the innocence and naiveté of the student teacher who cites the causes of and solutions to problems which have persisted for several years in spite of the best efforts of several competent and seasoned teachers. This is a situation which experience quickly corrects; by the third or fourth week, few student teachers will have easy solutions for complex problems.

The student teacher's role, in the beginning phases of student teaching, is that of learner as well as teacher. (Indeed, isn't every good teacher also a learner for as long as he teaches?) The learning will, however, be more effective and more efficient if the student teacher does more than sit. Active and early involvement in the learning and teaching experiences in the classroom will be of great benefit to the student teacher and will help give meaning and purpose to his observations.

The Cooperating Teacher's Role

The observation period is the most frustrating part of student teaching for many cooperating teachers. It generally takes an aspect of being supervised by a bright, attractive, up-to-date young professional. Even the most secure cooperating teacher has twinges of inadequacy, of wondering whether those critical eyes are pleased or appalled by what they see. The cooperating teacher needs to remind himself, frequently, that he has been selected because he is a superior teacher and has the ability to guide a young person through his first teaching experiences. An incident reported by Elizabeth Hunter serves to illustrate the cooperating teacher's dilemma:

Mrs. O'Brian greeted Jill warmly on Monday morning, and showed her around the room. "I'm afraid we won't be able to have a real conference until Wednesday," she said. "I have lunch duty all this week, we have a teachers meeting this afternoon, and tomorrow afternoon I attend a meeting of the mathematics committee. You see," Mrs. O'Brian added laughingly, "teachers are a busy lot. But if you are free on Wednesday, we can have a nice long conference after school."

"I am free on Wednesday," replied Jill, "and of course I'll stay."

"In the meantime," said Mrs. O'Brian, "you take as many notes as you like, and write down all the questions you have. I want you to feel free to move around the room and join with us in our informal activities, so that you get to know the children. I think you'll find that you fit into our room quite easily."

"Thank you," replied Jill. "I really do think I'll feel right at home here."

As Mrs. O'Brian watched Jill during the next three days, she was pleased by Jill's fine manner with the children. She seemed to know just when to join in any discussion, and she moved in to help whenever it was appropriate without having to be asked. "She's going to be excellent," thought Mrs. O'Brian.

Jill took frequent notes and was full of questions. As the sat in the back of the room, she thought, "Mrs. O'Brian seems to be very nice, but she certainly is old-fashioned! Gosh, the room is so quiet most of the time, it might as well be the morgue."

After the boys and girls had left for home on Wednesday afternoon, Jill and Mrs. O'Brian settled down for their agreed upon conference. Jill began:

"Well, I do have a few questions for you, Mrs. O'Brian, but I don't quite know where to begin."

"I'm glad you have a lot to ask about. That's a good sign," said Mrs. O'Brian. "Why don't you just run through them and then we can see which one we'll start off with."

"All right," replied Jill. "Now, for instance, why do you have the children raise their hands for speaking? Don't you think it would be better if they just joined in informally?

"And I noticed today in arithmetic that you didn't have them esti-
mate their answers before they began to work on the problems. Why
is that?

"Another question I have is, why do you use a spelling book? Don't
you ever use the words that come up in their daily living?

"And don't you think the classroom is awfully quiet? I always remember the remark I heard one teacher make, which struck me as
being awfully true—about a buzzing room being one where real learning was taking place."

Jill paused, "Shall I go on, Mrs. O'Brian, or would you like to discuss these questions first?"[1]

At this point, Mrs. O'Brian probably was sorry she had agreed to
work with a student teacher and was convinced children should be
reared *less*, not more, permissively in order that the exuberance of
future Jills might be curbed somewhat! Although it is little comfort,
it is a distinct compliment to Mrs. O'Brian that Jill felt she could
express her views so freely. If Mrs. O'Brian possesses the strength to
survive Jill's onslaught, she may suggest that Jill try managing a discussion group without hand raising and see how it goes. Mrs. O'Brian
may be surprised, but so may Jill.

Mrs. O'Brian's experience is not unusual, as any cooperating teacher
can testify. Although it's unfortunate that Jill's attack was so direct
and so extensive, Mrs. O'Brian can learn not to let concerns and questions wait for three days; she can learn to discuss aspects of her philosophy of teaching before the student teacher sooner so the student will
want to talk about problems related to her own teaching and will be
somewhat less critical of Mrs. O'Brian. It is to be hoped that with a
little more experience Jill will learn to be a bit less forthright and
more tactful. By responding to her questions calmly, objectively, and
with as much humor as can be mustered in a situation of this kind,
Mrs. O'Brian can help Jill grow as a teacher and can help her learn
a lesson in maintaining successful human relationships.

Not all student teachers are as critical as Jill; but in the beginning
days of student teaching, it is the rare cooperating teacher who
doesn't feel a bit uncomfortable while being observed. The student
teacher appears to be so eager to learn, so anxious for help with

---

[1] Elizabeth Hunter, *The Cooperating Teacher at Work: Case Studies of Critical Incidents* (New York: Bureau of Publications, Teachers College, Columbia
University, 1962), pp. 21–22.

methods, techniques, ideas. The cooperating teacher wonders, most of all, whether he's worthy of emulation—whether the example he's setting is good enough. That his example will be followed, that he will be influential, goes without saying. (Even Jill will be surprised to find next year that the "buzzing classroom" may not be as attractive as she thinks and that keeping the buzz from becoming a roar is no small task.) The wise cooperating teacher will not assume that he knows all the answers, or even all the questions. The approach, even during the observation period, will convey this message: "This works for me, with these children at this time. It may or may not work for you." The attitude will be one which will encourage questions and examination of techniques and methods. If the cooperating teacher is so sensitive that even implied criticism hurts, if he wants to hear only praise, he probably is not properly equipped to be a cooperating teacher.

A statement has already been made about the need for guiding the student teacher's observation, for doing more than telling the student to watch. I have maintained, too, that early involvement is very beneficial. This is also the position taken by Haines, who writes:

> Not all students will begin to teach in the same way. Every student teacher should, however, become involved from the beginning as a member of the class working along with the teacher. . . . The student learns more about the pupils and the class program, however, as he shares some responsibility in it. He may move about the room helping individual pupils while the teacher is teaching, enter into class routines as a co-teacher, or help a small group of pupils on his own. Some of these activities may be spontaneous; others may be carefully planned in advance.[2]

In selecting appropriate activities with which the student teachers might begin, two maxims might be suggested. First, let the student teacher's initial activities be in those areas in which he feels most secure. If the student teacher feels most confident in storytelling, in guiding dramatization or choral speaking, in doing a simple science demonstration, or in discussing the operations of a mathematical process—base two rather than base ten, for example—then, obviously,

---

[2] Alleyne C. Haines, *Guiding the Student Teaching Process in Elementary Education* (Chicago: Rand McNally & Co., 1960), pp. 99–104.

these are the activities with which he should begin. If the activities suggested above represent areas in which the student feels insecure and lacks confidence, then the wise cooperating teacher will permit and encourage delaying work in these areas at least until the student teacher feels at ease with the children and in the situation as a whole.

Second, be flexible. There is a danger that the student teacher will have a list of "things to do on the first day," and the cooperating teacher will have in mind certain beginning experiences which were successful for another student teacher. It may well be that neither list will be appropriate and will prevent both the student teacher and the cooperating teacher from observing the situation as it is now, from considering the student teacher's individual strengths and competencies, and from selecting activities which are fresh, interesting, and right for the teachers and the children.

The Cooperating Teacher as Observer

From the first, although the student teacher may not be aware of this, the cooperating teacher is observing as well as being observed. The student teacher's informal remarks to the children, the facility and speed with which names and routine procedures are learned, the interest shown in individual children and in the teaching materials in the classroom—all help to give the cooperating teacher some initial impressions of the student teacher and his readiness for professional tasks. The student teacher takes notes; so, also, should the cooperating teacher. These can form the basis for a productive first conference, at which time it can be tactfully pointed out to the student teacher that she didn't notice Marcia's missing tooth, even when Marcia extended the hand which held the tooth, that Bobby was running behind the swings on the playground and could have been seriously injured and that, again, the student teacher didn't notice. It is to be hoped, of course, that the notes relating to positive aspects of the student teacher's behavior will far outnumber the negative ones; but both types of notes, recorded examples of specific behavior traits, can certainly help the cooperating teacher guide the student teacher more effectively.

Will it make the student teacher nervous to know he's being observed and that the observations are being recorded? Probably so; it should be pointed out that one purpose of student teaching is to ascertain the prospective teacher's competence, skill, and general readiness to enter the profession. Making judgments and evaluating the work of the student teacher are inevitable parts of the student teaching process.

It should be mentioned that the notes can also serve as the basis for conferences between the university supervisor and the cooperating teacher.

The First Conference

It is the cooperating teacher who bears much of the responsibility for conducting the first conference in such a way that it will produce results.

We have seen that one of the problems illustrated in the account of the conference between Jill and Mrs. O'Brian was the delay in holding the first conference. The very basic and fundamental questions Jill was asking should not have been held for three days. The cooperating teacher and the student teacher should have arranged their schedules so that a conference could have been held after school on the very first day of student teaching. This should be informal, with the cooperating teacher almost anywhere but behind the desk; and the student teacher should feel free to discuss anything which has concerned him, assuming this discussion proceeds tactfully and with due regard for maintaining a constructive friendly relationship. If each participant in the conference acts with honesty, candor, and due regard for the feelings of the other, the professional growth of both participants will almost surely result.

The College Supervisor's Role

A brief visit, during the first or second day of student teaching, can assure the college supervisor that the student teacher is, indeed, on the job and can help the supervisor gain some insight into the developing relationship between the student teacher and his "critic." If it was impossible for the supervisor to visit the school before the student teaching period began, this visit will give him an overview of the facilities, the program, and the attitudes toward student teachers exhibited by members of the faculty.

Time should be provided for a brief conference with the student teacher and the cooperating teacher. Each should have the opportunity to present any problems which have arisen and to ask for the supervisor's help in assuring a good start for everyone involved in student teaching. In the great majority of cases, these conferences will be pleasant, full of the student teacher's delight with what he's doing and the cooperating teacher's happiness at working with such a bright, attractive young person.

On rare occasions, however, the conference is not this pleasant. When the student teacher indicates unhappiness with the teacher, the school, the children, or the student teaching situation in general and asks that he be removed from the student teaching situation, the supervisor is put in a difficult position. Removing a student teacher is a serious matter. Relations with the pubilc school personnel, and with the cooperating teacher especially, will be seriously strained. In the section of this chapter in which placements were discussed, it was pointed out that there is a disparity between the number of good situations needed and the number available. To transfer a student teacher to another situation will be difficult, especially after student teaching has been underway for some time. All of this should be explained to the student teacher, and he needs to be made fully aware of the serious implications of his request. If necessary adjustments can be made within the existing situation it will probably be better for everyone concerned. It should be clear, however, that the student teacher is entitled to a hearing, a full redress of his grievances; and there are justifications for changing the situation if relationships have become so poor that success in student teaching is impossible. Even less frequently, the cooperating teacher will request a change. In such a case, the same guidelines suggested above should apply. The problem should be aired, the student teacher's position made clear, and attempts made to solve the problem within the existing setting.

During this first conference, the activities in which the student teacher is engaged should be discussed with the student teacher and with the cooperating teacher. If the student teacher isn't being given a chance to do anything but sit, or if the best effort of the cooperating teacher to produce some activity other than sitting have met with little success, the supervisor has the responsibility of helping to resolve the problem, probably by initiating a three-way conference in which each participant gives his views. The student teacher and the cooperating teacher should understand, before student teaching begins, what activities will be typical of the first days of student teaching. It is the supervisor's job to see that the student teacher knows he will be expected to share a story or plan for some activity which will cause him to find a place in the group, and the cooperating teacher should be reminded that the student teacher will learn by example, of course, but, like the children, will learn most effectively by doing. During this first phase of student teaching, the college supervisor's role is that of listener, observer, and facilitator. If, after listening and observing, the supervisor feels sure that some drastic action must be taken, the greatest tact and diplomacy are required.

Much emphasis has been placed on the value of on-the-scene supervision. I disagree with those supervisors who say, "I don't visit during the first week; let them get settled and adjusted first." The college supervisor can do so much to ease the adjustment, to settle minor problems before they become big ones, and to let both the student teacher and the cooperating teacher know that the supervisor hasn't abandoned them but is concerned, interested, and eager to help. The first few days of student teaching are important, too important to be ignored by campus personnel. The college supervisor's role in the observation and participation phase of student teaching is not as active as and is perhaps somewhat less significant than the role of the cooperating teacher and the student teacher. He can, however, aid them in performing their duties more effectively and efficiently.

When Does the Student Get to Teach?

By discussing together two aspects of student teaching—observation and participation—which many writers and practitioners separate, I have attempted to underscore the close relationship between the two, to point out that the two proceed together and that a sharp line of demarcation ("During the first week you'll observe; the second week is when you'll participate.") should not exist in good student teaching situations.

Nor is there a clear and sharp division between observation and participation and "teaching." The student teacher who helps a confused fifth-grader with some social studies research is teaching. So is the student teacher who leads a discussion of a favorite composer and plays a recording of selections from his work. Teaching is not defined as the act of standing in front of a group of children with a textbook.

The cooperating teacher will gradually involve the student teacher more and more in deciding what areas of the curriculum to include in the work for the next day, or the next week, and in determining how these should be approached. ("What would you think of letting Joe's [a pupil's] group work on long division another day or so? Although the other groups seem to understand it, I don't think those six children do—do you?") Gradually, most of the suggestions become the student teacher's, more and more of the classroom management details are handled by the student teacher ("I'll go with the children to the library today, if you like, Mr. Jones; I wanted to ask Mrs. Martin about a book for storytime anyway.").

Telling a student teacher, "Tomorrow I want you to teach" will often have several results—none desirable; it will probably cause increased tension, fear, and less effective work with the children. How much better to be able to say at the end of a rewarding day, "Bob, do you realize that you were in charge for almost the entire day? I noticed that now the children are asking you instead of me for permission to leave the room. You are a teacher!" Far too much importance has been placed on the student's first experience before the whole class with the assigned task of presenting some new material in an understandable manner. This is not the total teaching process, any more than it is the total learning process. Working with the whole class and/or presenting some new material should grow out of other teaching-learning experiences in which the student teacher has taken part. The suggestion that the student teacher is ready to guide the children in a particular experience should, preferably, not come from the cooperating teacher but from the student teacher.

The student teacher who is showing normal growth and making adequate progress soon reaches the point at which he wants to have more responsibility. The cooperating teacher and the college supervisor welcome this, encourage it in fact; and if the gradual induction into the various aspects of teaching described in previous sections of this chapter has been characteristic of the student's activities, then the student probably *is* as ready for major responsibility as he thinks he is.

The two cases below detail the roles of the student teacher, the cooperating teacher, and the university supervisor in the decision to transfer major responsibility for the children's growth from the cooperating teacher to the student teacher.

The Anxious Student Teacher

As the supervisor is preparing to leave Highland School, Ann Johnson asks whether she can talk with him. "Of course," Dr. Edwards replies; could you leave now for lunch? I noticed a nice little restaurant down the street where we could talk and have lunch together." He is a little surprised at the request; Ann has apparently been making good progress. She was busily working each time he had visited, once with a remedial math group, another time helping to prepare a science demonstration. "She hasn't mentioned any problems, so what could be wrong?" he wonders.

His curiosity is soon satisfied. After they have placed their luncheon order, Ann comes right to the point: "Dr. Edwards, I've signed a contract to teach here in University Town. It's the grade level I want; and I'm very pleased, except for one thing—I don't know whether I can teach or not! I've almost begged Miss James to let me try all the reading groups and help with the independent study time too, because I know I'll have to do this next fall. She just smiles and tells me not to be in such a hurry! The three of us agreed on the things I could do to help learn about the children and what goes into a good day for them; I've done all this! I've read stories, taught games and songs, worked with every possible kind of small group—fast, slow, special interest. I've done each bulletin board twice. Well, Dr. Edwards, it's the end of the third week of student teaching. I think I'm ready to find out what I can do on my own. Can you help me?"

Ann's record at the university has been a good one, and Dr. Edwards has expected a high level of performance in student teaching from her. Although he hasn't been especially concerned, now that it is brought to his attention, he realizes that she isn't doing as much as he has expected she would by this time. In telling him of her problem, she hasn't been behaving immaturely or letting her emotions get out of control (she was obviously enjoying her lunch), and Dr. Edwards decides he'd better go back to Highland School with her and talk with Miss James.

Dr. Edwards' conference with Miss James leads to a successful solution to the problem. Miss James is sorry to learn that her desire not to push Ann too much has resulted in her feeling that she isn't learning. The next time Dr. Edwards visits the school, Miss James is not even in the building—she is visiting a classroom in the campus laboratory school. Ann is having minor control problems, but for the most part the day is going quite well. Ann was right. She was ready for this stage; she was ready to begin teaching on her own.

Of course, the student teacher's instincts regarding his readiness for major responsibilities cannot always be relied upon and are, in fact, far from infallible. This is the reason Dr. Edwards decided to check with Miss James and did not say, "Why, of course, Ann, you should have been in charge days ago; I'll speak to Miss James immediately!" There are many, many stories of student teachers who failed; and involved in the failure were attitudes of overconfidence and impatience. We are not born with the ability to be objective, and some of us never achieve this state; a student teacher must depend, in part, upon the guidance of those who are more mature and who have watched many other student teachers begin professional careers. Some student teachers do know their limitations and strengths and can assess their growth; *all* student teachers need to have a part in deciding when they start to teach.

The Reluctant Cooperating Teacher

Mr. Brown, the principal of Washington School, has observed Mrs. Wilson, a bright and attractive young teacher, for two years; she recently acquired her Master's degree and has requested that she be assigned a student teacher in the fall. The university director of student teaching relies upon the principal's judgment in these matters (the university places several hundred student teachers a year, and "screening" visits are not possible). Mr. Brown visits Mrs. Wilson's classroom one morning for the express purpose of noting her qualifications for working with a student teacher. She is an excellent teacher. Her classroom is neat, attractive, and stimulating; the children seem

happy and busy. There is a bit more moving around, more conversation, a more permissive atmosphere than Mr. Brown considers desirable; but on the whole he sees no reason for denying Mrs. Wilson's
request. A young teacher should profit a great deal from working
with someone who has so many ideas and who seems to be in touch
with all of the newer methods in education.

Imagine Mr. Brown's surprise when at the end of the next semester
the director of student teaching suggests that Mrs. Wilson not be
given another student teacher. What happened?

Ellen Brown is the unfortunate student teacher who was placed in
Mrs. Wilson's first grade. Ellen was delighted after the preliminary
visits—it was like a dream come true, and everything her methods
teachers had advocated was being put into practice! Mrs. Wilson had
such a warm, motherly manner with the children. She used lots of
materials; experience charts were everywhere! She seemed interested
in Ellen's farm unit, even mentioned a farm the class might visit.

Soon after student teaching began, Ellen started to feel that something was wrong. The children asked for permission to do *everything*,
and Mrs. Wilson seemed to encourage this. There was no evidence
that children's ideas were ever sought—Mrs. Wilson said first-graders
were much too young for any pupil-teacher planning. Ellen was
shocked when Bobby asked Mrs. Wilson where the tree in his farm
picture should be—and Mrs. Wilson told him! Matters soon became
worse. Mrs. Wilson became almost angry when Susan asked Ellen
whether she could use the office telephone. It was increasingly clear
that Mrs. Wilson wanted an assistant, not a student teacher. Ellen
wanted to skip one of the stories in the primer. It dealt with the Christmas holidays and it was then late March. She proposed developing
most of the vocabulary through a group-dictated story. The answer
was a flat, unqualified "No." Although Ellen had fully met what she
considered all the "preliminary steps" to working with the children
on her own, Mrs. Wilson never left the classroom for more than ten
minutes. One day, before a trip to a farm, Ellen asked the children to
draw farm pictures to show what they expected to see there. With a
triumphant smile, Mrs. Wilson quickly displayed a cardboard farm
scene which she had purchased at a local bookstore, and each of the
children produced a farm scene remarkably like the model. Ellen
could have cried—did, in fact, when she got back to the dormitory
that afternoon. That evening she called Mrs. Kent, her supervisor,

and told her everything. Mrs. Kent was appalled and was sorry something hadn't been done, or at least said, sooner. Unfortunately, Mrs. Kent was taking her preliminary exams that semester and hadn't made as many visits as she'd intended to. (Ellen smiled ruefully when Mrs. Kent apologized. Mrs. Kent had visited once, the first week, and had been so favorably impressed with the classroom and the superficial evidence of "newer methods" that Ellen was certain she had decided then that no further visits would be necessary.) Since it was the third week of student teaching, too late for a transfer (the state required eight full weeks of student teaching, and there were just barely that many weeks left in the semester), the decision was made that Ellen should continue her student teaching and try to do as much as she could. Mrs. Kent recommended to the director of student teaching that no student teachers be placed with Mrs. Wilson in the future. It was, of course, too late to help Ellen. One can only hope that she was able to manage her own classroom in the fall.

The principal has not been as observant as he should have been; or he has been unaware of the importance of selecting a cooperating teacher who will free, not restrict, the student teacher, who will treat student teaching as an internship, not an apprenticeship. Mrs. Wilson is to be pitied, of course, and so are the children she teaches, because they're not being guided toward independence as they should be. She is even more obviously unfit to guide student teachers, since, as Ellen soon discovered, she really wanted an assistant, one who would follow directions and do as she was told. Mrs. Wilson encouraged dependence, not independence; and the most modern "methods" in the world cannot disguise this.

The opposite approach, leaving the classroom completely when the student teacher enters, is equally disastrous. The student teacher who flounders helplessly, without guidance, because the cooperating teacher believes that "the sooner they try their wings the better" is as poorly prepared, or more so, than Ellen. Ellen at least had the benefit of a fairly good example of teaching techniques, and there was someone with whom she could test ideas. When the cooperating teacher abandons the student teacher, the college supervisor must, first of all, tactfully suggest to the cooperating teacher that the correct term is *student teacher*, not *substitute teacher*. Although it is perhaps unfortunate that some time must be spent in the classroom, rather than completing master's theses, term papers, or committee assignments, this is a responsibility which accompanies the acceptance of a student teacher. The college supervisor may also have to pay more frequent visits to the student teacher who is virtually alone than to the student teacher who can depend upon the cooperating teacher for some help, guidance, and suggestions. As with Mrs. Wilson, there should be a note to the director of student teaching that the deserter will not be used again! Student teachers deserve something better.

With each of the two extreme and unusual cases described above, the problem of natural progression through a series of steps leading to almost complete autonomy for the student teacher does not exist. Ellen did not progress beyond the observation-participation stage and will not until she has her own classroom. In the second type of student teaching situation, the student was plunged immediately into teaching, without any preliminary observation and participation. In both cases, the students did not get the guidance and help which they deserved from the cooperating teacher. In both cases, the cooperating teachers were unworthy of the trust and responsibility placed upon them.

SUMMARY

In this chapter there has been an effort to detail the cooperating teacher's responsibilities in guiding the student teacher through the early phases of student teaching and toward full responsibility and readiness for a classroom of his own. The college supervisor also bears a responsibility for this part of the student teaching experience. In the conferences and communications which occur before student teaching, the supervisor can inform the cooperating teacher of what is expected, help him define his role, and explain that eventually the student teacher must show he can stand alone, independent and competent. Otherwise, the university, and ultimately the state, *cannot* and *should not* certify the prospective teacher.

If, as in the cases detailed in the preceding section, serious mistakes are made in placement, and the mistakes are discovered too late to be corrected by transfer of the student teacher to another classroom, the college supervisor must attempt to fill both roles. He must cause the student who is being smothered to question, to disagree, and to discuss—even if he can't try them—alternative methods, materials, and techniques not approved by the cooperating teacher. To the student teacher who is receiving no help at all, the supervisor attempts to make more frequent visits, even if they must be short visits, and to stand in for the cooperating teacher in conferences following a lesson taught by the student teacher. In such situations the supervisor may even do a bit of demonstration teaching, since the student teacher has no other teacher to observe. The supervisor will probably make certain that the building principal is informed of classroom teachers who use student teachers as substitutes; this is a tactful way of suggesting that he avoid this practice himself!

The observation and participation phases of student teaching are not completely separate and distinct groups of activities, and the wise cooperating teacher will involve the beginner in both types of activities almost from the beginning. The position has been taken that the sharp divisions which appear to exist between observation and participation in a few student teaching programs, and as described by many writers, should not and do not, in fact, exist in good student teaching situations. The student teacher will learn most as he has an opportunity to test, to try, to become thoroughly and completely involved with the group.

The observation and participation phase should lead, gradually but directly, into major responsibility for teaching. Again, there is no sharp dividing line; but through guidance and involvement in the planning the cooperating teacher does, the student teacher will come to recognize his readiness for increased responsibility and will request it. The college supervisor may need to encourage more freedom for the student teacher or more vigorous activity on the part of the student teacher. Neither task is formidable, if relationships between the cooperating teacher, the student teacher, and the supervisor are of the quality described throughout this chapter.

The decision to accept major responsibility for teaching should be the student teacher's, although he may need to be encouraged or delayed a bit, if his judgment of his readiness is not supported by that of the college supervisor and/or the cooperating teacher. The acceptance of major responsibility is based upon successful performance in work with small groups and individuals as well as adequate knowledge of the pupils, their program, and the available materials and facilities for teaching.

The ultimate question asked by the teacher education institution and the state certification officials is: Can this person perform his professional duties competently and independently? The student teaching situation must provide an opportunity to answer this question. If the supervisor never visits the classroom, the college or university must be in some doubt about this matter. If the cooperating teacher never removes himself physically from the classroom to let the student teacher discover for himself what his abilities are, no one is very sure how this vital question should be answered.

If, however, the induction into teaching has been gradual, based on adequate participation and observation, and if the student teacher has been helped, through frequent conferences with his "critic" and his supervisor to look objectively at his strengths and weaknesses, the first major teaching assignment can almost surely be completed successfully.

Suggested Activities for Student Teachers

1. Gather data, as specified below, about the children in your student teaching classroom. These data may be collected in a notebook for sharing and discussion at a group meeting, for the perusal of the college supervisor, and to serve as a basis for conferences with the cooperating teacher.
   a) Refer to your text in educational psychology for guidelines for anecdotal records. Collect a few of these for each child in your student teaching group, or select several children for more thorough study.
   b) Survey the children's cumulative records and note scores on tests of academic achievement and intelligence.
   c) Ask for a copy of the cooperating teacher's daily program or schedule. Discuss with him the basis for the organization of the day, and the role of specialists (such as the music teacher or art teacher).

2. Prepare a list of things to do for the first day of student teaching. The purpose of these activities should be to help you gain a place in the group, to establish yourself as a teacher. Select a book to read, a game or a song to teach; prepare a bulletin board or a demonstration. Discuss these with your supervisor and cooperating teacher, and compare your suggestions with those of other student teachers.

3. Begin keeping a journal, log, or diary, in which you reflect objectively and positively upon the experiences of a day or several days. Such a journal need not be shared with other student teachers but may give insight and guidance to the supervisor and/or cooperating teacher.

Selected References

Burr, James B., Harding, Lowry W., and Jacobs, Leland B. *Student Teaching in the Elementary School.* New York: Appleton-Century-Crofts, 1958, Chapter 2, "Learning From Your Observations;" Chapter 3, "Extending Your Participation."

Concern for the Individual in Student Teaching. (Forty-second Yearbook.) Cedar Falls, Iowa: The Association for Student Teaching, 1963.

Goltry, T. Keith, and Dewey, Joseph C. *A Guidebook in Observation and Student Teaching.* Minneapolis: Burgess Publishing Co., 1953, Unit I, "Learning to Know the Pupils;" Unit II, "Getting Acquainted with the Room and Its Equipment."

Haines, Aleyne. *Guiding the Student Teaching Process.* Chicago: Rand McNally & Co., 1960, Chapter 1, "Student Teaching Situations;" Chapter 2, "Teacher Education Institutions and Public Schools Share Responsibility."

Hunter, Elizabeth. *The Cooperating Teacher at Work: Case Studies of Critical Incidents.* New York: Bureau of Publications, Teachers College, Columbia University, 1962.

————, and Amidon, Edmund. *Student Teaching: Cases and Comments.* New York: Holt, Rinehart & Winston, Inc., 1964.

Teacher Education and the Public Schools. (Fortieth Yearbook.) Cedar Falls, Iowa: The Association for Student Teaching, 1961.

Wingo, G. Max, and Schorling, Raleigh. *The Elementary School Student Teacher.* New York: McGraw-Hill Book Co., Inc., 1960, Chapter 2, "A Successful Teacher at Work."

4

Planning in Student Teaching

The roles of the three major participants in the student teaching experience must come clearly into focus in any discussion of the several types of planning for which a student teacher assumes responsibility. It is, or should be, obvious to the student teacher, the college supervisor, and the cooperating teacher that the prospective teacher's success or failure will be due in no small measure to his ability to see clearly the objectives, procedures, and resources which will result in the types of learning experiences from which pupils will derive the greatest benefit. In this chapter are detailed some of the major responsibilities and concerns of the student teacher, the college supervisor, and the cooperating teacher as they relate and interrelate in the long-range and day-to-day planning for and with a group of pupils. The roles of each of the major participants in the student teaching experience will be discussed, as each relates to helping the student teacher more effectively.

THE COOPERATING TEACHER'S ROLE

There are many ways in which the cooperating teacher can help the student teacher plan more effectively. One is through the example

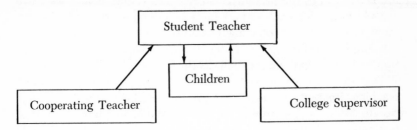

FIGURE 5. PARTICIPANTS IN PLANNING

set by the manner in which the cooperating teacher plans and by the types of planning he does. It would seem wise for the cooperating teacher to show the student teacher samples of his plans quite early in the student teaching experience. This will help the student teacher gain much more from the observation period than he could if he were unaware of the teacher's objectives and of his reasons for using certain procedures and materials with various groups of children. It would also seem wise to help the novice become acquainted, during the first week of student teaching, with accepted planning procedures: For what periods of time are plans made, and when does this planning occur? Is there a special format for written plans, which administrators expect the writer to follow? Are plans of a certain type to be handed in to your principal at a specified time each week or month? These are details which are seldom discussed in any college methods class. If lesson plans are handed in as a part of the work of a language methods class, for example, they are necessarily broad in scope and are often devised without any specific group of children in mind. The importance of helping the student teacher in this area cannot be overestimated.

Assisting the student teacher in becoming acquainted with one type of planning does not imply that this is the only way in which planning can or should occur. This should be made clear at the outset. At the time of the first conference about planning, it should be pointed out that although this method and these techniques seem appropriate in the situation in which the cooperating teacher works and for the methods he uses, other methods and techniques may be best for the student teacher. It seems honest and forthright to state, "The principal asks that we keep a plan book of this type. Carbons of our plans are handed in to the principal's office every Friday before we leave school." Elementary school principals are often forced to this requirement as a means of protecting substitute teachers and children, and it is hardly fair to keep the student teacher in ignorance of a regulation with such wide implications as this.

Two extreme positions are frequently operative in the student teaching situation. In one, the cooperating teacher states, in hopeless resignation, "There's nothing we can do. We have adopted series of textbooks, each with very explicit teachers' guides, and a principal with very definite ideas about teaching procedures. My planning consists of deciding which reading texts to use with which reading group and determining how many pages a day to cover in other subject areas. This is a matter of dividing numbers of pages into numbers of instructional periods. Even these are specified in our curriculum guide." This position can hardly be encouraging to the young student teacher about to enter a profession obviously held in so little respect by a practitioner. At the opposite extreme is the cooperating teacher who tells the neophyte, "Feel free to do anything you like! This is your room, now!" A statement such as this leads to frustration as deep and serious as that which results from the first position. It is really worse, because it is essentially dishonest. No teacher in the employ of a board of education, working as a member of a teaching faculty, is entirely free to do anything he likes. No prospective teacher should leave the student teaching experience with the impression that such freedom exists.

The answer to the first question, "How closely should the student teacher be expected to follow my plans?" would appear to be this: as closely, at first, as the student needs to follow them. It is, however, part of the professional responsibility of the cooperating teacher to encourage independence, self-reliance, and creativity in the student teacher. The fact that the cooperating teacher has been asked to work with a student teacher indicates that he is regarded as a highly competent professional. It should be clear, however, that the student teacher is a different person, with different strengths and weaknesses. He could not teach as the cooperating teacher teaches or plan precisely as he plans, even if he wanted to. It is part of the cooperating teacher's responsibility to show him that this would not be desirable even if it were possible.

Most student teachers are well aware of the fact that they are, essentially, guests in a school, that developing totally new areas of the curriculum and rearranging the classroom schedule are somewhat outside their limited areas of responsibility. A commonly expressed attitude is, "Oh, but I couldn't try that—could I? It isn't my classroom, you know." The student teacher's desire to please, to fit in, sometimes mitigates against creativity and the practice of his beliefs about education. The typical student teacher needs encouragement, and the cooperating teacher is in the ideal position to provide this encouragement.

It is my belief that planning in such large areas of the curriculum as a social studies unit should be a cooperative venture. Successful long-range planning is contingent upon extensive knowledge of children, their needs, interests, and previous school experiences. The student teacher can hardly be expected to acquire the same background of knowledge in a few weeks which the cooperating teacher has accumulated through a much longer period of studying each child and working closely with him. Even the student teacher who begins in the fall, soon after the opening of school, lacks the information which has been collected through conferences with teachers at the preceding grade level and through studying the cumulative records. Moreover, the cooperating teacher probably knows far more than the student teacher does about appropriate and available resources for a unit of work. He is familiar with the library resources and the school's policy regarding trips and outside speakers. Such information is invaluable in planning any major curricular venture. For these and many other reasons it seems prudent to plan as a team when planning all-important social studies, language arts, or science experiences. It may be appropriate to suggest that it is wise to involve administrators in planning of this type. Children will, of course, participate as their level of maturity and previous experiences permit.

The cooperating teacher has a definite responsibility in helping to develop the student teacher's competence in pupil-teacher planning. It is very important that the student teacher see the cooperating teacher work with the children in making plans. Planning sessions are probably a daily occurrence in his classroom. If so, the student teacher sees these as effective vehicles for teaching skills involved in democratic group processes. Watching may not be enough, however, for the student who has personally experienced little of this type of teaching and learning. With student teachers, as with children, one begins where the learner is. For example, one student teacher may learn quickly through watching the cooperating teacher listen to ideas, develop criteria, and reach decisions, all within a democratic framework which prizes the individual and his unique contribution. Soon the novice may be ready to try this approach himself. Another student teacher may see this as a good way of working with children and ask intelligent and perceptive questions about it but be unable to work in this way himself. Because of the cooperating teacher's maturity and experience, the student teacher will look to him for guidance; and the student deserves to receive it. The cooperating teacher will be able to see possible pitfalls in the plan: some important learning resources may not be available, or the question to be decided might be too large for this group to handle. Failure to steer the student teacher gently but firmly away from these danger spots may well result in the decision never to try pupil-teacher planning again, since "it obviously doesn't work"!

Another responsibility is that of providing the student teacher with as much information about the children as possible. This is not so much to protect the student teacher from unfortunate incidents which could have been anticipated as to help the student learn that the effective teacher knows his pupils and acts upon this knowledge. In a few school systems the cumulative records are locked in the principal's file and are not available to the student teachers. This is unfortunate and contributes little to the student's acquisition of professional attitudes toward confidential information.

Several principles have been stated and implied in the preceding discussion of the cooperating teacher's role in planning and in helping the student teacher to plan more effectively:

1. No student teacher can copy the methods and techniques of the cooperating teacher in planning. This should not be expected and would not be desirable even if it were possible.

2. It is the responsibility of the cooperating teacher to inform the student teacher of any limitations within which each will work and of any special requirements regarding planning. In no circumstances should the student teacher gain the impression that his professional freedom exists without accompanying responsibilities.

3. Student teachers will vary tremendously in their ability to plan. The cooperating teacher will take each student teacher as he is and will help him grow. This help will be in the form of good example,

from the first day of student teaching, and in the nature of questions the teacher asks which will cause the student teacher constantly to evaluate his objectives and his procedures.

THE COLLEGE SUPERVISOR'S ROLE

For a number of years, college supervisors have used the lesson plans made by student teachers as a basis for evaluating the student's professional effectiveness. Student teachers from one large university keep two sets of plans for each lesson to be taught. One set is *used*; notes are made on it during the lesson, and it is referred to as a basis for further teaching. The other set is typed very neatly and follows a rigidly prescribed pattern. Such plans are given to the supervisor for reference during each visit. This practice seems somewhat unrealistic, time-consuming, and of little value to the student teacher. It does, perhaps, condition the student teacher to accept dictation from an administrator regarding the form and content of lesson plans, but such conditioning can hardly be called desirable.

The work of the college supervisor provides many opportunities for in-service work with teachers. As a direct result of work with student teachers and their supervisors, the following changes were observed in the classrooms of cooperating teachers: Miss A is now trying a newer and more flexible approach to reading; Mrs. B no longer has the desks arranged in changeless rows; and Mr. C is doing some ability grouping in mathematics. These are concrete and desirable outgrowths of the student teaching experience and of work with the college personnel involved. This is not to say, however, that the role of college supervisor is identical with that of the curriculum coordinator or school administrator. Much as the student teacher is a guest in a school system, so is his college supervisor. If the presence of the supervisor is irritating, if he is constantly pointing to areas where he feels the educational program of a school or school system should be improved, little will be accomplished toward the major goal of helping the student teacher progress toward full membership in his chosen profession.

A broad spectrum of educational beliefs and practices is apparent today even to the nonprofessional. It is unavoidable that some practices in some school systems will be difficult for the college supervisor to accept. If a majority of the practices and policies of a school system are unsound and contrary to the findings of accepted educational research, it seems wise not to place student teachers there in the future. This is the province of the director of student teaching, in the larger institutions at least; and he will almost certainly accept, and act upon, the recommendation of the college supervisor. Once the student teacher is assigned, placed, and has entered upon at least the observation phase of student teaching, however, the role of the supervisor can no longer be that of critic or judge of the school system. The supervisor's primary responsibilities are those of helping the student teacher to grow professionally and of working closely with the cooperating teacher as he tries to achieve the same purpose.

It would seem essential to know the curricular framework within which the student teacher is working, what the cooperating teacher and the student teacher are free to do and what the may not do. The answer to the first question would appear to be, in part, that the planning done with and by the student teacher must be within the established framework of the school system selected as a student teaching center. The college supervisor has a tremendous influence upon the cooperating teacher's teaching methods and procedures, but this influence is wielded subtly and almost by indirection. Several examples of real curricular change which have resulted from conversations, discussions, and conferences between the cooperating teacher and the college supervisor have already been cited. The reader will undoubtedly be able to suggest many more. The supervisor is well aware that any question which begins "Mary [the student teacher] has indicated an interest in trying. . . ." is a loaded question, carrying with it the weight of the prestige of the college or university. This does not alter the fact that the role of college supervisor does not involve major curricular reform.

When the cooperating teacher suggests that the student teacher is spending a disproportionate amount of time in planning and that it might be better to rely upon the textbook guides for most of the planning, the supervisor is placed in a rather unenviable position. It would appear that a stand must be taken and that the professional growth of the student teacher will be enhanced if the supervisor's response is based on the following principles:

1. The best planning rests upon thorough knowledge of content (the guide can be very helpful here) and equally thorough knowl-

edge of the children in the group for whom the lesson is intended. The guide can be of little service in supplying knowledge of the group to be taught and of the individuals in a given group.

2. The student teacher lacks the experience and seasoned judgment of the classroom teacher. This makes selection of sections of the guide which are appropriate for the student teacher's purposes most difficult for him. Unless the student teacher submits to the discipline of writing plans, however brief, the selection is likely to be haphazard and based only upon the needs of the moment.

3. An important outgrowth of the student teaching experience would appear to be increased knowledge of teaching resources and materials, including not only the textbook but other resources as well—films, tape recordings, etc. Although a compatible relationship between the cooperating teacher and the student teacher is an important element in a successful student teaching experience, it is also essential that the student teacher grow toward effective teaching. Encouragement of textbook-centered teaching will only serve to perpetuate a number of educational ills.

Opportunities for developing the skills involved in teacher-pupil planning exist in almost every student teaching situation. The college supervisor and the cooperating teacher, working together, can help the student teacher recognize these opportunities and improve his methods and techniques of working with children democratically. Ideally, the student teacher has experienced involvement in setting goals and determining procedures from elementary school through each one of his professional courses, and he has watched the cooperating teacher utilize teacher-pupil planning many times. If the student teacher has this background, teacher-pupil planning will be an accepted part of his work with children. Unfortunately, many student teachers lack this experience, and the college supervisor must provide or help provide situations in which the skills which make pupil-teacher planning a truly effective classroom teaching procedure might be developed. There are a few student teaching situations in which the student teacher seldom sees the cooperating teacher involve children in planning. In such situations the college supervisor may help the student teacher survey lesson plans already approved by the cooperating teacher, with the purpose of locating appropriate opportunities for planning with children: Committee work is suggested for the social studies period. Could the children help decide what types of committees would function, and on which committees they wish to serve? A discussion related to room housekeeping problems is scheduled. Would it be more effective for children to choose their jobs (dusting, watering plants, etc.) rather than to have them assigned by the teacher? A trip is planned. Instead of having all details of the trip planned by the cooperating teacher and the student teacher, could the children help determine the questions they hope to have answered on the trip, the means of transportation, etc.?

It may be necessary to suggest that the student teacher observe pupil-teacher planning outside the student teaching situation. Of course, it is preferable for the student teacher to see the cooperating teacher use this technique and then to learn to use it with the group he knows best. Pupil-teacher planning, however, is so important that the supervisor may find it necessary to ask the student to take an "observation day" and visit a classroom where this method of teaching and working with children is in continuous operation. Values must be weighed, and occasionally a cooperating teacher may possess enough qualities associated with teaching skill to compensate for limitations in this area. Freeing the student to visit in another classroom may be one way of acquainting him with a procedure he cannot observe in his own situation.

The student teacher who is placed with a gifted and creative teacher faces a challenge and has a unique opportunity for growth. A strong student teacher will welcome the chance to watch such a person at work and will not be overwhelmed. A less capable student teacher will need the supervisor's help in developing increased self-confidence, identifying and building upon his own strengths, and adapting those of the cooperating teacher's methods that seem appropriate for his own use. The cooperating teacher will almost certainly be aware of the student teacher's feelings of inadequacy and will work with the supervisor in helping the student teacher develop a healthy professional self-concept. There will certainly be areas in which the student teacher is effective, and he should be helped to identify these. Perhaps the student who feels very inadequate needs to be left alone with the children, to test his own abilities, even more than the typical student teacher, and needs to be left alone sooner. This recommendation presupposes that the student teacher possesses at least minimal competence, identified by college or university personnel before placement, before, indeed, selecting the student to be enrolled in elementary education courses.

The principles that have been stated and implied in the preceding discussion are these:

1. One person's attempting to fill the roles of both curriculum consultant and supervisor of student teachers will usually contribute to ineffectiveness in both roles.

2. The student teacher should be helped to identify strengths in in his own planning methods and to recognize factors in the student teaching situation, which will contribute to further growth.

3. The college supervisor may at times have to insist on types of planning, by the student teacher which are not consistent with methods used by the cooperating teacher. Although the cooperating teacher may operate successfully using the various teachers' guides as the basis for most of his class work, this is not a practice which should be recommended for beginners.

4. If teacher-pupil planning cannot be observed in the student teaching situation, it may be necessary to suggest that the student teacher observe in a situation where this method is utilized. Needless to say, this will be handled in a most tactful manner ("I thought Joe might enjoy spending a day with Mrs. E.; I think it's good for student teachers to see different ways of teaching, don't you?").

THE STUDENT TEACHER'S ROLE

From the moment he enters the classroom in which he is to work, the student teacher is aware of the need for order, for routine, for planning. The more flexible the program is, the greater is the need for planning. Michaelis writes:

> Carefully prepared plans will help to make your student teaching more effective in several ways. Once you have analyzed the situation in which you are to teach and have made effective plans based on that analysis, you can proceed in the following manner.
>
> You can develop, organize, and use as guides in your teaching, practical and realistic purposes for a particular group of children. You can systematically consider ways to secure interest and attention, giving specific care to devising procedures and materials that will create a high level of motivation. You can achieve freedom from routine procedures, thus making it possible for you to give maximum attention to the direction of learning. You can avoid wasting valuable time, because activities and materials will have been carefully or-

ganized. You can meet the individual needs of children and make their experiences meaningful, because your plans will be based on study of the individuals in your class. You can achieve flexibility in your procedures, because you will have a framework in which changes can be made as special needs and problems arise. In addition, well-made plans will give you a feeling of confidence and security in the classroom, because you will have definite, appropriate experiences ready for your group.[1]

Figure 6 suggests the multiple considerations involved in the process we term with deceptive simplicity *planning*.

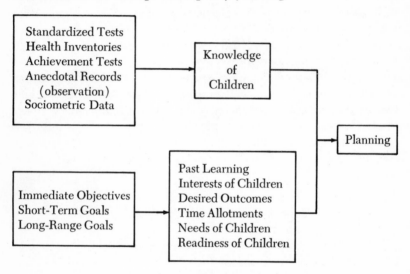

FIGURE 6. THE PLANNING PROCESS

As Michaelis suggests, the student teacher's planning occurs at several levels and is of several different types. Underlying this activity and guiding the student teacher as he plans with and for the children is the principle that successful planning rests upon a solid framework of child study. It is difficult if not impossible to plan intelligently without knowledge of the children for whom the plans are designed. These questions must be answered: (*a*) What are the intellectual

---

[1] John U. Michaelis and Paul R. Grim, *The Student Teacher in the Elementary School* (Englewood Cliffs, New Jersey: Prentice-Hall, Inc., 1953), p. 83.

characteristics of the children in this group? (*b*) What is their record of academic achievement? (*c*) What kinds of homes do these
children come from? Do the mothers of most of the children work
outside the home? What religious and socioeconomic groups are
represented in the community? (*d*) Are there special physical needs
a teacher should consider? Do any children have visual defects, hearing defects, or health problems which are not obvious to the observer?
(*e*) What information is available concerning the social relationships
within the class? Are any children rejected by most members of the
group? (*f*) What are the children's interests? Are they typical of
those of most children at this age and grade level? What special interests (hobbies, collections, etc.) are represented? There are several
ways in which the student teacher can gather this information. Con-
ferring with the cooperating teacher and carefully surveying the
school's cumulative records would be first steps. The following information is included in most cumulative records, and the student
teacher should consult the school nurse and physician, the guidance
counselor, and school administrators with the aim of gathering any
data not included in the cumulative records.

Standardized Intelligence Test Scores.   In the majority of schools,
group intelligence tests are periodically administered. In some school
systems, individual tests such as the Weschler Intelligence Scale for
Children or the Stanford Binet are given. Tests of this type are seldom administered every year, but it is helpful if the data are collected
more than once during the child's school career. Group intelligence
tests should probably be administered every three or four years, if not
more frequently.

Health Inventories and Physicians' Reports.   In addition to gathering
reports of immunization procedures, eye examinations, etc., many
schools are requesting that parents complete a health inventory, providing very helpful information about each child's eating and sleep-
ing habits, for example. It is general practice to include the name of
the family physician and an indication of the family's religious preference; this information may influence procedures the staff will follow
in the event of a playground injury to the child.

Achievement Tests.   Standardized achievement tests are adminis-

tered at least once a year in most school systems. This may be done
in the fall, soon after school begins, or in the spring, in order that the
child's achievement for that school year be recorded. This is not the
proper place for a discussion of the merits of once-a-year testing as
contrasted with twice-a-year testing, or for a discussion of spring
versus fall testing programs. The student teacher is referred to his
textbook in educational psychology for such a discussion. What is of
concern here is that the student teacher become familiar with the
testing program in the school system where he is working and consider
carefully the pattern of each child's scores and the range of scores
in the various subject-matter fields. If the cooperating teacher has
developed achievement tests to be used in mathematics, social studies,
science, or any other subject area, these too are valuable sources
from which the student teacher may draw more data about the children with whom she will be working.

Anecdotal Records. The student teacher will want to become acquainted with data regarding children's social behavior collected by
the classroom teacher. The college supervisor frequently asks the
student teacher to collect such data, realizing that evaluation and
child study are continuing practices engaged in by teachers who are
concerned with gearing the program to the evident needs and interests of children.

Sociometric Data. Figure 7 suggests the patterns of social relationships in one elementary classroom. Knowledge of such patterns is of
real benefit to the student teacher as he begins to work with children.
The cooperating teacher may have arranged the seating in the classroom according to the results of sociograms which he administered.
These data will be of interest to the student as he prepares to do
committee work, and the cooperating teacher may express a willingness to help him administer a sociogram and analyze the results.
Sociometric data should not be gathered without the permission and
guidance of the classroom teacher. The principal should probably be
consulted as well, and it is very important that these data be handled
most confidentially.

The types of information mentioned in the preceding paragraphs
are those which the student teacher will wish to have available before
doing any planning with or for the children. The supervising teacher,

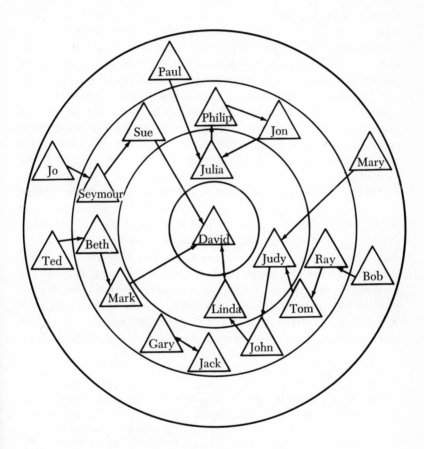

Figure 7. Pattern of Choices in Response to the Question, "Who Is Your Best Friend in Our Group?"

the school administrators, guidance personnel, nurses and physicians will almost certainly be willing to assist the student teacher in collecting necessary data and interpreting it.

Long-range planning for the student teacher means determining curricular objectives and procedures involving the major portion of the student teaching period. The student usually enters an ongoing program, and plans must be made with this fact in mind; however, even within this somewhat limited frame of reference, the student teacher can still plan toward major goals and objectives. This planning may be done in terms of curricular objectives: What do I hope to accomplish in reading? What do I hope to accomplish in mathematics? Plans may also be thought of in terms which are less subject-centered, and more child-centered: How can I meet the needs of the group of children who are quite successful in reading but lack interest and motivation to read beyond stated assignments, do not use the library, and in general think of reading as a "subject" confined to certain periods of the school day? How can I help the children who appear to have learned long division as a rote process and do not understand the concepts involved?

Whether the major consideration is how much curricular ground to cover or how to meet the identified needs of various groups of pupils, the student teacher must look ahead and see the entire student teaching period in terms of major goals, objectives, and procedures. Planning for a six-, eight-, or ten-week period makes possible the optimum use of learning resources, alerts staff members who will be asked to serve in a consultant capacity, and speeds the clarification of roles (supervisor–student teacher–cooperating teacher) which is so important in the early stages of student teaching. Burr, Harding, and Jacobs suggest the following guides for long-range planning:

1. State the goals you hope to achieve.
2. Organize your proposals about areas of curricular experience.
3. Indicate clearly the time sequence of proposed activities.
4. Provide for flexibility so that the children's readiness and progress may determine your timing and pacing.

Although your own long-range plans will be limited to the term of your student teaching, they will aid you in several ways. You will find that they broaden your perspective on the total program for the year, emphasize important goals, clarify problems needing special attention, and help in maintaining a balance in daily and weekly planning.[2]

---

[2] James B. Burr, Lowry W. Harding, and Leland B. Jacobs, *Student Teaching in the Elementary School* (Copyright © 1950, 1958, Appleton-Century-Crofts), p. 96.

It is important, therefore, to confer with the cooperating teacher quite early in the student teaching experience and, in terms of the accepted curricular framework and your knowledge of the children with whom you will be working, set the broad objectives toward which you will be working in student teaching, the procedures you will use to achieve these goals, and the techniques appropriate for evaluating the extent to which the objectives have been achieved.

The following is an example of the long-range planning done in various curricular areas by one student teacher:

Long-range Plans for Student Teaching—Grade One

Language Arts

Reading—Follow the groups as they will be established when I begin. Nothing can be planned ahead until the teacher wishes me to begin working in this area. I have read the children's books.

Writing—Whenever I am asked to begin working with writing, I shall integrate the activities with the science and social studies activities as well as reading.

Speaking—Because of the presence of several speech problems among the children, I shall plan activities which the entire class, as well as the individuals needing assistance, will find helpful. This will involve auditory discrimination.

Spelling—The children in this group have no formal spelling program, but I hope to help them with words they need for their writing.

Arithmetic

I have no idea as to what program is being followed by the school, but I would hope to follow a program similar to that developed by the [name of currently popular math program].

Science

Since this is an area in which I am free to choose my own program, I have selected Weather as the unit for the first part of November, followed by Getting Ready for Winter. Within this framework I wish to integrate social studies, art, writing, and reading, where possible. I would wish to allow some latitude in planning so that the children could, in part, determine the direction of the unit, although it will be outlined with concepts to be developed and possible directions in which it might go.

Social Studies

This will be very limited, because the teacher uses a social studies text as a supplementary reader. She emphasizes what my social studies methods prof. calls social living.

Music

There is a music teacher who comes twice a week. Mrs. B. has indicated that she has some records which involve rhythms which she wishes to have us use with the children.

Thanksgiving

There always seems to be some holiday activity for a week or so before the vacation. If this is to be part of my planning, I would like to try to depart somewhat from the usual concepts to present different facets as much as can be done at this grade level. This is a social studies area—our dependence upon each other for our needs and our appreciation for the work men do, as well as appreciation for the bounties of the earth.

Physical Education

A teacher takes the children once a week for gym. I shall have some games and exercises ready for rainy days and in case I am allowed to have any organized games during recess time.

Bulletin Boards

Where possible I would want to bring in the children.in planning and executing these. The science unit gives much opportunity to make use of the space not only in displaying the children's work, but in expanding their concepts and arousing their curiosity.

The plans of this student teacher are somewhat general and are almost entirely lacking in suggested procedures. They are included, however, as typical of the cooperative planning frequently done before student teaching begins. It is to be hoped that in discussing these plans with the cooperating teacher the student will clarify his role and see some of the teaching procedures by which his objectives might be achieved. The college supervisor should point out to the student that the plans indicate a desire to conform, to do "what she'll let me do," which suggests little creativity and less vision. The comment in the social studies section is particularly alarming. Student teachers should certainly expect to have at least minimal experiences in each curricular area.

Another type of planning for which the student teacher assumes responsibility is weekly planning. This can be more specific, in its reference to procedures, methods, and resources, than the long-range planning previously discussed. Michaelis states:

Weekly plans are most helpful if they are brief, flexible, and designed to provide for a smooth sequence of experiences. Their use affords an opportunity for the teacher to anticipate difficulties, secure essential materials ahead of time, make needed arrangement for the use of resources, and consider the sequence of steps to take in teaching a particular topic or series of related topics.[3]

One type of weekly plan—for a subject area, in this case spelling—follows:

Monday:
1. *Pronounce* each word and have the children "echo" after each.
2. Write these *extra words* on the board:
   orbit, element, neutron, nucleus, proton, molecule, nuclear
   Check on their meanings.
3. Assignment: Write one sentence each for all of the words from the spelling book, with the exception of the abbreviation *Nov.*
4. Hand in papers before arithmetic tomorrow.

Tuesday:
1. *Return* papers of sentences.
2. Pick out *major mistakes* and put on the board and discuss.
3. *Dictate prepared sentences* with the following cautions:
   margins, both left and right
   punctuation, including periods, commas, question marks, etc.
   spelling!
   capitalization

Wednesday:
1. *Return* yesterday's sentences for remarks but collect again for sample of student's work.*
2. *Dictate* the first writing of all 25 words.

Thursday:
1. *Return* yesterday's papers, tell range of scores.
2. Those who made perfect scores may use this time for study.

---

[3] Michaelis and Grim, op. cit., p. 89.
* These sentences indicate types of errors typically made by the pupils:
   Nor he knowed me.
   I could here your voice.
   We lenthen chains.
   The pin has lots of ink.
   I injoyed his program.
   I've have been to more than two states.
   We are going to have a Thanksgiving day porgram.

Those who missed words *write each word missed* six times and bring to my desk to be checked.

Friday:

1. Those who made perfect scores on Wednesday may use this time for study.
2. *Dictate* the second writing of all 25 words.

Evaluation: Their work on both Monday's and Tuesday's assignments was very careless, and I plan to work on their awareness of mistakes. Judging by the two test sets, on which scores were unusually low compared to former weeks' results, I didn't do a very good job of teaching the "extra" words. Mr. Jones (college supervisor) suggested writing the words several times on Thursday, but obviously that wasn't enough and/or the right kind of help.

It should be pointed out to the student teacher who prepared this plan that nothing is suggested as a motivating device and that it might be noted on the plan that *neutron, proton,* etc. were words added to the week's spelling list as a result of a study of atomic energy. In discussing these plans with the student teacher, the co-operating teacher will probably ask the following questions: (1) Since spelling is, essentially, a writing process, what purpose is served by having the children echo the words as they are pronounced? If correct pronunciation is associated with correct spelling, will you be able to hear individual errors when the echoing is a group process? (2) Will writing each word missed six times result in improved ability to spell it, in context, when the word is needed? What is your evidence for this?

Although the student is to be commended for evaluating the success of his plans, certain weaknesses are apparent. The plans would have been strengthened, of course, by a brief statement of objectives. There appears to be no reason for studying this week's spelling list, aside from "covering the material in the book." It is obvious that the student teacher included the words related to the study of atomic energy in an effort to help children identify spelling as being related to work in other curricular areas and as basic to success in communicating through writing, and a simple statement of objectives would have noted this.

There are other types of plans for a week's work. One type with which the student teacher should become familiar involves filling in blocks in a plan book:

> Monday:
>
> > Reading:
> >
> > > Group One: Streets and Roads,
> > >   pp. 24–26
> > > Group Two: More Streets and Roads,
> > >   pp. 1–6
> > > Group Three: Individualized Conferences
> > >   with Jeff, Sue, and Bob

The disadvantages of this type of lesson plan should be obvious. It is very difficult to note objectives, procedures, and resources, and to make some attempt at evaluation, within a ruled space of this size. This type of plan outline needs to be supplemented by much more detailed planning, particularly for the inexperienced student teacher. It is this type of weekly plan, usually included in a plan book of some type, which in many elementary schools is to be turned in to the principal's office.

What can the student teacher do when he is expected to complete plans according to a prescribed outline of this type? The most appropriate procedure would appear to be to use this as an outline and to supplement it with plans of a more complete nature.

Day-to-day planning is the most detailed type for which the student teacher is responsible. The objectives stated in such plans are those which one hopes can be achieved as a result of the particular day's work in a given subject area. Procedures are detailed, specific, and applicable to the work of that day in that area of subject matter. The long-range plans, and the plans for the week, will be referred to before one details the plans for the day. Long-range and weekly plans will be adjusted in terms of the accomplishments and problems encountered as each day's work progresses; and the more general plans, in turn, provide a helpful framework within which a day's work may be planned. One student teacher's plans for a day may look like this:

Wednesday, October 16

Planning Session:
8:45–9:15

1. Schedule time for reports from group doing research on pioneer housing in Indiana.
2. Recreation group—schedule time with Miss Y. (music consultant) for square dance practice.
3. Also schedule time (right after lunch?) for presentation of *Charlotte's Web*—Ann's group has illustrated portions of this and wishes to show a sequence of pictures and read the associated selections from the book.
4. Schedule Individualized Reading Conferences:

   1.   4.
   2.   5.
   3.   6.

9:15–10:15

Reading, related language arts activities.
Conferences—as scheduled.
Skill Group—Betty, Bob, Fred, Alice—work on syllabication principles—use example from _____ (p. 14).
Independent Work:

1. Complete poetry started yesterday.
2. Committee reports ready?
3. Any incomplete worksheets assigned to skill groups (groups needing a specific kind of help in reading)?
4. Read in books selected for Individualized Reading.

10:15–10:30

Recess.

10:30–11:15

Mathematics.
Bobs' group—work on base-five number system; check papers, proceed to number systems based on two and, if time permits, eight.
Sue's group—work on "patterns;" (finish work sheets discussed and distributed Tuesday).
Bob's group—work on understanding processes involved in long division; _____'s text should help with this (pp. 110–12) check before school to be sure there are enough copies—need eight.

11:15–11:45

Time provided for those who wish to share original poetry—if time permits, several children had selections they wished to read aloud from their Individualized Reading choices.

Lunch

1:00–1:30   Story—either *The Hundred Dresses* (Eleanor Estes) or share pictures and selections from *Charlotte's Web*—decide this in a.m. planning session.

1:30–2:15   Social Studies.
Committee Reports.
Recreation committee (Andy's group).
Food and Shelter Committee (Betsy's Group).
Film *Indiana's State Parks*—relate to recreation committee's findings.

2:15–2:30   Recess.

2:30–3:15   Science—begin study of Ice Age, glaciers, effect on soil and topography in Indiana. Recall differences in topography of land at Spring Mill State Park and Pokagon State Park, noted in film. Check with Miss C. (librarian) for books she said she'd assemble for us; this afternoon's session is mainly exploratory—might use sections of _____ text, which all the children have in their desks (pp. 12–15).

3:15–3:30   Evaluation—compare what we've accomplished today with plans made in a.m.

These plans are illustrative of the student teacher's concern for adjusting to individual differences and his efforts to involve the children in planning. Much of this planning is done with the children in the time provided for planning at the beginning of each day. Children gain security, much as the teacher does, from knowing in general what's going to happen today, and when.

Three general types of planning have been now suggested—long-range planning, weekly planning, and daily planning. All types are essential to give necessary breadth and scope to the student teacher's work and to help him develop the self-confidence which results when materials are at hand, goals are clearly established, and procedures are geared to the needs and interests of the group of children with whom the student teacher is working.

STUDENT TEACHING PLANS INCLUDE TIME FOR GIVING HELP
WHEN HELP IS NEEDED

Figure 8 suggests the manner in which daily, weekly, and long-range plans are interrelated. The student teacher will want to observe the methods of planning used by the cooperating teacher, and the types of plans used. It is to be hoped that the student teacher will not copy this method, nor the specific procedures recommended by the college supervisor, without asking:

1. Does this method seem appropriate for me and my way of teaching?
2. Are the types of planning recommended and followed the best types for these children and the materials we have to work with?

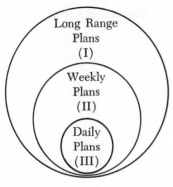

I. Social studies units, the literature program, major units in mathematics, for example, geometry.

II. Map reading, folk lore, measurement of a circle.

III. Specific aspects. For example, reading a global projection map, folklore of a particular region, some understanding of terms such as *diameter*.

FIGURE 8. KINDS OF PLANNING

3. Are the types of planning used by the cooperating teacher and recommended by the supervisor consistent with the philosophy upon which this school operates?

The answers to these questions will help the student teacher adapt and adjust the types of plans he will make and the methods he will use.

A major problem confronting the student teacher is suggested in the preceding statements about planning. The student teacher recognizes the need for establishing some professional autonomy, to be freed to be his own best self. He also recognizes that he will, almost certainly, receive a letter grade at the conclusion of student teaching. When his views about planning conflict with those of the cooperating teacher and/or the college supervisor, ambivalent feelings are sure to result—"Do I stand up for what I believe, and receive a lower grade; or do I follow instructions, in violation of what I believe?"

Of course it is to be hoped that this cleavage will not exist in connection with planning or any other aspect of student teaching. The team approach has been emphasized throughout this chapter; and members of a team can work out slight differences in objectives and procedures without the sacrifice of anyone's autonomy, particularly the student teacher's. If differences in objective and method are not slight, but serious, the solution to the student teacher's dilemma might be a three-way conference, in which all participants frankly but calmly discuss their points of view and resolve their differences. In such a conference, it is important that the student teacher have a role which is not subservient and that he be treated as a professional with his own contribution to make and with a right to his own opinion.

Fortunately, an increasing number of universities are not assigning a student teaching grade. The complex of experiences that make up student teaching and the variety of personalities involved make the assignment of a meaningful grade difficult if not impossible. Personnel officers for school systems have indicated an awareness of this problem and frequently place more importance on the written recommendations of the cooperating teacher and college supervisor than on a letter grade.

It would appear, then, that in the rare situation where disagreement about planning occurs, a discussion or conference can do a great deal to settle the differences and that the differences should be settled in such a way that the student teacher's professional self-concept and feelings of worth will not suffer. It should also be clear that a grade, when given, provides a very inadequate and limited index of the student teacher's learning in a rich and worthwhile student teaching situation.

Pupil-teacher planning is of such importance that it has been recommended that the student teacher be given the opportunity to see it in operation outside the student teaching situation if not within it. The student teacher learns how to do pupil-teacher planning by, first, having experienced it himself as a pupil; second, believing that pupils will learn more if they are involved in the learning process at all stages; and, third, by watching a teacher effectively utilize the techniques of planning with children. The following anecdote illustrates the manner in which one student teacher gained increased competence in this area:

Last week I talked to Dr. B. about how I might begin a study of Mexico without using the "turn to page 176 in your Geography books" approach. We discussed several ways, and I decided to read a story about Mexican children. Dr. B. thought the children might add some information, and we could, perhaps, summarize the first session by listing some things we would like to learn about the country. Dr. B. also suggested that I do some review reading in preparation for the project and gave me the names of several helpful books.

This morning . . . I read the story of Pedro and Petra in the Mexican market place. Two members of the class had traveled in Mexico. They had many interesting experiences to relate, and the class asked many questions. I relaxed. We were off—just as the books predicted. Soon other children were describing gifts from Mexico which relatives had brought them. It was not at all hard to guide the discussion into what we knew about Mexico. Words tumbled over each other as the class listed other things they wanted to know about this fascinating country.

. . . .

Monday afternoon I was worried about the varied topics the boys and girls listed and how they might be categorized. When I asked Dr. B. about the problem, he replied, "Put the entire listing on the board and get the children's idea of a solution. They can do it if you give them a chance." He sounded so confident.

Tuesday morning before school I copied on the board all the things they wanted to learn about Mexico. Believe it or not, before the social studies class got underway, several children asked how they were going to find out about so many things. . . . One attentive boy who had been silent came up with this, "We've got too many things for us all to learn. Why don't we divide into groups? Then each group could study about some of the things we've listed and tell us about them." Another pupil countered this statement with, "There are too many things; we can't have that many groups." Finally, the class decided it would be best to combine some of the things into one group as "The group that's going to study about people might just as well study about food, clothing, homes and amusements, because all that is about people." Children never cease to amaze me.

We did combine the separate items into six related areas. Then each child chose his area for work. . . . Each group met and chose a chairman.[4]

The student teacher had an objective—to give the children something more meaningful in social studies than a page-by-page perusal of the text. Working with his college supervisor and the cooperating teacher, the student teacher decided to begin with a story, which he hoped would stimulate discussion and questions. The ideas are not revolutionary, and they have been successfully tried by teachers for a number of years. It should be clear, therefore, that there is no magic involved. Pupil-teacher planning works, if the teacher has rather clearly established objectives, if he has faith in children's ability to participate effectively in determining some of their own learning experiences, and if he has the subject matter background necessary to help children make intelligent choices and decisions.

---

[4] Alberta L. Lowe, *The Value Approach to Student Teaching* (Cedar Falls, Iowa: The Association for Student Teaching, 1960), pp. 15–16, 20.

It would seem wise to devote a period of time at the beginning of each school day to planning, with children, the areas which need to be covered and determining individual and group responsibilities. Children may be involved in planning at many stages and at many times throughout the school day, as their past experiences and maturity levels suggest. Obviously, planning with first-graders is of a different nature (for shorter periods of time, for more direct and easily achieved purposes) than it is with fifth-graders planning a social studies unit such as the one described in the anecdote. Answers to questions related to the *how* and the *when* of pupil-teacher planning may depend upon the maturity of the children. The *why* of pupil-teacher planning depends, at all levels, upon the faith of the student teacher in the democratic process and his concept of the rights and responsibilities of its participants.

It is rather difficult for a student teacher to gain even a generalized notion of the types of planning which are done for an entire year. The student teaching period is necessarily shorter than a year and often begins after the school year has started and stops before the school year ends. The length of the student teaching experience varies from several weeks to a few months, at the most. There are several steps the student teacher can take, however, to learn something of this very important kind of planning: He can confer with the school administrators and members of the curriculum committee regarding curricular patterns established for the school system as a whole and for the specific grade levels. (The curriculum guide will help in surveying such long-range objectives and major goals.) He can survey the cooperating teacher's plans for the year and talk with him about them. He can survey the textbooks and other learning resources which will be used during the year. He can explore, with the cooperating teacher, the manner in which the student teacher's plans will coordinate with, supplement, and further the plans already made for the year's work. Finally, it will be particularly useful to the student teacher, in preparing for his own teaching, to confer with the group's previous teacher. It is helpful to know where the children have been, what they have done, in order to plan future experiences more intelligently.

Summary

It would be difficult to overestimate the importance of successful planning in student teaching. This planning rests upon a healthy relationship between the three major participants in the student teaching experience and upon a shared understanding of the limitations within which each works. In this chapter, some principles that should guide this cooperative effort have been suggested:

1. Although the college supervisor has many opportunities to make suggestions and dispense advice, his role as supervisor supersedes that of "curriculum consultant." An overcritical attitude will only serve to alienate school personnel and will not aid the student teacher.

2. The cooperating teacher can show the student teacher examples of his plans and discuss planning techniques with him, but he should not expect the student teacher to adopt these plans and methods uncritically and without changing them to fit his own needs and abilities.

3. The student teacher must see his plans in relationship to the ongoing curriculum of the school system. His plans cannot represent an intrusion but should, rather, compliment and supplement the general plans already made. It is hoped, of course, that the plans will indeed be general and would not be unduly restrictive or prescriptive.

4. The cooperating teacher can help the student teacher develop some successful and practical techniques for child study. A thorough knowledge of children is considered essential for effective planning.

Still another, more general, set of principles has emerged, as the work of the student teacher in planning has been discussed:

1. It is clear that not one but several types of planning, each different but interrelated, will be required of the student teacher. The plans, from long-range to daily plans, may be placed on a continuum according to specificity of objectives, detailing of procedures and resources, and evaluative techniques.

2. Children can be involved in planning with successful results; and the majority of student teachers possess the experience and maturity necessary to begin planning with children. Guidance of varying amounts may be required, but it seems that an essential element would be observation of the cooperating teacher as he uses this technique.

3. Successful planning of any type rests upon thorough knowledge of the children involved. Methods by which the student teacher can accumulate this information have been suggested in this chapter.

4. In planning together with the cooperating teacher, the student teacher will profit most from being treated as a professional, whose capabilities, ideas, and personality are respected.

Suggested Activities for Student Teachers

Activities for this chapter will center upon devising, discussing, and putting into operation plans of various types. For example:

1. Make a plan for one lesson, for one period of a day; this may involve the whole group or part of a group. Ask for an evaluation of the plan from your supervisor and/or your cooperating teacher. After trying out your plan with children, write your own evaluation of the effectiveness of the lesson and of your method of planning. Keep this plan for comparison with similar plans you make later in student teaching.

2. After noting the big areas of the curriculum (e.g., reading, social studies, science) as organized in the classroom where you are student teaching, make some long-range plans, in terms of your student teaching period (six weeks, nine weeks, etc.). What do you hope to accomplish in language arts? In mathematics? Discuss these plans or, ideally, develop them together with your cooperating teacher. Check these plans periodically, noting your progress and making necessary adjustments.

3. Follow a similar procedure with plans for an entire day, an entire week. Can these be as detailed as your plans for a reading lesson or spelling lesson? How will these plans differ from your long-range plans?

4. Discuss with your cooperating teacher his use of guidebooks, curriculum guides, and standardized planning forms.

5. Prepare a guide-sheet for use in pupil-teacher planning. What questions will you ask? What are your objectives? How will you plan to involve many children, followers as well as leaders? How will you gauge your effectiveness?

SELECTED REFERENCES

Burr, James B., Harding, Lowry W., and Jacobs, Leland B. *Student Teaching in the Elementary School.* New York: Appleton-Century-Crofts, 1958, Chapter 5, "Planning Your Work."

Curtis, Dwight K., and Andrews, Leonard O. *Guiding Your Student Teacher.* Englewood Cliffs, New Jersey: Prentice-Hall, Inc., 1954, Chapter 7, "Learning to Plan."

Haines, Aleyne C. *Guiding the Student Teaching Process in Elementary Education.* Chicago: Rand McNally & Co., 1960, Chapter 7, "Using a Planning-Evaluating Process."

Lowe, Alberta L. *The Value Approach to Student Teaching.* Cedar Falls, Iowa: The Association for Student Teaching, 1961.

Michaelis, John U., and Grim, Paul R. *The Student Teacher in the Elementary School.* Prentice-Hall, Inc., 1953, Chapter 4, "Making Plans for Teaching;" Chapter 5, "Planning the Unit of Work."

5

Working with Children

The isolation of the material in this chapter from that in the chapters dealing with planning and the initial phases of student teaching is, in a sense, very unrealistic. The student's first experiences in his student teaching situation and the effectiveness with which he completes the tasks involved in planning have much to do with the success he will achieve as he works with children individually and in groups. Nonetheless, there is a point at which plans must be put into action and a time for moving from observation and participation into the acceptance of major responsibility. It is to be hoped that the break will not be a sharp one, that the dividing line will be almost unseen; but at some point in student teaching, the cooperating teacher and the supervisor must communicate, by their behavior if not through words, that the primary responsibility can no longer be theirs but must be accepted by the student. They will, of course, continue to advise, support, guide, and help, but the student teacher must, at some point in the student teaching process, become the teacher. If this point is never reached, if the children continue to ask the cooperating teacher for help and look to him for leadership, if a child says to the student teacher, "We don't *have* to *mind* you; you're only a student teacher!" then the student's qualifications for certification can be seriously questioned, and there is reason to doubt his ability to succeed in his first year of teaching. Of course, there may be extenuating circumstances, and the student teacher may not be entirely to blame for his inability to make the transition from student to teacher; but the student teacher ordinarily reaches a point where he can and must prove his ability to succeed on his own, to do the job he's learned to do, without an unusual amount of help and support.

Elements in the preparation of the student teacher which will abet or inhibit his success as an independent, professional person have already been identified. They need only the briefest review here:

1. The student teacher has been well prepared by his college or university to accept the responsibility which accompanies student teaching. He has successfully completed the so-called professional and general education portions of his teacher education program, and the laboratory experiences leading up to student teaching have been both productive and rewarding.

2. He has had the opportunity to become well acquainted with his supervisor, his cooperating teacher, and his student teaching situation, including facilities, resources and personnel.

3. He has been helped to identify the needs and interests of the children in his classroom and to make various types of plans with these needs and interests in mind. He has learned to make plans that indicate cognizance of society's expectations (as specifically reflected in the school community where he is doing student teaching) and due recognition for the structure of each of the disciplines for which the elementary school assumes instructional responsibility.

4. In the student teaching situation, he has been helped to progress, easily and naturally, through observation and participation to the point where assuming major responsibility seems to be the logical next step.

Inadequacies in any of the procedures suggested above, whether due to institutional, administrative, or personal shortcomings, can result in serious delay in the student teacher's acceptance of the role of teacher. The college supervisor and the cooperating teacher attempt to provide the necessary guidance, direction, and help as the student teacher progresses toward his goal, building on strengths and compensating for or eliminating weaknesses.

Each of these steps is complex, and this brief summary is not intended to oversimplify or underestimate their significance. The focus here is on the part each step plays in preparing the neophyte for full membership in his chosen profession. A major "test" prior to that membership is proving one's ability to guide children's learning effectively and independently.

GUIDING GROUP WORK

As the student teacher accepts increasing responsibility for directing the learning activities of children, the emphasis shifts somewhat from developing a background of data about children, information about and understanding of the school and its role in the community, and working with the cooperating teacher as he plans, to concern for acting upon the basis of all of the accumulated information, attitudes, and understanding. It is as though the question now has become: So what? What difference does all of this make as you teach, as one acts and reacts with a group of children? If those charged with the responsibility of directing and guiding the student teacher do not ask this question, directly or indirectly, then the student teacher must ask it, critically and continuously; for it is as the student teacher works with children that his philosophy, his beliefs about human beings and the manner in which their behavior can be changed, is tested. It is as he relates to the class, individually and collectively, that the impact, or lack of it, of all his previous educational experiences becomes apparent. It is no longer possible for the student teacher to convince his supervisor or cooperating teacher that he truly believes in involving children actively in the learning process if they never see him operate on this belief. Effective performance with a reading group or adjusting a predetermined spelling list to meet better the needs and capacities of a child means so much more than the A one received in a language arts methods course. These statements are neither creative nor highly original; each participant in the student teaching process knows the basic truth upon which they rest. They are included for the purpose of underlining the importance in student teaching of productive and increasingly more effective performance as the student teacher assumes more and more responsibility for directing the learning experiences of children.

In the following pages, the student teacher's work will be dealt with in three phases: his work with the entire class, his work with committees and small groups, and finally his work with individual children.

THE STUDENT TEACHER WORKS WITH THE ENTIRE CLASS

It has been previously noted that many people define teaching as the act of presenting a body of significant material to a large group of pupils, then testing their understanding and grasp of the material presented. It should be clear to the reader that the definition of teaching upon which this book operates is somewhat broader than this, but it is nonetheless true that there are occasions when this is an accurate reflection of the teaching act.

THE COOPERATING TEACHER OBSERVES THE STUDENT TEACHER'S
FIRST WORK WITH THE CLASS

With all that has been said so far about studying children and adjusting the school's program to meet the needs of the learners whenever this is possible, how can one ever justify standing before thirty or thirty-five children and presenting material with the intent of having it digested and assimilated by each child? Any student who has had even minimal exposure to educational psychology knows the tremendous range of differences, intellectual and emotional, which are present within any group of children. (These differences are minimized only to some extent and only in one area even when children are grouped homogeneously, one might add.) Different home backgrounds, different educational expectations, goals, objectives all present major problems in motivation. To repeat then, why is a teacher ever justified in working with a class as a whole?

The first answer to this question is a practical one: Divide the number of pupils in a class by the number of minutes in a school day, then multiply this by the number of areas of the curriculum which the teacher is responsible for covering, and it becomes clear that a completely individualized program is impossible, at least, with the school day and the school year constituted as they are now. Then, one is tempted to suggest, use the magical three groups. Three groups in math, in spelling, in reading, in science, in social studies, each meeting with the teacher for only twenty minutes a day, becomes almost unmanageable even on paper, much less in practice.

Even if it were practical to devise a completely individualized program (and team teaching and programmed instruction are making this somewhat more practical than it was thought to be even a few years ago), it seems logical to assume that there are some benefits the learner can derive from operating in large groups at certain times of the day. If one abandons the concept of each child taking from a "lesson"—be it a demonstration, a film, or whatever—the same facts or generalizations, then large group instruction becomes less fearful.

Much of the learning which occurs when a film is shown to a large group takes place in the discussion which follows the film; this is also true of a science demonstration. Presentations may be effective with large groups, groups larger than class size, in fact; but to be effective they should be followed by smaller discussion groups. For example:

Officer Smith agrees to talk to both groups of second grade children about the equipment used by local policemen; both groups are studying the policeman as part of a larger "Community Helpers" unit. After his presentation, which lasts about twenty minutes and for which both Officer Smith and the children have carefully prepared, Officer Smith answers questions asked by any of the fifty or sixty children assembled to hear him. Miss Brown, student teacher in one of the second grades, then provides a "break" for the children in the form of an active game. Back in the classroom, one group of children draws pictures of the officer and the equipment he demonstrated. Another group compares the equipment Officer Smith brought with him with that shown in the books about policemen they have for just such reference purposes. A third group meets with Miss Brown to check their questions with Officer Smith's statements. Miss Brown has tape recorded the presentation for future reference, in case some point has been missed. (Other possibilities for a small group project would be inspecting the cruiser in which Officer Smith arrived, writing reports of the talk, and/or writing thank-you letters to him.) With the single exception of the question period following the discussion, in which the size of the group might inhibit certain children and prevent questions, it is difficult to see how the presentation could have been more effective for thirty than for sixty. Although this is a controversial point, especially when discussing large group instruction for young children, there is an admitted saving of time—the policeman's and the children's—and it does not seem to me that the resulting learning would be seriously diminished.

The point to be emphasized here is that presentation is not teaching; the information imparted must be related to previous learnings, must be organized and reorganized as the information is discussed and the learner becomes aware of some of the implications and applications of the raw data. This is where the skill of the teacher is utilized, and it is doubtful that a teaching machine which can help the child do this has yet been devised.

A similar approach can be used even in one-textbook situations. The student teacher can carefully develop the vocabulary and attempt to provide some motivation for silent reading. The silent reading can be followed by one of a host of activities, all of them more effective than the usual rereading, aloud, of the same material which has just been read silently. For example, children can find related material in trade books or reference books; outlines can be developed indicating the major points developed in the text; maps or charts can be constructed; or the science experiment described can be demonstrated in the classroom. Letters can be written requesting additional information; the new vocabulary can be checked in a dictionary, or children's own definitions developed, on the basis of the teacher's introduction and in the context of the material read. If nothing else is practical, children can be asked to read for specific information and to relate this information to the class. Whole-class work does not necessarily mean dull, routine work: "Open your books to page 27; the lesson deals with simple machines. Read it silently—the new words are on the board. [Five-minute pause—children "read," teacher puts examples on board for math class.] Bob, read the first paragraph, please; Susan, the second. . . . " *This would represent poor teaching whether one child or fifty were involved.*

In each subject or curriculum area, there are certain fundamentals which the school accepts responsibility for teaching. For example, the ability to divide words, correctly, into syllables is of direct benefit to both spelling and reading. It is a skill which children should acquire. Even the proponents of individualized reading recommend that some basic elements of syllabication can be introduced to an entire class, with the full knowledge that the concepts will not be grasped equally well by all children, that reteaching will be necessary, and that the presentation will be followed by or include discussion and opportunities for the children to apply the skill under consideration in functional situations. The individualization of instruction can follow the introduction of this concept. At that time it will be apparent that a few need no additional work, that many will profit from the use of work sheets which will check their understandings of the process or concept, and that a few lack readiness for this skill and cannot be taught it for a while. Of course, it can be argued that the brighter students should not have been bored with something they already knew (perhaps they did, but to what depth?) and that the slow learners could have been more profitably occupied working at a task at their level; but there is, nonetheless, some security which comes from the student teacher's knowledge that the children are operating from the same broad base. He can then assume exposure, at least; and in the usual press and rush of planning for many groups, even this assumption may not be justified.

In summary, it might be said that the student teacher will of necessity spend some time working with the children as a total group.

WORKING WITH AN ENTIRE CLASS CAN BE REWARDING AND BENEFICIAL

Although this has its disadvantages, and none of the arguments favoring attention to individual differences is being denied or rescinded, it does not necessarily follow that nothing good, nothing creative, can occur in a large group. Large or total group instruction can be used to introduce a major topic, to motivate interest in a unit of study, or to conserve time and resources; and if it is followed by attention to differential learning rates, a high level of learning may result.

THE STUDENT TEACHER WORKS WITH SMALL GROUPS

Very frequently, the student teacher will work with small groups of children rather than with the whole class. These groups of youngsters are gathered for any of a number of purposes. Groups will be organized for the purpose of providing specific help needed by each member of the group. For example, even though the children regularly read in the familiar reading groups, the teacher may note that two or three members of each group have difficulty in reading aloud in an interesting, enjoyable manner. These children meet with the teacher for several sessions with the purpose of improving their oral reading skills. When oral reading skills have improved, the group will no longer meet. Such groups organize for the purpose of solving a specific problem, members may represent several ability levels, and the group will dissolve when the problem is solved. Figure 9 illustrates two types of groups and summarizes the purposes for which small groups are organized.

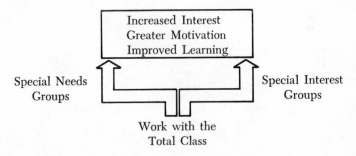

FIGURE 9.   WHY USE GROUPS?

Grouping on the basis of ability is such a common pattern that it needs only brief description here. On the basis of standardized tests, survey tests, and records of achievement in preceding grades, the teacher organizes groups for instruction at appropriate levels. This form of grouping is most commonly used for reading instruction at the primary level, but it is occasionally used for mathematics and spelling as well and at the intermediate and upper grade levels. These groups will probably be formed when the student teacher arrives, and his task will be the selection of appropriate methods and materials for each group and the continuous evaluation of the progress of the children in order to determine whether changes would be beneficial. It is interesting to note (and this could be some valuable "action research" for the student teacher) how much more frequently children are moved *up* than *down* and how really inflexible these groups often become.

THE STUDENT TEACHER HELPS A READING GROUP SOLVE A PROBLEM

Groups may be organized for the purpose of pursuing a particular interest shared by several children. Most often, this relates to a unit or topic already being discussed, but it can also serve as a motivating device, a stimulus to greater interest among the whole group. For example, three boys with a specific interest in the Civil War may prepare a report and a display which contributes a great deal to interest in this aspect of American history, or some children may display coin collections that relate to a country being studied or to a period of American history.

The student teacher may have little to say about the patterns of grouping used by a cooperating teacher. He may suggest changes in placement in ability groups, he may recognize the importance of forming a special need group, and he can provide encouragement and stimulation to children who exhibit special interests which relate to classroom activities or may create interest in a new unit or project. The wise cooperating teacher doesn't resent suggestions of the type outlined above but, rather, utilizes them, just as the student teacher accepts similar suggestions when he has major responsibility for teaching.

Providing the right amount of direction for the types of groups discussed in the preceding paragraphs is not as difficult as guiding the work of committees. The groups are organized either for purposes which are very clear to the teacher, as in the case of ability and special need groups, or because children have exhibited a high level of interest in a topic. In the latter case, the teacher's job is that of helping the children relate their special interest to the concerns of the group and decide how they might best share their information. Motivation may be something of a problem with the ability groups, as even the most casual survey of a teacher's guide will suggest. When children have little involvement in setting the goals, or have difficulty in seeing the purpose of what is going on, extrinsic motivation must be substituted for the absent intrinsic motivation for learning.

Ordinarily, in student teaching, opportunities to work with a small group will precede working with the total group, although I have known several student teachers who were unable to challenge the children in a bright reading group and therefore lost control of the group; but these same student teachers were much more successful in working with the class as a whole, for reasons which could only be surmised.

Small group work, aside from committee work which will be discussed in a later section of this chapter, can accomplish much which cannot be done when the total group is the teaching unit: Teacher-child rapport may be improved because the teacher-pupil ratio is lower; the teacher is more sensitive to learning problems and can adjust his teaching techniques almost immediately. The methods and materials selected can be those which are best suited to the learning levels, needs, and interests represented by the group.

Pupil participation is usually better in a small group; children will

WORKING WITH A READING GROUP CAN BE REWARDING

ask questions, make comments, and in general take greater interest
in the learning activity.

Providing Help for the Student Teacher as
He Works with Small Groups

The cooperating teacher can help the student teacher identify
changes which should be made in ability groups and can aid in locating specific problems which might be solved through the organization of temporary needs-oriented groups. He helps the student teacher
plan for his work with small groups and evaluate his success (or lack

of success). He also helps by suggesting, or assisting the student teacher to select, appropriate learning resources for use with the groups and significant activities for children who are not working directly with the teacher.

The college supervisor is in an excellent position to help the student teacher see the many opportunities for work with small groups, those which may be observed in the student teaching classroom and those which must be studied vicariously. Background reading might be suggested, observations in other classrooms might be arranged, and seminars or group conferences can be scheduled in which problems common to many of the student teachers might be discussed and possible solutions suggested. Teachers of methods classes might be asked to discuss grouping as it affects learning in their areas of competence, and the supervisor would probably accept responsibility for arranging such discussions (although an agenda committee, made up of student teachers and in charge of planning each meeting or seminar, can make detailed arrangements, with the result that supervisory time will be saved and student teachers' growth enhanced).

Work with small groups, organized for a variety of purposes and existing for various periods of time, is an important part of a teacher's task; and a rich student teaching experience will provide many opportunities for work with smaller-than-class-size groups. Work with small groups will not stop when the student teacher demonstrates competence with whole group teaching but will continue throughout the student teaching experience, because of its value and significance in children's learning.

Committee Work—A Real Test of Strength

In this section, problems specifically related to committee work will be discussed. Committee work differs from other small group work largely because of its genesis: the pupil may have little or nothing to do with identifying the need for a small group or deciding which group he'll join. In contrast, for successful committee work, needs and interests must be recognized by the children and purposes clearly stated in terms they can interpret. The distinction is a fine one, however; and many of the techniques and suggestions which apply to successful small group work of other kinds also apply to successful com-

mittee work. There is little need to be concerned whether children
charged with responsibility for cleaning the aquarium or adding periodically books to the room library form a "committee" or a "group."
The major difference is in the children's identification of an objective
as their own rather than as the teacher's.

One very effective and creative teacher was observed while guiding
committee work in her fifth grade for the greater part of an afternoon. At the conclusion of the visit, the observer thanked the teacher
but admitted some disappointment, adding, "I had hoped to see you
teach." The reader may smile at the naiveté of such a remark, because
most teachers and student teachers are well aware of the high level
of competence required for the guidance of committee or small group
work with children. In fact, it is occasionally recommended that the
student teacher avoid committee work because it is so difficult to guide
without directing, to suggest alternatives and let children decide
which is to be preferred, and to help groups select from a variety of
learning resources rather than to do this for them. Committee work
rests upon faith in the democratic process, and it occasionally involves
letting children learn by the mistakes they make. A few teachers will
say committee work takes too long; that it promotes unacceptable behavior (since the teacher is not in direct and complete control); and
that the results, whether a mural, a dramatization, a display, or a
written report, are bound to be mediocre and will seek the level of
the poorest member of the committee. Other teachers say that the
individual should not be submerged in the group, that committee
work slows the gifted and frustrates the slow. Committee work appears, however, to be more than justified, on several counts. Very
capable student teachers, at least, would profit a great deal from experience in guiding committee work, for these reasons: Committee
work enables children to pursue topics of special interest which might
not be of interest to the whole group; learning is enhanced when it
is motivated by interest. Work in committees with a follow-up discussion or compilation of the findings of each group makes it possible to
investigate a topic in greater depth than would be possible if the
group of thirty pursued a topic together. For example, in a fifth grade
study of the westward movement in the United States, one group
might explore the means of transportation and the various routes
taken, another the recreation or protection people provided for themselves as they journeyed west, and so on. It would not be possible

to do justice to these aspects of the unit working as a total group—time is too short.

Work in committees helps children learn leadership skills and some of the qualities essential for good "followership" as well. Although it is true that we normally associate with those who are intellectually and socially similar, it is nonetheless important to learn how to work with those who are different. The briefest list of the church groups, charitable groups, and political groups to which many of us belong should reinforce the claim that we need to learn to operate effectively in these groups and that the elementary school has some responsibility for providing opportunities and guidance for this learning.

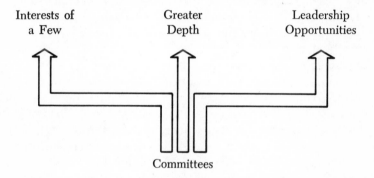

FIGURE 10. WHAT COMMITTEES PROVIDE

Purposes for which committees are organized are indicated in Figure 10. In the chapter on planning, it was suggested that the student teacher might visit a room where pupil-teacher planning could be observed, if he could not see it in his own situation. The same suggestion applies to committee work. A cooperating teacher may have been selected for any of a number of good qualities and demonstrated competencies. The ability to guide committee work effectively may not be among these. If this is the case, it will be of some help to a student at least to see this in operation, to see concrete evidence that it does work. It could be argued that one observation will do little good and that it could, in fact, be harmful, if the committee work for that particular day were less than fruitful and productive. Much depends, of course, upon the attitude with which the student observes, the faith of the teacher in the democratic process and in committee work as a part of it, and the conference between the student and the teacher following the visit. In favorable circumstances, even one visit can be helpful in demonstrating the "how" and "when" of committee work. It is far better of course if the student can gain direct experience in guiding committee work with the children he knows best and in the situation with which he is most familiar. Under what conditions might the student teacher help children organize committees? The following illustrative situations are merely suggestive; many more will occur to the reader:

A fourth grade exhibits strong concern for safety in and around their school building following a series of playground and hall accidents. They organize groups that gather data and interview the principal and the school nurse, and they devise a series of safety posters and bulletin boards to serve as reminders. Finally, they organize "safety teams" to visit classrooms and lead discussions designed to make the pupils more safety-conscious.

A second grade has been awarded $25 by the PTA to spend for books to be added to their room library. Following a trip to the public or school library, committees are organized to select books in the following categories—animal stories, science books, books about community helpers (their social studies unit), and a category they call "other good books." The lists are combined and discussed, and the purchase order is completed after each group has reported.

A sixth grade is involved in a study of Latin America. They need up-to-date and accurate information on events and the political situation in Brazil. One group surveys newspapers and news magazines. A second group writes carefully composed letters to the Brazilian embassy, the Organization of American States, and the Pan American Union. A third group writes to the American Under Secretary of State for Latin American Affairs and locates all the available official statements about the present political climate and state of affairs in Brazil.

The following is a guide sheet for committee work that a student teacher developed with some help from pupils and distributed to each committee member for reference while his committee worked.

Plan for Committee Work

Committees:

[Children signed up for committees representing their major in-

terest. The student teacher occasionally set limits concerning the
number of members appropriate for each committee.]

1. temperature
2. precipitation
3. air pressure
4. wind speed
5. wind direction
6. relative humidity
7. cloud cover and formations
8. charting weather information

Things to Consider

[These were developed with the children after their topics, listed
above, were selected.]

1. What instrument is used to gather and measure information
   about our topic?
2. How can we make the instrument or one that measures the
   same thing?
3. Why and how is our topic important in weather study and
   forecasting?
4. How does it influence daily weather?
5. What special vocabulary is needed to talk about our topic?
6. Is history important in studying our topic?
7. What experiments or demonstrations could be used to illustrate
   our information?
8. How can everyone in the group contribute to its success?
9. What materials can be brought from home to make our study
   more interesting?
10. How can we best summarize our information for the class?

What generalizations can be drawn from the illustrations above?
First, committees were not organized for the purpose of organizing
committees. There was a job—or several jobs—to be done, and committees appeared to be needed in order to complete the task or tasks
with speed and efficiency. The major job was subdivided into tasks
that one could reasonably expect children to be able to handle. Each
group knew very well what it was expected to do and was aware of
its responsibility to the total group and the solution of the larger
problem. One can only suppose what teaching techniques were utilized as the committees organized themselves, worked, and reported;
but the teacher's role almost certainly included the following:

He helped to identify and narrow the problem so children could
manage it and eventually solve it.

He helped with the identification of needed committees—subdi-
viding the larger problem, helping children decide which area or

aspect interested them most, and determining the best size for each group. This may or may not have involved the administration of a sociogram ("Name three children with whom you'd most like to work") so a child would have the chance to select those children with whom he can work most effectively. The membership of committees should be determined primarily on the basis of interest, but certainly group dynamics is an important consideration.

The teacher helped locate necessary resources (books, newspapers, reference books, school stationery for the important letters, etc.) and gave such instruction in how these should be utilized as seemed to be necessary.

The teacher helped children organize their information by asking important and leading questions. He did not, however, tell them what they had learned. This is part of their task.

The teacher helped in the presentation of each committee's findings. It is most important, if children are to gain breadth as well as depth, that those who are sharing information do so in an interesting and instructive manner and that others accept the responsibility for intelligent and creative listening. Dioramas, puppet shows, charts, displays, dramatizations—all will serve to make a report more appealing and hold the interest of the group. Reading a report which has been carefully copied from an encyclopedia indicates little learning on the part of the reader, will be boring to the listeners, and should be avoided.

Problems in Guiding Committee Work

A student teacher asks what to do when Jeff wants to prepare a separate, individual project rather than join a committee; what to do when Sally and Beth ask, for the fourth time since student teaching started, to serve on the same committee; and how to handle Bob, who is bright, quick, and tends to dominate any committee he joins. Understanding each child, his drives and motivations, should give the student teacher his answer. If Jeff *always* wants to work alone, then it may be necessary to be rather firm in suggesting that he involve himself in group work of some sort; however, if he has an idea and wishes to pursue this idea on his own and if he normally does not object to group participation, he probably should be permitted to do what he wishes. Little would be accomplished by forcing his participation in a committee project that doesn't interest him.

Sally and Beth obviously feel more secure when they work with each other. Insisting upon separate projects would produce insecurity, but might also result in more independence in social relationships. It would seem they should be encouraged, but not forced, to select different tasks. A first step might be the assignment of very different kinds of jobs within the same general committee. Bob might benefit from hearing a tape recording of his performance on a committee or from observing and taking notes on the operation of another bright child who is somewhat more skillful in group relations. He might also be helped to select a particularly challenging aspect of the committee's job which would give him somewhat less time for bossing, overdirecting, and ridiculing contributions less impressive than his.

Easy formulas cannot be provided, however, for meeting the many problems which occur as student teachers work with committees. The solutions to these problems lie in thorough knowledge of the children in the group, adequate understanding of the subject concerned and of the available resources, and, above all, faith that the learner does have something to contribute to the learning process and that more learning will result from his involvement.

Adjusting the Program to Meet Individual Differences

The fortunate student teacher enters a classroom where individuals are respected; where individual differences are respected, not decried; and where every effort is made to help each child achieve at his level, pursue his special interests, and satisfy many of his unique drives. This statement hardly represents original thinking; all the participants in the student teaching process have seen or heard similar ideas expressed many, many times. What are the implications of such faith in the worth of each individual? What are the practical applications of respect for individual differences?

First of all, the teacher and the student teacher are aware of the characteristics which make each child different. In a classroom where individual differences are respected, there is a wealth of evidence about each child. The results of intelligence tests, achievement tests, interest inventories, sociometric measures, and pertinent anecdotal records are included in the child's cumulative record; and this record is immediately available to the teacher. Records of parent conferences and of the child's achievement in preceding grades will be included in such cumulative folders, along with any other information which will enable the teacher to know each child better and to work with each child more effectively.

Second, it means that facilities and resources are adequate for the necessary adjustments of the program. It is somewhat naive to suggest to the student teacher that he take individual differences into account in planning his reading program if the classroom in which he works is equipped with straight and uncompromising rows of desks extending from the coatroom in the back to the chalkboard in the front except for room to stand and the space provided for the teacher's desk. Proper attention to individual differences is also difficult if the reading materials consist of grade level editions of the adapted reading series, and nothing more. Even the most dedicated and creative student teacher would find it difficult to do much in such a situation.

Probably the most significant aspect of attention to individual differences is the relationship which exists between the teacher and each pupil. When one child was heard complaining that his teacher "went so fast I couldn't keep up," the child's mother suggested that the child inform the teacher of his problem. The child sadly shook his head, "He isn't *that* kind of teacher, Mother." The most complete cumulative record and the most up-to-date facilities and learning resources will accomplish little or nothing in the classroom of a teacher who attempts to teach every child the same facts at the same time, whose program consists of lock-step "progress" through the adapted textbook for each subject area. Even in the absence of adequate materials, an alert teacher, and one who is concerned for children, can adjust his pacing. In fact, such a teacher will find the materials, somewhere, somehow, if his belief in the importance of helping each child grow at his own rate rather than an imposed rate is strong enough.

It may be helpful to note what constitutes individualized instruction in each of the major curricular areas—what does individualized instruction mean in reading and language arts, in mathematics, in science, and in the social studies?

If individualized instruction is practiced in reading and the language arts:

Children will be given wide latitude and freedom in selecting reading materials, whether or not these are included in or supplementary to the basal program.

Work on word analysis skills will be adjusted to each child's needs. Needs will be considered in assigning drill or practice material, and it will not be considered essential to finish every exercise on every page in a workbook.

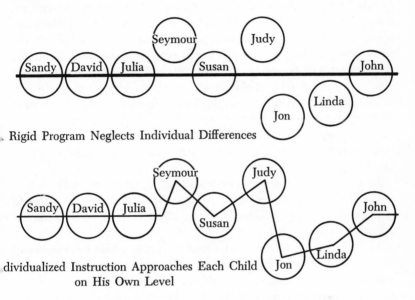

Rigid Program Neglects Individual Differences

Individualized Instruction Approaches Each Child on His Own Level

FIGURE 11.   INDIVIDUALIZED INSTRUCTION

Spelling lists will take into account words individual children have missed in writing stories and reports. The number of words each child is expected to master each week is also adjusted in terms of the teacher's knowledge of what is reasonable. Perhaps a basic list, a spelling workbook, is used; even so, it is not considered the entire spelling program.

Children will not be expected to exhibit handwriting which is identical to that in the copybook. The teacher works for legibility, neatness, a reasonable rate of speed, and somewhat even slant; but Mary's W doesn't have to be exactly like that in the manual. In making the transition from manuscript to cursive writing, the teacher may make some general, introductory comments to the entire class; but children will understand that the change is gradual, that each will receive all the help and encouragement he needs, and that it isn't "bad" still to use manuscript writing when nearly everyone else is using cursive writing.

The creative writing experiences children have will stem from their experiences, not be dictated by instructions from the textbook (in the better textbooks, of course, topics or ideas are *suggested*, and the authors of the textbook depend upon the teacher to use the ideas imaginatively). For young children, especially, the length of the story or report will not be a primary consideration; time limits for the writing will be interpreted flexibly; and no child, at any grade level, will be forced to make public a story or poem he has written.

The children recognize that the language they bring with them is neither "good" nor "bad" but that it is theirs. The work which is done to change substandard English to a socially more acceptable kind is done to help the child, not to condemn him or his linguistic background.

In mathematics, the individualized instruction means that:

The child won't be expected to move from concrete examples to numerical abstractions before he can make this move easily and confidently.

The teacher recognizes that there are many roads to Rome, and that a method of developing understanding of algorism which makes sense to Mary may or may not make sense to Susan. There is flexibility in method and process; and the emphasis is always on understanding, not rote memorization.

The child is not expected to move to a more advanced process (moving to two-digit multipliers from one-digit ones, for example) before the teacher is fairly certain that a sound foundation has been laid. As in the language arts, practical material is assigned with individual needs in mind, and a thorough program of diagnostic testing keeps the teacher fairly well informed concerning fundamentals which children do and do not understand.

The teacher is careful to use vocabulary, in mathematics, which is accurate and specific, but which is clearly understood by the child with whom he's communicating. Some children use terms such as *associative law* confidently and easily, but simpler language may be needed for others.

Even if this means consulting with a specialist whose knowledge and understanding of mathematics exceeds his, the classroom teacher will make sure that each child is *growing*, is challenged, and that *grade level* doesn't suggest a ceiling any more than it suggests a floor.

In science, individualized instruction means that:

Children will be encouraged to pursue individual interests, to find ways of answering questions which are of special concern to them. The science experiences of the whole group should expand individual interests, not confine them, and should stimulate individual projects and experiments, not inhibit them.

As in mathematics, the bright child will be encouraged, and the teacher will not hesitate to say, "I don't know, but I know where we can find out!" The teacher will not assume grade level knowledge, whatever that is, but will find out what children know and don't know and will develop his program accordingly.

Children will not be afraid to make mistakes, and no question will be considered a stupid question. There are abstractions in science which are difficult for some children to grasp, and the teacher, as well as brighter children, will patiently accept this fact. Concrete examples, demonstrations, and experiments will be used as long as they help to build understandings, concepts, and generalizations. (It would logically follow from this that each child would not necessarily have to participate in each demonstration or project.)

If individualized instruction is provided in social studies:

Children will be helped to understand abstractions. This problem —in connection with such concepts as *peninsula, legislature, democracy*—occurs here as well as in the areas previously discussed, and direct experience cannot be relied upon to the extent it can be in science and mathematics. Films, filmstrips, and reading material written in a simpler style and with a more limited vocabulary can help develop some of these generalizations, and so can frequent discussions in which children express their understandings in their own terminology.

A variety of materials will be used. Newspapers, news magazines, pamphlets, and other reading materials in addition to the text can certainly help the teacher in guiding each child in the formulation of important concepts and generalization. Field trips and resource people can perform this same function.

Children will have freedom, within the structure of a social studies unit, to pursue individual interests. For example, as part of a study of the Civil War, a child may wish to gather biographical data about General Grant or find out more about battle equipment. These individual projects will have real meaning for the child because he has selected them; and if the child carefully organizes his data and reports it in an interesting manner, the class, too, can gain much.

Work on map skills, research skills, and other skills will be planned so that each child feels he is learning and accomplishing something. A concept may be introduced to the entire group to conserve time, but the teacher follows this with as much individual help as each child needs.

The separation of these curricular areas, for purposes of discussion, should not be interpreted as an indication that relationships are insignificant, that the integration of knowledge is an outdated and discarded educational goal. The teacher who attempts to plan a program which takes into account individual differences in intelligence, socioeconomic background, etc. will do this not in one area but in as many areas as time and materials make practical. The examples suggested in this section are merely illustrative; the alert, creative, sensitive cooperating teacher or student teacher will think of many more as he adds to his knowledge of his children and his particular teaching situation.

Methods instructors with specific responsibility for a curricular area can contribute much to a student teacher's ability to adjust programs to better meet children's needs. This help could be provided through individual conferences or through discussions with seminar groups. An alert college supervisor will not overlook the contribution methods instructors can make, and will draw fully on their expertise.

When the Cooperating Teacher Is Indifferent or Disagrees

Can the student teacher adjust his program to meet individual differences in the face of the cooperating teacher's indifference or opposition? At first thought, the answer to this question appears to be rather clearly, "No!" If the student teacher enters a situation in which the approach is "every child on the same page at the same time," it seems rather foolhardy to suggest that he try individualized reading,

INDIVIDUAL PROJECTS CAN BE CHALLENGING

grouping in mathematics, a variety of science experiments dealing with properties of air, or rewriting some of the social studies material so it can be read by some of the poorer readers.

In fact, however, isn't this an improper question to ask? Would a classroom teacher who is rigid and inflexible in his teaching philosophy and methods be selected as a cooperating teacher? If conditions were ideal this would not happen, but the readers of this book are well aware that conditions are not ideal and that selection of cooperating teachers is sometimes made on the basis of insufficient evidence. Student teachers are, not infrequently, assigned to teachers who have little or no feeling for individual children or the unique learning problems each one presents. Can nothing be done, except in the area of helping the student teacher adjust to this sad state of affairs? The college or university supervisor can be of tremendous service here. First of all, if the supervisor is alert, such a teacher will not be selected! Much can be done, however, even if mistakes are made, if the cooperating teacher is interested in helping the student teacher and does not assume his way is the only way. The following dialogue suggests one approach:

DR. ARTHUR (college supervisor): Miss Collins, Jane is certainly enjoying her work in your classroom. She feels she has learned so much, and I'm sure this is true after listening to her contributions in our seminars. Several of the student teachers have mentioned individualized reading, and Jane seems to be very interested in trying it. I notice you have a very good school library, and I wonder whether you and Jane might select three or four of your brighter youngsters with whom Jane might try this approach to reading?

MISS COLLINS: Well, I suppose so—individualized reading involves conferences, doesn't it? What would the other children be doing while Jane had her conferences?

DR. ARTHUR: Oh, any of the usual "seatwork" could be used; or you could proceed with your regular reading activities while Jane holds her conferences out in the hall, where she wouldn't disturb your class.

This sounds a bit directive, and you may be sure such a dialogue would occur only after much evidence of disappointment and frustration on Jane's part. Dr. Arthur was obviously using his position and the status it gives him as a lever (a club, if you prefer) to make a change, even a small one, which is important for the growth of the student teacher. He didn't suggest reorganizing the reading program, or using multiple texts for reading, or anything which would have seriously threatened the classroom teacher—even such a small change as that suggested was traumatic, but it was at least within the realm of possibility.

Visits to classrooms where teachers are demonstrating adjustment to individual differences can be arranged, again, under the firm and kindly auspices of the supervisor, who may say, "Miss Collins, I'm sure you wouldn't mind if Jane visited Mrs. Boland's class, would you? I'd like to give Jane the chance to see older (or younger) children."

The student teacher may not have such able support, however. What can he do in the event he is on his own? The student teacher can show his interest in the children by giving special help before school, after school while a few are waiting for the bus, or at any other free moments during the day. This is asking a great deal of the student teacher, it is true, but it may be the only possible way for him to show his awareness of individual differences and his concern for meeting them adequately. The student teacher can bring books, magazines, newspapers, or pamphlets to class for use as materials supplementary to the text. If possible, class time should be provided for the use of such materials; at least, children can use them during free periods and take them home to read. The student teacher can encourage individual projects to be completed at home. If the student teacher shows interest in collections, hobbies, science experiments, etc. and through skillful questions and comments stimulates the child to persevere even though he is not required to for a grade, both the child and the student teacher can learn.

These suggestions seem quite small, and the results may be equally small. They do not substitute for an effective classroom program. They can help the student teacher see the possibilities, however; and he will not leave student teaching assuming that the approach and organization he sees is the only way or even the best way.

Incidentally, college methods teachers can be of real service if they will take time to discuss specific teaching problems with student teachers who return to campus for seminars and conferences and if, in their courses, they will not be dogmatic about techniques of teaching. Student teachers who find a philosophy of teaching totally different from any they have been led to expect sometimes feel lost ("If I can't do it the way Mrs. Brown said to, in math methods, I don't know what to do"). College instructors need to accept some responsibility for helping prospective teachers become open-minded and willing to try different approaches.

When the Student Teacher Does Not Try to Individualize His Program

The fault is not always the cooperating teacher's when a student teacher fails to attempt individualized instruction; lack of effort to adjust to individual differences can sometimes be traced to the student's laziness, timidity, or lack of knowledge. The following comments are illustrative:.

SUSAN: Mrs. Jacobs, why is it so important to use a different text for each reading group? My time is so limited; I just haven't enough time to make all those plans and charts and things. Besides, these children are third-graders, and I think they ought to be able to handle third grade material. We all read out of the same book when I was in the third grade, and it didn't hurt me!

CAROLE: Dr. Jones, Mrs. Evans wants me to study the arithmetic papers the children did today and see what kind of mistakes they're making. Then she wants me to make up some worksheets and help those who are having a lot of trouble. I just don't think I can do it—won't the children resent it if I single them out and treat them like dumbbells?

BILL: Miss Brown, I've watched you do a dozen individualized reading conferences, and in language arts we did lots of reading about this. I just know my questions would be "picky" and I'd make the child feel he was taking a test. I just don't think I can do it! I should be able to, but I can't.

After the initial feeling of despair passes, the cooperating teacher and college supervisor can answer these student teachers, and the answers can be phrased in such a way that the student teacher's growth is enhanced. First, each should make a mental note to inform the other of these comments and the attitudes they reflect. The cooperating teacher might suggest to Susan that she look again at the intelligence test scores and the achievement test scores. This should be ample evidence that the children in the class differ and that different learning experiences must be planned for them. She should also be asked to examine thoroughly her motivation for teaching. A student teacher who exhibits as little enthusiasm and expends as little energy as this gives cause for deep concern. It might be better if she chose another profession, one which is physically and emotionally less demanding than teaching.

Dr. Jones might first suggest to Carole that she survey the math papers and note the errors, as requested. Then she might develop some worksheets for those who showed little understanding of the process or processes involved; these would, of course, be used after additional explanation and further instruction. He might also suggest that she develop some worksheets for other ability levels, each representing a skill not mastered or a concept not grasped. These would also follow explanation and instruction and might help Carole feel better about singling out the "dumbbells" for extra work. This will probably not solve the basic problem, however. Because Carole seems to have trouble accepting slow learners, she may be assuming the brighter youngsters in the class have this trouble, as well. If the level of human relationships in this classroom is high, the children will accept each other as worthwhile human beings, with strengths, weaknesses, competencies and shortcomings, and academic competence, or lack of it, will not attract undue attention. Carole needs to examine her concepts of learning and her beliefs about the type or types of pupils the public school should serve.

How can the cooperating teacher and the supervisor help Bill, who says he just doesn't know how? First of all, something could be done to help build his confidence, perhaps by reviewing briefly the things he's done successfully and which at one point he felt he couldn't do. Then he might make, along with the cooperating teacher, a detailed lesson plan, perhaps for a sharing time—for example, a discussion of books (such as mysteries) all of which relate to one area. With such a detailed plan and with knowledge of the books to be shared, he can move gradually toward effective individual conferences. Because he might feel the sharing was of a little less significance to successful individualized reading than the conference, he might consider it less threatening.

Neither the cooperating teacher nor the college supervisor should feel he has each of these situations to handle by himself; desirable changes will be effected much more quickly if the cooperating teacher and the college supervisor work together and toward similar goals. Each must use the knowledge he has of the student teacher, and each must apply the principle of individual differences to student teachers as one does to children. Each student teacher's rate of growth is unique; the methods and techniques which work with one will not be successful with another. The three-way conferences which have been referred to several times can be very useful with student teachers who need help and guidance in adjusting the program to meet individual differences.

The student teacher may not be aware of some learning resources which might help him in adjusting his program. The cooperating teacher should certainly be expected to know the library, the films, the tapes, all the facilities which might be used to enrich learning and to reach each child more effectively.

The College Supervisor's Role

The college supervisor can help the student teacher who wishes to adjust his program to meet individual differences. The supervisor should not try to do this alone, but should work as part of the student teaching team. The individual conferences, group meetings, and seminars mentioned before are of value in solving problems related to the individualization of instruction. Another useful technique is the preparation of materials for use by the student teachers: tips, suggestions, ideas, and lists of resources which will be of present and future value to the student teacher.

SUMMARY

Success in college course work, professional and general, is an accepted prerequisite for student teaching. A certain minimal prior acquaintance with the student teaching situation and the personnel involved is assumed and will unquestionably contribute to productive and rewarding student teaching. The student teacher's performance will also be enhanced by a gradual although active induction into teaching and by help which supports without diminishing the student teacher's self-reliance or independence. All of this, however, is designed to prepare the student teacher for the acceptance of major responsibility for the growth of a group of children; and outstanding success in these pre-student teaching phases of professional preparation cannot begin to compensate for incompetence and ineptitude with a group of children. The purposes of this chapter have been to suggest, first, the significance of that portion of student teaching in which the college student becomes the teacher and is accepted in this role by the children as well as by school personnel and, second, to provide some guidelines which may help the student teacher and those who guide his growth toward independence and self-reliance.

Whole Group Instruction

The position has been taken that work with an entire group of children or with more than one class need not be unproductive. If the introduction of new topics to an entire class is followed by attention to individual learning rates and variations in interests and experiences, genuine learning may result. Whole group instruction of a worthwhile nature goes far beyond the "every child on the same page of the same text" concept upon which some teachers have operated for too long. It seems that some phases of the learning process can be carried on with entire classes, with beneficial results. At any rate, in an era when educators are faced with a double explosion—the explosion of knowledge and the population explosion—it makes sense to search for more effective and creative ways of working with large groups.

Small Group Instruction and Committee Work

The student teacher's first opportunities to work with children will probably be either individual help of some kind or supervision of a small group of children or a committee. Groups of children may be organized on the basis of needs, interests, or level of academic achievement. In general, groups organized on the basis of achievement levels are organized by the classroom teacher before the student teacher arrives, and the student teacher's role includes suggesting changes in the groups and providing interesting and challenging materials. The essential difference between small group work and committee work is that children's purposes and objectives are central to successful committee work but may or may not be identified for small group work. In both types of organization, the student teacher assists by providing guidance, help, and other resources of many kinds; in committee work the leadership role is assumed by one or more of the children.

Individual Instruction

Since his days as an elementary school pupil, the student teacher has been increasingly aware of differences in learning rate, motivation, interests, and achievement. It is to be hoped that he begins student teaching with the understanding that some attention must be given to these differences if maximum learning is to result. He becomes a student of children first and learns as much as possible about them, their strengths, weaknesses, problems, and concerns. Then he turns his attention to the structure of the various areas of the curriculum. A third concern is what society, as reflected in the school community, expects the school to accomplish. Each of these—knowledge of child development, the structure of the disciplines, and society's goals for its schools—must be considered in planning for a group or for an individual child. There appears to be a decreasing emphasis on considering the nature of the child in planning his learning experiences; but this can hardly be ignored even if one's first consideration is the structure of a subject, because the rates at which different individuals can comprehend succeeding levels in an organized discipline will vary a great deal. Ignorance of individual differences, or failure to act upon the knowledge of such differences, will result in learning which is mediocre at best. In the section of this chapter which dealt with making curricular adjustments in terms of individual differences, specific suggestions were given for work in language arts, science, social studies, and mathematics. Permitting—indeed, encouraging—individual study of a topic was recommended, as was pacing progress through text material on the basis of rates that are appropriate for individual children, and not by dividing the number of textbook pages by the number of teaching days.

Help Provided by the Cooperating Teacher and the College Supervisor

These two participants in the student teaching process should not feel their jobs have been completed when the student teacher demonstrates some competence and independence in guiding individuals and groups of children, small and large. They may suggest new methods, new techniques, and resources which the student teacher may not know about. They will continue to support the student teacher, to hold conferences and meetings which deal with problems and concerns of the student teacher. The student teacher may need an extra amount of encouragement or stimulation, and the supervisor and "critic" are in the best positions to provide this. It is very important that the supervisor and cooperating teacher work together, and it is unfortunate when the student teacher must receive all the help he gets in attending to individual differences from his cooperating teacher or has to visit another classroom to see effective committee work.

Suggested Activities for Student Teachers

1. Examine copies* of the schedule or daily program developed by the cooperating teacher. For each area of the curriculum, develop some possible techniques or methods for utilizing small group instruction, possibly including committee work.

2. In areas of the curriculum in which the approach is almost without exception centered on the whole group and on the textbook, develop some worthwhile follow-up activities which will make individualizing instruction practical. These might include, for example, worksheets which would be assigned individually or lists of additional "enrichment" procedures for bright children.

3. Invite a methods teacher, or a panel of methods teachers, to work with a group of student teachers in attempting to solve instructional problems in his, or their, areas of competence. It is probably most helpful if one area at a time can be discussed; but if crowded days and busy schedules prevent this, the panel approach (a math methods instructor and a social studies methods instructor, sharing a two-hour seminar, for example) should be of some value.

4. Early in the student teaching experience, a list of long-range goals was developed for each curricular area. Examine these goals now, preferably with the cooperating teacher and the supervisor. Prepare a brief and simple statement of progress.

Selected References

Burr, James B., Harding, Lowry W., and Jacobs, Leland B. *Student Teaching in the Elementary School.* New York: Appleton-Century-Crofts, 1958, Chapters 6, 7, and 8.

Byers, Loretta, and Irish, Elizabeth. *Success in Student Teaching.* Boston: D. C. Heath & Company, 1961, Chapters 6, 7, and 8.

Concern for the Individual in Student Teaching. (Forty-second Yearbook) Cedar Falls, Iowa: The Association for Student Teaching, 1963.

---

* It is most beneficial if the teacher is given the opportunity to *try* these approaches, after such lists have been developed. This may not always be possible, however; and some benefit should be gained by directing the student teacher's attention to the possibilities that exist.

Michaelis, John U., and Dumas, Enoch. *The Student Teacher in the Elementary School.* Englewood Cliffs, New Jersey: Prentice-Hall, Inc., 1960, Chapters 7, 8, and 9.

New Insights and the Curriculum. (1963 Yearbook) Washington, D.C.: The Association for Supervision and Curriculum Development, 1963.

Wingo, G. Max, and Schorling, Raleigh. *The Elementary School Student Teacher.* New York: McGraw-Hill Book Co., Inc., 1960, Chapters 3, 4, 5, and 8.

6

Using Learning Resources

As the student teacher works with children, in groups and individually, he will gain an increasing awareness of the importance of the materials available for his use. One hopes that this lesson will be learned as a result of having a broad range of films, filmstrips, tapes, slides, models, and other media available. Unfortunately, too often it is the lack of such learning resources in the face of obvious need which impresses the student teacher. Why are learning resources so important? Is it intended that a teaching machine someday replace the teacher? Clearly, this is not the intention even of those most heartily supporting programmed learning! Rather, learning resources which supplement the textbook are important because:

1. They can help the teacher adjust the program to meet more adequately the needs of each of the children in his classroom; a film, a filmstrip, a tape recording can often help the teacher reach a child who has not been reached by verbal symbols, written or spoken.

2. They enable the learner to identify more easily with persons, ways of life, and ideas which are different from those he has known. Direct experience has no substitute; but time and other practical limitations prevent traveling to Africa, visiting Congress in session, or

observing the first U.S. moon shot in person. Direct participation in important historical events, such as the signing of our Constitution or the first session of the United Nations General Assembly, is impossible. Seeing these events on film, traveling to faraway places through television, filmstrips, or tape recordings will give added meaning to the social studies and science programs, enrich the literature program, and add life and vitality to the entire curriculum.

3.   They present points of view which contrast with and may even contradict those presented in the textbooks or by the teacher. In a democracy, such divergent views are to be encouraged. They stimulate critical thinking and problem-solving abilities, attributes desperately needed by every citizen today, and by those preparing to lead our nation tomorrow. At the very least, a carefully selected film causes a reorganization of facts, opinions, and concepts; at best, it can stimulate a change of opinion, a reorientation toward a group of people or another way of life.

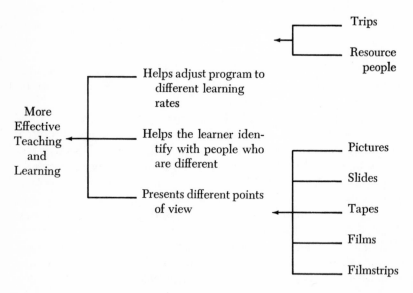

FIGURE 12.   USING LEARNING RESOURCES

Figure 12 illustrates and summarizes these reasons for using adequate learning resources. These are also some of the reasons for dissatisfaction with the single-textbook approach to teaching. No text-book, however well it is written, is adequate by itself; learning can be immeasurably enriched through the selective and judicious use of trade books, slides, maps, films, filmstrips, models, exhibits, bulletin boards, records, and tape recordings. In fact, as the student teacher is well aware, most textbooks include references to appropriate supplementary resources of many varieties. As Chandos Reid writes, "It is through the use of a wide range of media both for furthering the quest for learning and for reinforcing and expressing ideas already learned that we can best help children learn constantly from the world about them."[1]

It is hoped that before student teaching, one will have learned how to thread and operate a standard movie projector, filmstrip projector, and tape recorder. If these skills have not been acquired, then the supervisor may suggest that arrangements for instruction be made so that the student teacher will have demonstrated competency in these areas before he leaves campus. The student teacher should not be dependent upon his cooperating teacher or the school's audio-visual coordinator for such instruction, although it is better to ask for and receive their help than not to use audio-visual aids because of ignorance of operating procedures.

During the initial visit to the school, the student teacher should attempt to acquaint himself with the range of materials available. Such questions as the following are appropriate:

Where is the audio-visual equipment stored? How does one arrange for its use?

Are films shown in the classroom, or is there a room other than the classroom which must be scheduled when a film is shown?

Is there a catalogue, file, or list of films and other materials which are owned by the school system and are permanently available? How may such media not owned by the school system be ordered (if at all)?

Where is the school library? Is there a trained librarian? Do the children visit the school library regularly as a group, or as the need arises? If the public library is used, how many books may be checked out at once, and for how long may they be kept?

---

[1] "Children Learn Through Many Media," *Childhood Education*, February, 1960, p. 254.

Are textbooks at several levels available for use in one classroom, or is a teacher limited to the use of only third grade textbooks in the

STUDENT TEACHERS WORK TOGETHER TO CHECK AVAILABLE RESOURCES

third grade? Where are textbooks kept? Is there a book room or central repository for books? Does each teacher have "his own" textbooks? If so, may these be traded with other teachers?

Other questions will occur to the student teacher as he learns more about his situation. The cooperating teacher may well anticipate some of his concerns and include important information in the first conference, if it is not in the guidebook developed by and for the teachers of a school or school system.

Types of Audio-visual Aids and Resources

What types of audio-visual equipment should the student teacher know how to use and hope to find in his student teaching situation? It is inappropriate to include a lengthy and detailed description of projectors, films, chart types, etc. in a book of this nature. For such a list the student teacher is referred to sources listed at the end of this chapter; however, a brief and suggestive list of commonly used equipment and resources is included here as an aid to the student teacher who wishes to review and reinforce his skills and knowledge in this important area.

Films and Film Projectors

Children respond positively to the sound and movement of a film (as well as color, when provided); manufacturers are attempting to provide projectors which are simple to operate. The student teacher should not assume, however, that he knows how to operate the type of projector owned by the school system, which may differ somewhat from the one he learned to operate in a course in audio-visual materials. Obviously, any film shown to children should be previewed first; and young children, especially, should not have to wait very long for the projector to be threaded, the screen to be raised or lowered, and other preparations to be made. It is far better if everything is prepared while the children are on the playground or perhaps during the lunch period, so that getting started is merely a matter of flicking a switch. Replacement bulbs should be easily accessible, again to avoid long delays.

Filmstrips and Filmstrip Projectors

Filmstrip projectors have the advantage of ease of operation, and the films they use are lower in cost. Filmstrips lack the attraction of motion, but can be stopped for any length of time while the class discusses a particular frame. Children can learn to operate filmstrip projectors, freeing the teacher to give his entire attention to the discussion of the filmstrip and to observing the reaction and response of the children. Most filmstrip projectors can be adapted for showing slides. Slides which the teacher has collected on various trips can be a very valuable aid to a social studies lesson. Again, it is a wise precaution to be sure that an extra bulb is at hand and that the screen, projector, and other paraphernalia are arranged before the attention of the children is expected. Previewing a filmstrip is somewhat easier than previewing a film, and small individual projectors or viewers for this purpose are available.

Overhead and Opaque Projectors

These projectors make it possible to show small maps, pages of a book, flat pictures, and overlays to a large group. Many teachers have found such projectors invaluable aids in helping children construct large maps from those of smaller scale or in showing steps in a complex scientific process by using plastic overlays in different colors. Opaque projectors are quite large, cumbersome, and difficult to move. Overhead projectors are smaller and easier to move, and because the bulb produces less heat it does not damage the material being projected. Either projector, or both, can serve well in making single copies of valuable material available to the entire class.

Television

A few school systems have their own television stations and offer courses planned by groups of teachers, with outstanding teachers from the school system providing the instruction. More frequently, television lessons come from corporate enterprises such as the Midwest Program on Airborne Television Instruction. Advantages of television instruction are fairly obvious: First, teachers who have demonstrated competence are selected as television teachers. Second, a great deal of time can be devoted to preparing a television lesson, or series of lessons, and an almost limitless number of aids or amount of materials are available. Third, children can experience vicariously that which it would be difficult for them to experience directly. "Trips" to distant art museums, an automobile factory, a congressional committee hearing become meaningful learning experiences for children through effective use of this medium.

Television instruction has some obvious disadvantages, however: First, it is inflexible. A science lesson is telecast at a given time each day, or several times a week. This may or may not be the best time for a teacher and a group of children. Second, television lessons, in social studies especially, are quickly outdated and are expensive to replace or update. Finally, there is a tendency for classroom teachers to neglect areas of the curriculum in which the children are receiving television instruction. They may abdicate responsibility for instruction in music, for example, rather than working with and supplementing that which is presented on television. A story, unfortunately true, is told about a group of foreign educators touring elementary schools in our country to observe foreign-language instruction. In every elementary classroom they entered in one school system, the television set was turned on, and the lesson was proceeding. The teachers were absent and there was complete lack of attention from the children; in fact, the conditions observed by these educators were chaotic. More and more television lessons are being put on kinescopes, which can be rented or purchased by schools or school systems and used when the classroom teacher wants to use them and in the manner he deems most appropriate. A plan such as this minimizes the disadvantages of television and permits the teacher to make effective use of this resource.

Maps and Globes

These should be available in a variety of sizes and with subject matter from the simplest (outlines of continents, or large, simplified maps of the U.S. with only the names of the states) to the most complex. For beginners, simplicity is so important that it deserves emphasis here. Most globes and maps try to convey far too much information for a third- or fourth-grader. It cannot be assumed that even fifth and sixth grade children can interpret legends without some instruction. There is a need in the upper grades for maps which portray different kinds of data—physical maps, political maps, product maps, or population maps, for example. Although a globe, of course, is a more accurate representation of the earth's surface than a map, and every map contains a few (or many) inaccuracies, maps are necessary for showing detail and are especially useful for representing a relatively small geographical area.

Charts

Commercially prepared charts are frequently used in teaching such things as phonics, sentence diagramming, or organization of governmental units. These conserve teachers' time and are usually attractive. It might be suggested that charts made by the teacher or by the pupils and the teacher provide more depth of learning and a closer relationship between the learner and his curriculum.

Models, Realia, Dioramas

Teachers and children can profit from the development of these types of learning aids, which represent a means of illustrating ways of life different from that which the children know, of bringing a literary scene almost to life, of making learning interesting, and facilitating the retention of important generalizations.

Bulletin Boards

Attractively arranged bulletin boards can do much to brighten a classroom and to reinforce or supplement more highly verbal learnings. Displays of children's work (not always just the best) or of book jackets, bulletin boards related to seasonal events or holidays—all these and more have been used effectively by elementary teachers.

Many significant learning resources other than those just named might be listed, of course. There is great variation from school to school and from classroom to classroom in the number of these resources which are provided, and the student teacher will almost certainly wish to make a thorough examination of the equipment and resources available to him.

Assuming (optimistically) a wealth of resources, how does the student teacher select? What criteria govern the selection of this film but not that one, of this tape recording before that one? *Appropriateness* is one of the first criteria. Is the aid or resource appropriate in length, approach, and subject matter or content for the group for which it is intended? A second criterion is *value*. Does the film or filmstrip contain some truly valid and useful ideas, and do these relate to some area of study in which the children are presently actively engaged? (Surely the practice of herding large groups of children into an auditorium to see a movie—any movie—can no longer be defended!) Included within the limits of this criterion would be such important considerations as the date the material was published or produced, the authoritativeness of the material, and the additional help provided for the teacher, in the form of a guide, manual, or outline. A third criterion, closely related to the first two, is *interest* or *attractiveness*. Will this aid or resource capture and hold the attention of the children? Significant material, geared for the grade level or levels under consideration, will serve no purpose at all if it is presented in a dull, uninteresting manner.

The cooperating teacher can be of real service to the student teacher in applying these criteria and in making the careful preparations essential to effective use of any aid or resource. The material will be previewed, if at all possible; and the student teacher will determine how it should be introduced. It may or may not be necessary to remind children of the unanswered questions, the unsolved problems, which have provided the reasons for viewing, or reading, or listening. A discussion following the presentation can serve to pinpoint major concepts and clear up misconceptions, and it can reveal questions which are still unanswered and problems which are still unresolved; an effective teaching aid is as open-ended as an effective discussion. Together the cooperating teacher and the student teacher decide why the aid will be used, what purpose it will serve; determine how it will be used and when; and select appropriate introductory and follow-up activities. Although this may not be necessary, the cooperating teacher may also tactfully remind the student teacher of the importance of following established school routines and policies in scheduling, care of equipment, loan periods, and other details which can easily slip the mind of a beginner.

What about the situations in which there is no school library, no A-V coordinator (*media specialist* or *materials specialist* is a newer title), and only a limited number of textbooks? The public library has already been mentioned, and the following sources may also be utilized: (1) Paperback book clubs—Scholastic magazines and *My Weekly Reader* both have such clubs, making paperback books available to children at prices from thirty-five cents to a dollar. (2) Children's magazines and newspapers—*Highlights for Children, Jack and Jill,* and *Children's Digest* are only three of the very good magazines to which many children subscribe; *My Weekly Reader* and Scholastic periodicals are both published almost every week during the school year, and at every level, Grades 1-6. (3) Books owned by the children—If these are properly labeled to prevent loss, many children would be happy to bring them to school. (4) Although such practices are hardly to be encouraged, it is a well known fact that dedicated teachers do spend a great deal of money, their own money, on supplies. Money spent on books probably yields greater returns than money spent on construction paper, crêpe paper, cutouts, gummed seals and stars, and the other items teachers commonly buy. Schools ought to be supported at a level which makes such expenditures unnecessary; but at the present time, in many communities, teachers must buy the "extras" which are, in reality, so very important for enriched learning.

FIELD TRIPS

One of the most valuable learning resources available to the student teacher is the field trip, an organized, purposeful class visit to an industry, community service, or governmental agency. The field trip is also a learning resource fraught with danger for the inexperienced teacher, or student teacher! Nowhere is planning more important or the student teacher's ability to guide children effectively put to a more severe test. Many field trip problems result directly from the student teacher's tendency to consider any trip a good trip, any extra-school activity worthwhile. Guidance from the cooperating teacher and supervisor can and must cause the student teacher to examine carefully the reasons and purposes for any proposed trips and their relationship to the educational program. The student teacher is seldom fully aware of the impact of a trip upon school-community relationships. A poorly organized trip, taken by children who aren't very sure why they're leaving school but are delighted and exuberant over the change of routine, can do great damage to the school's reputation in a community. On the other hand, it is true that a well-organized, purposeful trip, taken by children who are seriously concerned with getting answers to significant questions, can be of tremendous benefit to the school's reputation in the community.

Some teachers have had such terrible experiences on a field trip that they vow never to venture from their classrooms again. There are also a few teachers who regard a trip as a lark, a vacation, a release from routine, and underplay or completely neglect the educative possibilities inherent in a field trip. If a trip is the best way of providing significant and lasting learning experiences, both children and teachers should recognize this and devote the necessary time and energy to insure its success. The following guidelines may help:

1. Children must be involved in planning the trip if it is to be successful. This planning proceeds through identification of purposes, broad and specific; logistic planning (when, where, and how); contacts with personnel at the location to be visited; and follow-up evaluation. Children in the upper grades, obviously, can take more responsibility for planning at every level than can those in the primary grades; but fifth- and sixth-graders will show the results of previous efforts to involve them in planning. Effective participation in any phase of the democratic process must begin before a child is ten or eleven. The teacher and student teacher are well acquainted with their groups and should be competent judges of the level at which the children for whom they are responsible can be involved in the arrangements for a trip. It is enough to say here that some degree of involvement beyond the level of simply telling children they're going to take a trip is fundamental to the success of a field trip.

2. The developmental levels of the children must provide a basic framework for a successful trip. Jane, a student teacher, wished to take her first-graders to a zoo. The bus trip took one hour, and Jane had neglected to plan any activities for the children while they rode on the bus. Result: a disorderly, ill-mannered group of six-year-olds who became the despair of the bus driver and the zoo guide alike.

Susan took her second-graders to the small suburban post office which served the school community. The children were eager to see and learn, but facilities were so arranged that not all thirty of them could see or learn very well. In fact, Susan herself had to wait outside with five or six children who could not even get inside the post office door. While these children had a brief, condensed version of the tour the others received, the larger group waited with the mothers who had provided transportation; and the mothers were not prepared to control the behavior of children in such a large group. Result, a less meaningful learning experience than should have been provided and could have been provided if Susan had acted upon her understanding of the seven-year-old and his needs and interests. Poor facilities were also at fault here, of course; but the group could have been divided for two trips, comparing notes after all had had an adequate tour of the post office.

3. Logistics—involving the movement of children to and from the school; guide service at the destination; food and rest room facilities, if the trip is to be a long one—is a mundane consideration; but failure in this area almost certainly guarantees failure of the trip as a learning experience. The school bus is usually to be preferred as transportation, in contrast to private cars; and the student teacher or teacher should drive only as a last resort. Insurance regulations and liability laws should be checked. Most school trips are entirely uneventful, fortunately; but the wise student teacher will be certain that every precaution is taken and will avoid any mistakes which can be traced to carelessness or poor planning. His parents' written consent for the trip will be a necessary prerequisite to a child's participation. It seems cruel to deny a child the chance to go to the museum simply because she "forgot" her note; but it is very possible that her parents didn't want her to go and would be most unsympathetic in the event of an accident. If the notes are sent home soon enough but not so soon that they are lost before the day of the trip, if children understand that no note means no trip, and if parents understand the importance of the trip, then there should be no problem. Admittedly, the note does not absolve the school or the student teacher from legal responsibility; but the existence of such notes is proof that the parents understood something of the nature of the activity and the risk involved.

4. The student teacher has foreseen the strong drive children have to be directly involved, to see, to hear. It may be necessary to divide the children into several smaller groups, with several guides, seeing

the same things at different times. A visit by the student teacher to the trip destination before the group's visit makes it possible for any problems of this nature to be resolved and will help convince the hosts that this trip is for business as well as pleasure.

5. Specific questions, sent in advance to the guides, will serve to focus the visit, to give it added meaning and purpose. Of course, the children will see and hear much more than they expected to; but their trip is fundamentally for the purpose of getting answers to their questions, and this point should not be lost on the teacher, the guide, or the children. Older children may wish to take notes on the trip; and even some young children may wish to record a percentage, a date, or a name. If the student teacher expects this, the pencils, pads, copies of the questions, and other materials should be easily available, not left at the place where the wraps were deposited as the group entered the building.

6. Discussions, dramatizations, murals, dioramas, written and oral reports may all serve as effective evaluation techniques and help the children better organize what they've learned. A trip is, for young children especially, almost an overwhelming experience; and skillful guidance by the teacher is essential if pupils are to recall the significant, not the trivial, the worthwhile as well as the unimportant. (For one group of children, third-graders, the most vivid recollection of their first train ride, taken as part of a transportation unit, was the drink each one got from the water fountain on the coach!)

None of the preceding remarks is intended to discourage student teachers who wish to plan field trips. They are included in order to underscore what the student teacher already knows, that a field trip is not to be taken without a great deal of thought, planning, and assessment of its values, potential and realized. The supervisor and cooperating teacher should not suggest a trip simply as a learning experience for the student teacher. Unless the children see and identify with the purposes of the trip, the learning for the student teacher will be negative, and he may determine never to try a trip when he has a classroom of his own.

THE RESOURCE PERSON

Frequently, a dentist, a fireman, or other person with specialized knowledge of some type is invited to the classroom to talk with the children, to answer their questions, to give demonstrations or exhibit a collection or pieces of equipment. These are well-meaning, interested persons or they would not have volunteered their time; but they need to be tactfully cautioned about the length of their presentation, the handling of questions, and the level of their approach. The children, too, need to plan and to know something of what to expect. Questions sent to the speaker in advance of his visit, a warning concerning the attention span of the group, and inviting the visitor for a period in the day when children will be relaxed and eager for his presentation will add to the impact the resource person will have and will make his contribution more meaningful. Children may suggest the name of a resource person, or the cooperating teacher may know of someone who can make an important contribution to a particular study. In many elementary schools, a resource file is kept. This file usually consists of a series of cards, carefully selected and kept up to date, on which are listed the names of resource persons who have been effective in the past. The areas of competence are specified, and there is a note on each card concerning the place where the person named may be reached. Such a file is very valuable, and the student teacher should know of its existence and make use of it. A similar file related to field trips is equally valuable.

One knows before student teaching begins that a single textbook is, by itself, inadequate; it is to be hoped that in his student teaching situation he will find learning resources of many varieties, a philosophy of teaching and learning which supports their use, and guidance and direction in their selection and utilization.

THE ROLE OF THE COOPERATING TEACHER AND THE COLLEGE SUPERVISOR IN THE SELECTION AND USE OF LEARNING RESOURCES

The cooperating teacher and the college supervisor encourage the student teacher to involve the children in many types of learning experiences, to use a wide variety of resources at appropriate times, and to accomplish specific purposes. They can insist that objectives be stated prior to the use of a resource, acquaint the student teacher with the resources available to him, help in applying criteria which will aid in selecting the best or most appropriate resource, and aid in evaluating the learning which results.

The responsibility of the supervisor and cooperating teacher for providing instruction in the operation of film projectors and other equipment has been referred to; it is sometimes true that the student teacher has had little or no prior experience with such equipment; and although it should not be necessary, such instruction must be provided within the student teaching experience or the student teacher will begin his teaching career unable to operate or function effectively in the field of learning resources of which audio-visual aids represent such an important part.

It might be added here that the supervisor who is also a methods teacher can help the student teacher a great deal by demonstrating in the college methods class as well as in meetings and seminars the significant contribution to learning which results from what has been called the multi-media approach.

SUMMARY

As the student teacher works with children, in groups and individually, his work will be made more effective if he makes full use of the learning resources which are available to him. In addition to the textbook, these include trade books; films, filmstrips; tape recordings; slides; maps; globes; and community resources, including speakers or other resource people. The student teacher needs to become familiar with the operation of the major types of audio-visual equipment and with the procedures to be followed for scheduling their use in the building where he is student teaching. Specific recommendations have been made for effective use of field trips and resource people, special emphasis has been placed on the planning which must precede trips or presentations if maximum learning is to result.

If the student teacher demonstrates the ability to guide groups of children effectively and includes all types of learning resources in order to help them learn more efficiently, he has successfully achieved a major goal. Although the supervisor and the cooperating teacher have at this stage assumed a less active role in the student teaching process, their support and guidance are still essential to the student teacher's greater independence.

Suggested Activities for the Student Teacher

1. Make a checklist of the audio-visual equipment owned by the school,

and make arrangements to learn to operate any equipment with which you are unfamiliar.

2. Check sources such as *Free and Inexpensive Learning Materials*, available from George Peabody College of Education, Nashville, Tennessee, for a list of the films, slides, and filmstrips available for use in the science or social studies unit you have planned or as a supplement to the chapters in the textbooks used in the classroom where you are student teaching. If your state department of education or your school system has such a list, consult it as well.

3. Consult the following sources for general trade books which might enrich units (science, social studies, etc.) or supplement the texts you are using.

    Eakin, Mary K. *Good Books for Children*, compiled by Mary K. Eakin. Rev. ed. Chicago: The University of Chicago Press, 1962.

    Mathes, Miriam Snow. *A Basic Book Collection for Elementary Grades*. Chicago: American Library Association, 1960.

4. Develop a lesson plan involving the use of a film; discuss with your supervisor and cooperating teacher whether the preliminary discussion, guidelines you set, and follow-up activities seem to be appropriate. If possible, try your plan and evaluate the effectiveness of your lesson.

5. Discuss with your cooperating teacher and the principal of the school the regulations about field trips and appropriate procedures in planning a trip; and, if possible, plan a field trip in connection with some major learning experience you are guiding during student teaching.

SELECTED REFERENCES

Boutwell, William D. *Using Mass Media in the Schools*. New York: Appleton-Century-Crofts, 1962.

Burr, James B., Harding, Lowry W., and Jacobs, Leland B. *Student Teaching in the Elementary School*. New York: Appleton-Century-Crofts, 1958, Chapters 11 and 12.

Dale, Edgar. *Audio-Visual Methods in Teaching*. New York: Dryden Press, 1954.

Educational Media Index. New York: McGraw-Hill Book Co., Inc., 1964. Volume 1, *Pre School and Primary* (Grades K–3); Volume 2, *Intermediate* (Grades 4–6).

Reid, Chandos. "Children Learn Through Many Media," *Childhood Education*, February 1960, pp. 248–54.

Wingo, G. Max, and Schorling, Raleigh. *Elementary School Student Teaching*. New York: McGraw-Hill Book Co., Inc., 1955, Chapter 10.

7

Discipline, Management, and Control

Probably no problem looms as large—or is more vexing to the student teacher, the college supervisor, and his cooperating teacher —than the problem of discipline. No amount of demonstrated competence in planning, working with individual children, or success in managing the attendance slip and the milk money can compensate for ineffectiveness before the whole group or, worse, evidence of disrespect and ridicule from the children. Martin writes: "Although many problems confront the student when he begins directed teaching, discipline in the classroom appears to be the one of major importance. Almost without exception student teachers express a doubt about their ability to handle a class.[1] The magnitude of the discipline problem is underscored by Brembeck, who writes: "No single problem is mentioned more frequently by these student teachers. No other problem made greater demands upon their growing skill, yet they demonstrated their ability to learn fast, and most of them emerged

---

[1] John E. Martin, "Discipline, the Student Teacher's Nemesis," *The Educational Forum*, January, 1961, pp. 213–14.

from teaching feeling confident to handle most problems in control."[2] Further documentation relative to the size of the problem and evidence that the problem can be solved could be presented but the readers of this book are almost certainly well aware of the importance of control—of *discipline,* if you will—in successful student teaching. The question which needs to be answered relates to the steps through which one progresses from anxiety to confidence, from inadequacy and timidity before a group to poise and competence.

To claim that the problem is susceptible to solution in three easy steps is to invite ridicule, and rightly so. Discipline problems have their roots in complex interpersonal relationships, influenced and shaped by many past experiences. The child recalls other student teachers and transfers to Miss Smith some of the attitudes and feelings which affected his behavior toward Miss Johnson. Obviously his feelings toward his "regular" teacher, and toward teachers in general, will be involved in the behavior he demonstrates toward student teachers. Finally, he'll be influenced by the behavior of others in the group, and this is true even of young children not normally considered very group-conscious. The discipline problems of student teachers assigned to him in the past will affect the way in which the cooperating teacher works with the student teacher. One report, from a principal, that a former student teacher has had severe discipline problems as a beginning teacher can affect the cooperating teacher's first remarks to the student, and the freedom the student teacher is given to handle behavior problems in his own way. The college supervisor's attitudes toward the student teacher's control problems will reflect his experiences as a classroom teacher and his concept of control and discipline. The individual child, the group of children, the student teacher, the cooperating teacher, and the supervisor may each approach the student teaching experience with different expectations, different concepts of acceptable and unacceptable behavior, and different methods of achieving the goals each has set. To say that all behavior is goal seeking is to repeat a truism, but it is vital to the success of the student teaching experience that this truism be accepted as applying to all those concerned with student teaching. It is unreasonable and unrealistic to expect that the student teacher, the cooperating teacher,

---

[2] Cole S. Brembeck, *The Discovery of Teaching* (Englewood Cliffs, New Jersey: Prentice-Hall, Inc., 1962), p. 21.

and the college supervisor will have identical concepts of self-discipline, although all three will verbalize this term as the ultimate goal. Nor will all three participants agree on the precise nature of unacceptable behavior. A child's comment may well be defined as "cute" and "clever" by one, "sassy" and a bit impertinent by another, and extremely rude and intolerable by the third. The plea for communication, honest and forthright, has been voiced many times in this book. Frequent communication provides the only way divergent views on children's behavior can be resolved and the student teacher freed to develop some techniques, methods, and approaches which will be effective for him.

DISCIPLINE IS NOT A SERIOUS PROBLEM WHEN CHILDREN
ARE BUSY AND LEARNING

The Student Teacher Prepares to
Work Effectively with His Class

In his initial visit to the school, the student teacher will almost certainly observe very carefully the methods and techniques used by the cooperating teacher in providing guidance as children change activities and move to the playground or lunchroom. He will note whether or not children are free to move about the room during independent study periods, whether or not children are permitted to converse naturally as they remove their wraps or work together in small groups. The permissiveness, or complete lack of it, will almost certainly impress the student teacher; and he will learn very quickly the type of classroom atmosphere to which he is expected to adjust and the limits within which he will be expected to work. If the student teaching situation is a desirable one, the atmosphere will be one which will encourage natural, easy relationships and courteous concern for every person in the classroom, and the limits will be those which are set by the demands of group living. If the class is very large, it is probably realistic and wise to expect that children raise their hands before contributing to a discussion and that rather definite routines be established for leaving the classroom, sharpening pencils, etc. These limitations, however, exist because they may make group living easier, and not because the teacher wishes to impose his will upon those who are too young and inexperienced to object. It is undesirable for the student teacher to try to imitate the gestures and small mannerisms which the cooperating teacher uses very effectively; however, it is hardly wise for the student teacher to condone violation of the rules imposed by the cooperating teacher or to encourage a level of behavior which the classroom teacher considers unacceptable. Early in the student teaching period, answers should be sought to the following questions:

1. What is normal and expected behavior before school starts, in the halls, during lunch periods? This behavior is often controlled in terms of what the principal expects, and the student teacher can hardly advocate disobedience and insubordination. He may decide to ask questions during job interviews which will help him to find a position in a school where there is a point of view more akin to his;

but in student teaching he learns and abides by the same policies and rules as do the other teachers in the building.

2. What kind of atmosphere does the cooperating teacher create in his classroom? Is the student teacher free to be somewhat more, or less, permissive, as his beliefs and understanding of children and teaching suggest? It is certainly undesirable for the student teacher to be forced to handle each routine (the distribution of textbooks and paper, for example) precisely as the cooperating teacher does. It would seem logical that the student teacher might set slightly different standards for behavior during transition periods when activities are changing, or that he might not be disturbed if young children make a few comments during the reading of a favorite story or poem. Ordinarily, children can make such minor adjustments in behavior easily, although, as was noted before, behavior with one teacher, or student teacher, certainly influences and affects behavior with other teachers. Within reasonable limits, however, the student teacher should be free to experiment, to try different approaches, and to develop his own ideas about appropriate noise levels and the amount of activity that should be permitted in the classroom.

3. Probably the most important of these questions is: What kind of children is one teaching? What are their attitudes toward school, toward teachers, toward learning, and toward themselves? From what kinds of homes do they come? What sort of relationships exist between each child and his parents; and what attitudes do the parents, in general, have about school? Careful study of the children's cumulative records, observation of and informal conversations with the children, and discussions with the cooperating teacher which focus on these topics should help the student teacher as he attempts to guide but not direct, to encourage initiative and the acceptance of responsibility rather than strict conformity to a rigid code of behavior. Conversations about children should be handled carefully and professionally, and any information imparted should be held in strictest confidence.

There comes to mind a situation in which two student teachers on a public bus were discussing children in their class. One said, "Mrs. Ames says not to bother trying to handle Bobby G.; he's impossible, and his parents just won't cooperate." Unfortunately for all concerned, especially Bobby, friends of Bobby's parents were seated immediately behind the student teachers, and there was a great deal of unpleasantness for everyone concerned. The student teacher certainly should have known not to discuss children, by name, on a bus (or in any other public place); and he violated the trust placed in him by his university and the school system in which he was working. A comment of the type the cooperating teacher supposedly made was somewhat unprofessional too. The teacher is not entitled to the privilege of ignoring or abandoning any child, no matter how trying he may be.

There is another reason for not indulging in pessimistic gossip about children. The student teacher may be successful in working with a child who is very difficult for the cooperating teacher, just as a child may be much more difficult for the student teacher than he is for the cooperating teacher. Thus, it seems unnecessary and unwise to say to the student teacher, "You'll have trouble with Gregory; it's best to ignore his bids for attention," since the student teacher may wish to handle this attention getting in a different way. It is also possible that Gregory may not behave unacceptably with the student teacher. The cooperating teacher may wish to suggest specific measures for dealing with individual children after problems have arisen; but where child behavior is concerned, forewarned may not be forearmed. Information should be provided, by all means, and the student teacher should be guided away from major pitfalls; but prescribing specific remedies for anticipated ailments should probably be avoided.

4. It is essential that the student teacher know what usually happens as the result of unacceptable behavior. Is the offender isolated? For how long? Where? What level of misbehavior results in being sent to the principal's office? Is physical punishment ever used? If so, who administers this? Is a child ever kept after school? If so, for what kind of offense? Are children ever deprived of recess? Is group punishment ever used? In what circumstances? Although absolute compliance with rules which seem oppressive or even cruel is not advocated, the student teacher can find himself in real difficulty if his attitude toward rule infractions is markedly more lenient (or more strict) than that of the cooperating teacher.

Before and during the first few days of student teaching the student teacher will attempt to gain adequate knowledge of the children he will be teaching, and he will assess the attitudes toward children's behavior exhibited by his "critic," other faculty members, and administrators. He will want to observe and carefully note the specific limits placed upon children's behavior by the cooperating teacher and the typical consequences of misbehavior, not for purposes of imitation but for purposes of understanding the general level of behavior he'll be expected to maintain. Throughout the student teaching process, the student teacher, the cooperating teacher, and the college supervisor will work to establish, protect, and maintain easy and effective means of communication.

Definition, Goals, and Objectives of Discipline

It would seem wise, at this point, to define goals and objectives in connection with discipline and control; what is it that the student teacher is attempting to achieve? Byers and Irish write: "The modern educator aims for democratic control. He thinks of discipline and control as a way that children live together to develop self-control, character, and orderliness. He guides children to consider and plan the conditions under which they will work together successfully and happily."[3] Two other writers, Michaelis and Dumas, define discipline as follows: "Discipline . . . refers to that behavior through which a child can live harmoniously with both the children and adults in his social group and through which the purposes of educational activities can be achieved. Ideally, such behavior should be intrinsically motivated."[4]

What can the student teacher do to achieve control which is not externally imposed? How can he guide his group toward self-discipline? The following guidelines are designed to help the student teacher find answers to such questions.

Discipline Is Not an End in Itself

There is no virtue inherent in a quiet, orderly classroom. The virtue lies, rather, in the possibilities for learning that exist in a reasonably orderly, quiet classroom and that do not exist when uncontrolled

---

[3] Loretta Byers and Elizabeth Irish, *Success in Student Teaching* (Boston: D. C. Heath & Company, 1961), p. 86.

[4] John U. Michaelis and Enoch Dumas, *The Student Teacher in the Elementary School* (Englewood Cliffs, New Jersey: Prentice-Hall, Inc., 1960), p. 118.

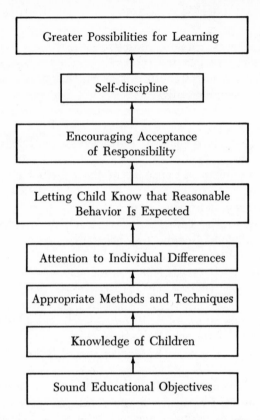

FIGURE 13. BASIS, DEVELOPMENT, AND AIM OF DISCIPLINE

noise and chaos prevail. The student teacher should not be blamed for feeling successful when he is merely authoritative; principals, supervisors, professors of education courses, all have contributed to the growing myth that discipline, even self-discipline, is a goal worth achieving for its own sake. Discipline is a means to an end—improved learning for children—and not an end in itself.

The Basis of Effective Discipline

Effective discipline rests upon the teacher's (or the student teacher's) thorough knowledge of the children he's teaching, sound and reasonable educational objectives, and appropriate methods and techniques for working with children. This is simply a restatement of that which is common knowledge to the student teacher, the college supervisor, and the cooperating teacher; but it is nonetheless true. More specifically, the following suggestions can probably be of some help as the student teacher attempts to work with children in increasingly more effective ways:

1. It is essential to plan in terms of the developmental levels represented by the age group taught. The attention spans of the children will be of primary concern; so will their expressed interests and needs. Committee work, prolonged periods of sitting and listening, work involving details and control of small muscles probably will not be attempted with most first grade groups, because they are not ready for such experiences.

2. Careful planning, with and for children, and the knowledge that all necessary materials are ready and arrangements made will give the beginner much-needed poise and a sense of security. This is not to say that flexibility and a willingness to make adjustments as a class period progresses are not important. These qualities and abilities are *quite* important; however, adequate pre-planning will do much to free the student teacher to give full attention to guiding the children effectively.

3. Children who are aware of the purposes of an activity and who have been involved in some of the planning which preceded the activity are not likely to exhibit behavior which will endanger the success of the enterprise. There are individual differences to be taken into account here, of course; and no single activity is going to be equally interesting, appealing, and significant for each child in a class. When, however, children are made aware of the importance of an activity to the group as a whole, if not to each individual in the group, they are much more likely to be cooperative than if the activity is imposed upon them for purposes known only to the adults concerned.

4. Children differ, intellectually, emotionally, and physically; and fewer discipline problems will result if the student teacher takes into account these individual differences when learning activities are planned and instructional materials are selected. This section of the chapter has included a discussion of the limitations within which the student teacher works. Nowhere are these limitations more obvious than in the area of teaching materials. To suggest adapting the read-

ing program to the varying abilities represented in a class is not very realistic if the student teacher is provided with thirty copies of one text, in a school which has no library. In most situations, however, there are opportunities to use a variety of materials, and the creative student teacher can almost certainly vary his methods and the rate at which he "takes" the individuals in the group "through the material." When children feel they are learning, when they have feelings of pride and success, they normally do not get into trouble. Many discipline problems are caused by bored children and by children who feel the learning task at hand is impossibly difficult.

5. It is to be expected that a few children will cause most of the trouble in a classroom. The most careful planning and conscientious attention to individual differences will not guarantee success with each child in the group. The great majority of children will respond positively to kindness, concern for their needs, and an interesting program; but a few children, for a variety of reasons, cannot be reached. This is very frustrating; but it is a fact, nonetheless, and the wise co-operating teacher and college supervisor will help the neophyte focus on the children who are responsive and cooperative, and those with whom the student teacher is succeeding. Occasionally the student teacher does make real progress in guiding difficult children; in a few cases the student teacher succeeds where others have failed. For these reasons, the student teacher keeps trying, and even slight progress is cause for rejoicing.

6. It may be appropriate here to define more precisely what is meant by *self-discipline*. It is a term which is used quite frequently, yet there may be little real understanding of the term or common agreement concerning its practical aspects. There is evidence of self-discipline when a child finishes his part of a committee's task without urging or pressure; there is evidence of self-discipline when a child continues to work on a project whether or not the teacher is directly supervising him. Self-discipline is the acceptance of responsibility without external controls. Although few adults possess this quality in a very high degree, it is a goal toward which educators work, steadily, and persistently. The smallest progress toward self-control is praised, children are expected to control their behavior and usually behave accordingly. There are two rather specific steps which the student teacher may take toward developing self-discpline among the children: encouraging children who do accept responsibility, and

displaying an attitude which conveys the expectation of reasonable behavior. There follow other suggestions that will also help in the development of self-discipline. These relate to working within the limitations of a child's developmental level and to providing a carefully planned and interesting program.

Problem Children

When the student teacher has problems with a few children, he must act quickly, consistently, and with understanding. Most student teachers know what the limits are and have successfully guided the behavior of most of the children within these limits; however, a child or a few children may "test" a student teacher, may behave in a way or ways which are unacceptable. Much of the whispering, giggling, and similar minor infractions can be handled with a frown, a disapproving glance, a shake of the head, or a knowing wink or smile. Children occasionally forget, and a simple reminder may be all that is necessary. The student teacher will be more concerned about willful disobedience; complete lack of concern for the comfort, convenience, or feelings of others; and behavior so aggressive that children's safety is endangered. What can be done in such situations?

1. As already noted, the first guideline or cue is that which is typically done in such situations. Johnny leaves the classroom without permission and stays out a long time. He is well aware that in his classroom in his school this is out-of-bounds behavior. The student teacher will probably ask for an explanation; then, if it seems proper, he will proceed to ask that work missed be made up, will isolate the child for a specified length of time, will refer him to the principal's office for a conference about the problem, or will take other such measures. Because the possible consequence of one's behavior should help to guide that behavior, it seems especially important that the missed work be made up or a substitute found for it, if it means returning early at noon or remaining after school for a few minutes. The "punishment" should fit the "crime;" beyond this, an established pattern should probably be followed, and the student teacher will wait until he has a classroom of his own to try an approach which seems to him to be more humane, reasonable, or fair.

2. The student teacher will not neglect to follow through. If a child

is warned that certain action will result if certain forbidden behavior recurs, then it is very important that the behavior be followed by the promised action. If the student teacher tells Mary that further interruptions of the reading group will result in her being asked to sit right beside the teacher until the group adjourns, then this is exactly what must happen if Mary interrupts. It logically follows that the student teacher will be very careful not to propose any action which can't actually be initiated. If the class knows the principal is out of the building for the day, it is not very sensible to threaten sending a child to his office in the event of any more kicking under desks, or pushing in line, or whatever the undesirable behavior happens to be. They know this can't happen, and the student teacher's authority is diminished.

3. The student teacher should be consistent in determining the punishment which should result from a given aspect of misbehavior. Mary's punishment will be the same as Susan's, regardless of how the student teacher feels about the two girls. This seems to contradict the advice previously given to treat each child as an individual, but the individual guidance can follow the direct action which must be taken very soon after a misdemeanor. Consistency demands that concern for the group, temporarily at least, take precedence over concern for an individual child. Unfortunately, such choices must be made by every teacher. The children can't be expected to take into account Mary's immaturity, or her broken-home background, or the new baby at home, any of which can produce attention-getting, negative behavior. They see only that the teacher sent Susan out of the reading group when she was naughty, but that Mary got to stay. In rare cases, the student teacher may send a child from the room on an "errand" and explain that he especially needs the group's help, and the teacher's, now and, in terms children can understand, why special and temporary allowances will be made for that child. For the most part, however, consistency and impartial treatment will be important aspects of the student teacher's efforts to help children achieve self-discipline.

4. The student teacher will try to gain the respect of the children, and this takes precedence over becoming their "friend." Far too many student teachers hesitate to act firmly or decisively because they fear they'll lose the affection of the children. Of course, it is very human to want to be liked; but in the case of a student teacher concerned

with guiding a high level of pupil behavior, respect is more important than affection. These two qualities are not mutually exclusive, at any rate, and most student teachers are both respected and liked. There is a real danger that the young student teacher will behave too informally with older children, and will lose their respect by becoming their "buddy" or "pal." Still, dignity does not mean austerity, and respect does not mean fear. There can be a relationship between the children and their teacher which exemplifies warmth, ease, and friendliness but still assures the teacher the respect and dignity which must adhere to him in his role as leader.

5. Physical punishment—spanking—should never be undertaken lightly or become the routine reaction to misbehavior. The student teacher should be very sure that spanking is the only way of solving a particular problem and should recognize that he's treating symptoms, not causes. Physical punishment seldom produces better attitudes toward the teacher or the school, and the best that can be hoped for is less tension in the classroom atmosphere and a child who is at least temporarily submissive. Of course, the student teacher has informed himself about school regulations regarding spanking, including the need for witnesses, notification of parents, etc. It is to be hoped that the need for such drastic behavior will never occur and that the student teacher can use isolation, withdrawal of a privilege, or some other means of forcing compliance when a child lacks self-discipline.

6. Redirection of behavior, suggesting an acceptable activity to take the place of one which is unacceptable, and anticipating misbehavior before it occurs are valuable tools for the student teacher, and he should make full use of them. To prevent a playground quarrel, perhaps a game can be quickly organized. If one sees that two pairs of scissors are needed and that grabbing and similar egocentric behavior will result if something isn't done, then one can quickly suggest a substitute activity for one child or find another pair of scissors. It sometimes seems that the student teacher must see and hear everything and be two or three steps ahead of bright, quick children; and this is certainly true. It is often amusing to talk with mothers who have formerly been very critical of the level of behavior in the classroom after they have been Brownie or Bluebird leaders, Cub Scout den mothers, or taught Sunday school. In most cases, their perceptions have changed remarkably, and their respect for the managerial skill of the teacher has increased by several hundred per cent.

7. Parent support and cooperation should be enlisted, especially in dealing with stubborn and persistent discipline problems. Little will be accomplished if the school is working on one set of assumptions and the goals of the home are very different. For example, parents may be encouraging aggressive behavior at home, feeling that the child has been too meek and submissive. If the school can be informed of this, school personnel may not find it possible to be as permissive as they'd like to be, but they will certainly be more understanding. An increasing number of communities have counseling agencies to which families may go when problems appear to be too big for them or the school to handle. Larger school systems employ school psychologists who can be of invaluable assistance in gathering data about a seriously disturbed child and recommending a course of action which will help the child move toward group behavior which is acceptable.

8. Drastic action, including physical punishment and isolation from the classroom, should be taken with the full and complete knowledge of the cooperating teacher and, perhaps, the building principal as well. To banish a child from the classroom without specific directions concerning where he is to go and what he is to do is *most* unwise.

9. Finally, it should be noted that the student teacher is a human being and that mistakes will be made, through anger or stubbornness. Mistakes are to be expected, and they can be handled honestly and with a sense of humor.

In the preceding discussion of the goals and objectives of the student teacher's efforts to control, to direct, and to discipline, it has been noted that discipline is not an end in itself, that the only virtue of control is that it makes possible a higher-quality learning experience for an individual and a group. It has been pointed out that another goal of these efforts is the achievement of self-control which will cause the child to direct his own behavior toward constructive ends, both when he is working independently and when he is part of a group, small or large. The teacher's objective is to make outer restraints and imposed limitations unnecessary most of the time with most children. One hopes that when restraints and limitations exist or must be imposed it will be for the purpose of furthering a high level of group activity, not because the teacher or administrator wishes to exercise the power of his position. Several suggestions have been provided for the student teacher who encounters a child or children who seem unwilling or unable to control their own behavior. Some guidelines for the student teacher were suggested: Discipline problems will be minimized when the program is related to the learner's needs and interests and when the learner is well aware of the objectives and purposes of a particular activity.

Something should be said about the special problems presented when the student teacher is placed in what is commonly termed a culturally deprived neighborhood or community. The outward signs are below-average dwellings, inadequate recreational facilities, above-average incidence of crime and misdemeanors, and little or no interest in the schools of the community. Occasionally, school halls must be patrolled by policemen, and teachers are not permitted to remain in the building after a certain hour in the afternoon. Ordinarily, such communities are located in large metropolitan areas, and student teachers are not placed in the schools of such communities; however, many student teachers who possess a strong social conscience and unusual skill and ability in working with people of all types request such placement. What about discipline in schools of the type just described, where knives are brought to school as commonly as pencils and where teachers often fear for their personal safety?

First of all, the student teacher must not expect miracles. To speak of developing self-discipline in such a situation is more than a little naive. The student teacher is in the school for only a short time, too brief a period of time to change pupils' attitudes and established patterns of behavior completely. The student teacher must be especially careful not to go beyond the well-established limits; at first, at least, liberty may be interpreted as license. Fairness and objectivity in the treatment of children who have not known fairness is very important. Sympathy can become maudlin. The problems of these children must be left at the school, if the student teacher is to retain reasonable mental health! Setting reasonable expectations for discipline and making special efforts to adjust the program (materials especially) to fit the needs of the youngsters should pay large dividends to the student teacher. A spirit of hopelessness, or an attitude of not caring because "these people" don't want to be helped, will accomplish very little. Unfortunately, many teachers assigned to buildings located in depressed neighborhoods exhibit one or both of these attitudes. Even in situations where antagonism has existed between pupils and teachers for some time, a student teacher who exhibits genuine concern (but not pity) for his pupils and who controls gently as well as firmly has been known to cause a marked improvement in the behavior of pupils and to help them take those first slow, halting steps toward self-discipline. Miracles? Probably not with these children; but progress is certainly possible, and the student teacher who successfully meets the challenge of working with underprivileged, disadvantaged youngsters deserves a great deal of credit. The results of his efforts will persist long after student teaching ends.

When the Student Teacher and the Cooperating Teacher Disagree on Classroom Control

It is not unusual to find the student teacher quite concerned at the end of the first or second day of student teaching that the children in his group are controlled more firmly, or that the classroom atmosphere is much less permissive, than he feels is desirable. Unfortunately, too many instructors of methods courses and educational psychology courses are rather far removed from the elementary school classroom and have not faced the realities of dealing with a group of children who, perhaps, are not interested in learning, are in school because they have to be, and find the school's program completely unrelated to their needs, present or future. It is easy to stand before a group of rather highly motivated prospective teachers and discuss the very guidelines which have been presented in the preceding section of this chapter. These are neither new nor original. It is obviously desirable to cause students whose background is one of a series of rigidly controlled classroom situations to consider methods and approaches which are more natural and pupil-centered, but such discussions often do little to ease the student teacher's practical problems in the area of discipline and may result in a great deal of inner conflict. This is healthy, and from such confusion over how much control and direction is wise can come an effective and productive way of working with children; however, before the conflict and confusion are resolved, the student teacher is often faced with the problem of adjusting to a program which is at least as rigid as any he knew as a child and which stands in direct contrast to the type of program he has learned to value and work for. Theoretically, the rigid disciplinarian will not be chosen to guide a student teacher, but every reader of this book knows that such cooperating teachers *are* selected. The divergence in points of view can take another direction as well. In rare cases, the cooperating teacher is more, not less, permissive than the student teacher thinks he should be. What can be done when either of these problems occurs? The following illustrative conference dialogues may provide some suggestions:

It is 3:45 in the afternoon, near the end of the first day of student teaching. Miss Arnold and Sally Briggs, her student teacher, have settled in a quiet, comfortable corner of the classroom to discuss the day's activities. Sally begins by reviewing her notes and inquiring, in a matter-of-fact manner, why Bobby was not permitted to go to gym class today. Miss Arnold replies that Bobby had misbehaved in reading group on Friday, and his punishment was to miss gym for two days. Sally inquires further concerning the nature of the misbehavior. It seems that Bobby had finished the assigned silent reading and rather than sitting quietly had begun disturbing children who were still reading—he grabbed their books, attempted to engage them in conversation, etc. Repeated warnings had been to no avail, and finally Miss Arnold told him precisely what would happen if he persisted in his disturbing behavior. What Sally saw today was the direct consequence of Bobby's own actions, Miss Arnold concludes; and she recommends similar procedures and techniques to Sally. It occurs to Sally that the basis for Bobby's problem is his superior reading ability and that some way must be found to let him progress at a faster rate. She comments favorably on several aspects of the day's activities— the children seem to enjoy their social studies work especially, and the reports they gave today were well organized and thorough. Then Sally inquires about the need for dismissal by rows, and for complete silence before a row's number can be called for dismissal. Miss Arnold replies that there is too much confusion at the coat room when all the children are dismissed at once. Sally agrees that this might be a problem; but today, because it was warm, the children wore no wraps and left the classroom as the rows were dismissed. She wisely decides, however, not to pursue this matter further. It will probably be best for her to follow the same routines, with perhaps a bit more permissiveness—even if the children have to be dismissed a few at a time, complete silence need not be required. Although not very much can be done about dismissal practices, Sally privately decides to do something about Bobby. He is a bright boy, and needs to be challenged.

Sally wisely applied several sound human relations principles during the conference. First, her positive comments were far more numerous than the negative. She left the impression that she considered Miss Arnold a very good teacher, and her questions were never allowed to become challenges. When she disagreed with Miss Arnold's approach, she decided for herself whether to conform to the established routine or to take a somewhat different approach. In the case of the child who was a behavior problem, she decided on a minor change—perhaps reading with him individually, perhaps discussing the story with him while the others are finishing, perhaps by dismissing him for a few minutes and asking him to rejoin the group when all are ready to discuss the story. In this case, a change of some type will be made. In the case of the dismissal routine, nothing in the nature of a major change can take place, so Sally decided to conform and to hope for a better situation when she has her own classroom.

In another conference, a student teacher and a cooperating teacher discuss the control established by the student teacher, and his disciplinary methods:

MR. JOHNSON: Bill, I feel the children are much too noisy while you're teaching. I think it's essential that you command respect and stop being so friendly with the children. For example, you asked for Joe's report on colonial farming tools three days ago. It still wasn't completed today. I know, better than you realize, that Joe's a "power" in this group, and it isn't easy to deal with him; but something should have been done to help him assume more responsibility. In fact, I think he's purposely put off finishing the report, just to see how far you'll let him go.

BILL: I think you're right, Mr. Johnson. I should be more firm with all of them, but especially with Joe. The class is watching this test of strength between Joe and me very carefully, I can tell. I'll lose the respect of many of the boys if I show that I'm not in charge and that Joe doesn't respect my ability to teach. What can I do?

MR. JOHNSON: First of all, I think a conference between you and Joe is essential, and long overdue. Get a final commitment from him about this report and hold him to it. Joe's very anxious to be the chairman of the committee working on farming and industry in colonial times; I believe I'd insist the report be done or not permit his name to be suggested when the chairman is selected. But that just takes care of Joe, Bill. The class is taking longer and longer when a shift in activities is called for. This morning, it took almost ten minutes for the math papers to be collected and the next lesson to get started. We haven't that kind of time to waste, Bill. It's getting worse, not better. Fully half the class was inattentive while you were reading *Treasure Island* this afternoon—did you realize that? What can you do to keep things moving, Bill; and can anything be done to improve the way in which children listen to you?

BILL: Well, that business of collecting papers bothers me; I guess I was still trying to help Marcie and Sue with division of fractions and didn't let the class know I wanted the papers collected quickly and efficiently. I won't make that mistake again. Mr. Johnson, I don't really like *Treasure Island* very well and I don't read it very enthusiastically, I'm afraid. I hope I can select a book I like better for the next storytime. If I like it better, I think the children will, too. You know, about this listening, I'm a poor listener myself. I don't really listen to reports or comments from the children. The only things I really listen to are questions. Could this be why they don't listen to me?

The problems discussed in this conference are major ones, and they will not be solved overnight; however, it seems that Mr. Johnson and Bill agree on the nature of the problems, and they apparently can work together, with mutual respect and concern for the feelings of one another to solve the problems. Bill was honest in his appraisal and made no attempt to blame someone else for his shortcomings. Mr. Johnson was perhaps a bit too directive; but he did focus the discussion immediately, and evidently he felt that it was essential to get to the point right away. Bill has made a mistake which is common to many student teachers; he places more importance on having the children like him than he does on gaining their respect. Somewhat more authority in his manner when he gives directions, and a thoroughly businesslike attitude when he's planning with the class (what *needs* to be done, not what do we *want* to do) will help. By his voice, his words, his manner, he must impress upon the children that he knows what he's doing, that he is in charge.

In this situation, Bill and Mr. Johnson did not disagree on ultimate goals; but it's clear that Mr. Johnson considered the problems far more serious than Bill did. What if they had disagreed? What if Bill had felt ten minutes for collecting math papers was not too long, particularly since he was trying to give some last-minute help to two pupils who had learning problems? Suppose Bill had taken the position that children who didn't want to listen to the story he was reading didn't have to? Mr. Johnson then might have let matters reach the point where Bill sought his help, and finally admitted that the situation was out of hand. By then, however, the situation might have deteriorated to the point where Bill could not regain the youngsters' respect, regardless of the drastic measures taken. Or Mr. Johnson could have said, arbitrarily, "Bill, I want Joe sent to the principal's office if his report isn't handed to you tomorrow morning. I want you to close your book and stop reading immediately when a child whispers or otherwise indicates inattention. I want you to use your watch, and any papers not sent to the front desk in each row by an agreed-upon time will neither be collected nor graded." In other words, he could have proposed solutions to each problem and insisted upon compliance with his wishes.

Neither of the approaches suggested would have produced or effected desirable growth and maturity on the part of the student teacher. In fact, until the student teacher himself recognizes a problem and wants to solve it, not very much can be accomplished which will be of lasting benefit to him. The student teacher who says, "They're as quiet as I want them to be." isn't ready for very much constructive advice; measures taken by the cooperating teacher will be for purposes of controlling children so they won't disturb other classes (or the principal), and the cooperating teacher will recognize that he's performing a holding action, not helping the student teacher.

The College Supervisor's Role When There Is Disagreement

It has been suggested that the cooperating teacher and the student teacher should have some common goals in mind with reference to classroom control. If this understanding of goals and objectives has not been established before the student teacher's first real "teaching" experience, then respect, honesty, and consideration for the other's position will be required as the problems are aired and solutions proposed. The objective of such a conference is the increase of the student teacher's competence to deal with future classroom management problems, not the adjustment of children's behavior to satisfy the cooperating teacher.

At times, the college supervisor must help each of the other two participants in the student teaching experience to identify the real nature of the problem and to protect the integrity of the student teacher or the sanity of the cooperating teacher.

In one situation, the classroom teacher, unusually permissive herself, felt things were completely out of hand. The student teacher seemed very satisfied with her progress, and her reports to the supervisor were quite different from those given by the cooperating teacher. The university supervisor, wisely, listened to both; but he never held a three-way conference in which some of the differences could be aired. The cooperating teacher gave up trying to point out to the student teacher that children's jumping up and down on top of tables and chasing each other with scissors and tools from the workbench were not entirely satisfactory educational activities and finally took over in order to protect the children from physical harm. If the supervisor had been perceptive and alert, an early conference involving the student teacher, the cooperating teacher and the supervisor could have prevented a poor situation from becoming impossible.

Further, the supervisor can ask questions, as he hears each side presented, which may cause each disputant to look more calmly and critically at the position he's taken and be more open-minded to the other position:

> Jane, I wonder if you realized that Mrs. Evans has had many phone calls from parents wondering what is going on. It's becoming harder and harder for her to defend you, even though she'd like for you to regain control of the class by yourself. Assuming things are out of control, Jane (and I'm afraid I agree with Mrs. Evans that they are), what can you do *now* to establish a more calm, workmanlike atmosphere, to regain control?
>
> Mrs. Brown, can anything be done to help Phil see that he could accomplish so much more if the children were better listeners, if they were more quiet? We see this; but I don't think he does, yet. I think he's rebelling against the rigid teaching he had, and he's overcompensating. Can you suggest an approach we haven't tried?

Another obvious technique which the college supervisor uses to the fullest is the seminar or group meeting, attended by all the student teachers with whom a particular supervisor works. I strongly recommend the establishment of an agenda committee, made up of student teachers who can get together for planning without causing undue hardship and who are responsible for surveying the other student teachers and selecting related problems for discussion at each seminar or meeting. Of course, the supervisor will add items to this agenda and will approach them in the manner he considers most appropriate. With specific reference to discipline, a problem almost certain to be listed, the supervisor may wish to ask the rigid disciplinarian to complete a case study of a particularly difficult child. The object of such a request would be deepening the student teacher's understanding of the complex nature of most behavior problems. Another approach would be to suggest a hypothetical classroom teaching situation, involving perhaps the defiant child. Through role playing, or simply through discussion, the approaches each student teacher would use can be compared and contrasted. The supervisor may also assign pertinent books or articles dealing with discipline to be reported on and discussed.

Incidentally, a meeting or series of meetings with the cooperating teachers, also dealing with discipline and means by which the student teachers could be helped most effectively, might serve to change the focus from "What kind of classroom atmosphere do *I* want?" to "How can I help my student teacher learn some methods, techniques, patterns, etc., which will be effective for *him* as he works with children?"

The college supervisor has an important contribution to make in the area of discipline; it is he who can most effectively help the student teacher translate the best of what he has read and heard into classroom practice and who can tactfully promote an attitude on the part of the classroom teacher which will free the student teacher to do more than imitate.

CLASSROOM CONTROL AND SCHOOL POLICIES

It is appropriate here to tell of a student teacher who took children for a walk in the school's neighborhood with no advance planning and without the knowledge of the cooperating teacher or the building principal. In order to give the student teacher the opportunity to teach by herself, the cooperating teacher had scheduled a morning of parent-teacher conferences in a room down the hall from the classroom. Imagine her surprise when she saw her brood, running, skipping, scattered, and yelling, crossing the street in front of the school—at will, not bothering to look for traffic. As she excused herself from the conference and left the room, she saw the principal in the hall. The principal said the best approach was to finish the conference and ask for a thorough explanation when the student teacher returned to the building, with, it was to be hoped, all the children safe and unharmed. Thoughts of lawsuits occurred to the teacher— and probably to the principal too—because the classroom teacher would probably be held liable for any accidents which occurred on such a venture. Fortunately, everyone returned to school safely; but the trip, with so little planning, resulted in very little learning for the children.

In another case, a student teacher brought candles for the children's jack-o'-lanterns and planned to light them, with kitchen matches, during the Halloween party. He had not bothered to check with anyone about fire regulations. If he had, he could have saved some expense to himself and much disappointment to the children, because he was not permitted to light the jack-o'-lanterns.

In both cases, the student teachers neglected to inform themselves properly regarding established school policies. They were, of course, also proceeding with major activities which had been planned inadequately. In the preceding chapter, it was suggested that a copy of the faculty handbook or the written policy statement which most teachers in a given system have available to them be given to the student teacher. In the absence of such a written statement, the principal of a building has the responsibility for informing student teachers of pertinent school board and state regulations regarding school trips, science experiments involving chemical agents and fire, the celebration of holidays, and other matters. A conference dealing with such established policy should be scheduled either before or early in the student teaching period.

The matters briefly mentioned above relate only indirectly, perhaps, to discipline. There are also areas of direct impact on the manner in which the children move about the building, on behavior during fire drills, and on other common matters, which are reflected in written and unwritten policies. Anyone who has visited several school buildings in succession is aware of the vast difference in atmosphere, discernible even as one enters a building. The building principal is a vital force in shaping this atmosphere, and the student teacher will be expected to adjust—conform, if you will—to the established patterns. In building A, the children do not talk in the halls, and the teachers escort the children, in double file, to the playground and to the buses. The principal of building A spends much time patrolling halls, and every classroom door is left open. Sympathy is extended to each student teacher who has had to suffer in building A; but, nonetheless, the student teachers can adjust and they leave this situation more convinced than ever that a reasonably permissive atmosphere and respect for the principal, without fear, is healthy.

"The teacher next door" is another force with which the student teacher should be familiar; this force can be beneficial for the student teacher, providing an opportunity for him to see a different teaching personality in action, different disciplinary standards discussed and applied; however, if "We must be very quiet, boys and girls, so we won't bother the class next door" is the overt and obvious outgrowth of the influence of one's professional neighbor, then this is less beneficial. Obviously one is concerned for the effect one's actions have on others—for example, older children who have a different recess time do not play right under the windows of primary classrooms, because this makes their work difficult or impossible. This is different, however, from maintaining a particular classroom atmosphere not because it's best for you and the children, but because it will ease relationships with one's professional neighbor, next door or across the hall. What does this mean to the student teacher, who must live with this but only temporarily? If the standards of teacher X, passed on through teacher B, to student teacher A, are artificial and unnatural, the student teacher will suffer. For example, behavior slogans (e.g., "A good third-grader doesn't bother his neighbor") may be imposed upon the student teacher indirectly, as described above. The student teacher may not feel that the use of such slogans is appropriate, and the wise cooperating teacher would not force the student teacher to use them simply to maintain friendly professional relations with his neighbor.

Communication and *understanding* are key words here, as they have been throughout this discussion of the student teaching process. The principal must accept responsibility for communicating to the student teacher the written and unwritten policies which govern group and individual behavior in the school. The cooperating teacher helps the student teacher interpret these policies and adapt them to better fit the classroom situation and the student teacher's personality, needs, strengths, and weaknesses. The college supervisor, as well, helps in this adjustment process and attempts to help preserve the integrity and individuality of the student teacher.

When the Student Teacher Loses Control

In rare situations, the student teacher is incapable of establishing himself as a group leader, the children demonstrate complete lack of respect, and their behavior deteriorates to the place where something must be done about it. It is most unfortunate when the student teacher loses control; and everyone concerned, it is hoped, has done his best to prevent this from occurring. In most cases of discipline trouble, there have been many conferences and observations in other classrooms to watch the methods and techniques used by other teachers, and none of these efforts has been fruitful. The focus now must shift from the student teacher to the children. No longer can the student teacher be permitted to stand before the group, vainly trying to keep minimal attention and to guide learning activities. That stage has been passed, and the teacher and supervisor must be guided by their answers to the following questions: If the situation were changed, if the student teacher were allowed to start all over again, would he be likely to achieve more success? That is, has he learned enough to justify a second chance? Has the student teacher's performance been so poor that he should not be permitted to teach under any conditions?

Almost without exception teacher education institutions are concerned with the selection of students who, as freshmen or sophomores, demonstrate the qualities generally associated with teaching success. College or university personnel involved in this selection process will readily admit that they are not entirely satisfied with the results of their efforts to screen and to weed out unlikely prospects. Occasionally, still too often, a student reaches the student teaching phase of his preparation with only limited abilities and chances for success. No one who has been involved in permitting this to happen should feel he has done the student a favor. It is no favor to encourage a person to enter a profession where he will be both unhappy and unsuccessful, and this is not taking into account the harm he will do to thirty children per year in his forty years of teaching. Every reader has had the sad experience of watching, or being in the class of, the bitter, dissatisfied, unhappy, and ineffectual teacher who might have had a more productive and rewarding life had he made a different professional choice. "Niceness," "sweetness" and similar desirable qualities are inadequate, by themselves, as guarantees of professional success. More will be said in Chapter 8 about this problem of refusing admission to our profession to those obviously ill-equipped for it. It is enough to say here that the college supervisor and the cooperating teacher must face, very honestly, the prospect of acting courageously and on the basis of their best professional judgment when the teacher loses control of his class. The welfare of the class being taught must be considered, and so must the welfare of future classes.

In answering the question concerning the value of a second chance either in the form of another student teaching experience or, with the lowest possible grade, entitling the student to state certification as a teacher, the following guidelines may be helpful:

Survey the notes taken during observations and conferences. Is there evidence of growth? Do the kinds of questions asked and comments made become more perceptive and more mature as the supervisor and cooperating teacher talk with the student?

Does the student seem to be aware of the severity of his problem? Does he recognize that he has lost control?

As the children are observed, do they seem to be insecure, continuing to admire the student teacher but unable to respond to his inept leadership, or are they openly and obviously rebellious, indicating both lack of respect and unwillingness to respond to the student teacher as a person? Has there been a change in their response to him? That is, once the problem is identified and the student teacher begins to try to apply the suggestions he has received, do things improve even a little, or is the gap between the student teacher and the children so wide that bridging it is impossible?

As the student discusses his problems, what solution does he propose? Does he feel he still wants to teach? One student teacher persisted throughout student teaching to work on this problem of control; and at the conclusion, his advisor said, as the only positive comment he could make, "Well, as least you showed up every day, and I know how much courage it took to do that!" Showing up every day is hardly enough, by itself; but retreat into psychosomatic illness causing frequent absences and other evidence of giving up are sure indices that the student is admitting a major mistake and that the help he needs now is some face-saving redirection and career advice.

The Student Teacher Faces Failure

What about Mary Evans, student teacher, as she realistically faces the fact that she has lost control, that the children don't listen to her, don't respond to her directions, are impervious to her threats of punishment? She can blame her "critic" ("My methods of discipline are more permissive than hers, and the children just couldn't adjust"), her college supervisor ("He made me so nervous that I just couldn't function while he observed me"), and her teacher education program ("We need a course in discipline! Those professors are so bookish, so idealistic, that their help is as good as nothing! How can they expect us to control children when they don't tell us how?") Obviously, there may be an element of truth in each of these accusations or all of them; however, such accusations are of little value, because they give the student teacher no guidelines to use in solving the problem which is present and pressing. The teacher education institution should continuously evaluate the professional courses it offers, and the cooperating teacher should evaluate continuously his relationships with his pupils; but the results of their deliberations will not help Mary, here and now, who is obviously in trouble. We must assume that Mary has tried; that sincere and conscientious effort has gone into every day of student teaching. We must also assume that proffered advice and assistance has been received graciously and gratefully. If Mary has not tried or has been stubborn or rebellious when others have tried to help, then the solution to her problems lies out of the province of this book. The first step, then, is to shift the focus of the student teacher from "Whom can I blame?" to "What are the best next steps, for the children and for me?" She too, will want to review the record, to assess her growth, to examine the nature and cause of her trouble, and to decide honestly whether or not teaching is important enough to her to justify the effort it will take to overcome her weaknesses and add to her competencies and strengths. She may ask what other career opportunities are open to her, what additional college preparation each would require; and the college counselor and her college supervisor can help in answering this question. Of course, such questions have been asked before; but the finding of answers has perhaps not been quite so crucial as it is now!

A third consideration will be the reaction of the student teacher's family—husband, parents—to her failure. It is to be hoped that they will be kind and supportive and that they will help in the rebuilding of a sadly damaged self concept. Even if these qualities will not characterize their response, however, Mary should not persist in working toward a career goal which is imposed upon her by others. Discipline problems may have their basis in lack of dedication to teaching as a career, or in serious questions about one's adequacy for teaching. Student teaching should help in discovering such indecision; and it is not to the student teacher's discredit to say, "I'm sorry I was so late in discovering this; but teaching, really, is not for me."

Suppose, however, that Mary does see progress, does feel her teaching strengths almost balance this one glaring weakness, and that with time and some effort she can learn to guide and direct children's learning. Mary's first job is to convince her supervisor and cooperating teacher of this and to suggest either another student teaching experience or that they make it possible for her to teach in her own classroom. This latter proposal should be with the clear understanding that she will need an extraordinary amount of supervisory help during her first year of teaching and that hiring officials will be informed of this fact. She must also face the fact that the final decision is not entirely hers but that the supervisor and cooperating teacher must take into account the influence she will have on the great numbers of children she'll teach during her career. Mary's decision will be right for her, it is hoped. Hundreds of youngsters will suffer if it isn't.

Some Final Thoughts about Discipline

It is unfortunate that creativity, sensitivity to the needs of children, academic competence, personal integrity—all of the qualities associated with superior teaching—cannot compensate for inability to control a group of children, to guide them efficiently and effectively as they proceed through a day's activities. Discipline, the ability of the teacher to help children live together calmly and harmoniously and accomplish learning tasks with a minimum of confusion and misdirection of energies is the student teacher's greatest problem and one which must be solved both to the satisfaction of the student teacher and of those responsible for guiding and evaluating him. It is essential to find a way of operating with children which is natural and easy for the student teacher and also is consonant with the policies of the administrators and teachers in the building in which student teaching occurs. The student teacher will benefit most if he is helped to find his own way and is not expected to use techniques, methods, and approaches which the cooperating teacher finds effective. From adequate planning and the thorough knowledge of methods and materials which will suggest the most appropriate techniques and resources will come the security and sense of direction which form a major part of the foundation for effective control and discipline.

There should perhaps be more room for divergent ideas and policies regarding acceptable classroom behavior than there is. Too often, the student teacher must be more authoritarian and rigid than he feels he ought to be, merely to convince his supervisor that the children aren't out of hand and that he can maintain the very quiet classroom so many teachers feel is essential for learning and for their own peace of mind. Although the college supervisor and the cooperating teacher provide guidance, assistance, and encouragement, and although the example set by the cooperating teacher is, one hopes, well worth emulating, the job of working with children in such a way that learning will not be impeded but promoted and children will relate to one another reasonably and calmly *is the job of the student teacher, and no one can do it for him.* His is the responsibility for learning enough about each child to work with him successfully, alone and in groups, and the task of selecting appropriate learning materials and methods. He must be aware of the limitations of his teaching situation and must demonstrate a willingness to conform, even while working for limits which seem to him to be more reasonable and just. Discipline presents a tremendous challenge to the student teacher and to those who help him; but it is a challenge which the vast majority of student teachers meet successfully, with the guidance and support of supervisors and cooperating teachers.

Suggested Activities for Student Teachers

1. Select three children, and during your observation period note the manner in which the classroom teacher directs or controls their behavior.
   a) Is his voice raised to the child? What type of response does a raised voice evoke?
   b) Does he issue direct commands? Are his suggestions subtle but, nonetheless, firm?
   c) Is this child handled differently from the others? (Is he watched more closely, given more freedom, etc.?)

2. Select one of these children for thorough study, through anecdotal records, sociometric data, and utilization of the data the school already has. Try, if possible, to arrange for a parent interview or a visit to the home. In a written summary of your study, make several specific suggestions which you feel would contribute to more effective self-control or self-discipline, if this is within the limits of possible achievement.

3. Prepare, for discussion with other student teachers, a statement of an example of your effective handling of a difficult situation. Stop before telling how you handled the problem, and ask the other student teachers to suggest appropriate solutions. Then, finish your description by disclosing how you, in fact, solved the problem or kept one from occurring.

4.* Interview a building principal and report to your group of student teachers his beliefs about beginners' discipline problems. He might answer questions such as the following:
   a) Do most student teachers have discipline problems? (If his answer is "Yes," ask him to give you his impressions as to why this is true.)
   b) What should student teachers know in order to minimize control problems?
   c) What kind of classroom atmosphere is desirable, from an administrator's point of view?
   d) How do you, as a principal, try to help a beginning teacher who is having discipline problems?

5. Interview three teachers, one relatively inexperienced, one who has taught five to seven years, and a teacher with more than ten years of experi-

---

* The college supervisor may wish to suggest the names of some principals who have the necessary experience and background to handle such questions. Inviting a panel of principals to speak to the student teacher might be an effective variation of this suggestion.

ence. Ask them to respond to questions similar to those you asked the principal or principals.

SELECTED REFERENCES

Anderson, Paul S. "Discipline in the Classroom Today," *Phi Delta Kappan,* December, 1959, pp. 114–17.

Brembeck, Cole S. *The Discovery of Teaching.* Englewood Cliffs, New Jersey: Prentice-Hall, Inc., 1962, Chapter 2, "The Tough Challenge of Teaching."

Brown, Thomas J., and Bavish, Serafina Fiore. *Guiding a Student Teacher.* New York: Harper & Row, Publishers, 1962, Chapter 4, "Discipline and Teaching."

Byers, Loretta. *Success in Student Teaching.* Boston: D. C. Heath & Company, 1961, Chapter 3, "Looking at Classroom Management" and Chapter 4, "Achieving Democratic Control."

Hymes, James L. *Behavior and Misbehavior.* Englewood Cliffs, New Jersey: Prentice-Hall, Inc., 1955.

Martin, John E. "Discipline, the Student Teacher's Nemesis," *The Educational Forum,* January, 1961, pp. 213–14.

Michaelis, John U., and Dumas, Enoch. *The Student Teacher in the Elementary School.* Englewood Cliffs, New Jersey: Prentice-Hall, Inc., 1960, Chapter 5, "Self Discipline and Group Behavior."

Muus, Rolf E. *First Aid for Classroom Discipline Problems.* New York: Holt, Rinehart & Winston, Inc., 1962.

Sheviakov, George V., and Redl, Fritz. *Discipline for Today's Children and Youth.* Washington, D. C.: Association for Supervision and Curriculum Development, 1956.

8

Evaluating the Student Teacher

It is perhaps unfortunate that books of this type must be organized in chapters. Such a division almost militates against the reader's understanding of the interrelatedness and the integration of a process such as student teaching. It has already been noted that there is no sharp dividing line between observation and participation phases of student teaching, nor is there one between participation and the acceptance of major teaching responsibility. The process of evaluation is similarly interrelated with other aspects of student teaching. Further, it might be stated that there is a strong relationship between the evaluation, in which the student teacher takes part, of children's progress and the evaluation of the student teacher's effectiveness and growth. That is, an appraisal of children's achievement will tell us much about the effectiveness with which they have been guided.

EVALUATION DEFINED

Alleyne Haines stresses the importance of the evaluation of a student teacher's effectiveness and underscores the responsibility of

180

public school personnel and representatives from teacher education institutions to perform the evaluative task with fairness and objectivity. She writes:

> Personnel of teacher education institutions and of public schools who work with Student Teachers have a responsibility to the teaching profession and to the community, as well as to the students whose progress in teaching they guide. They have a responsibility to the teaching profession and to the community for recommending as future teachers only[1] those students who are qualified to teach, who have demonstrated competence, and who have given evidence of probability of success in teaching.[2]

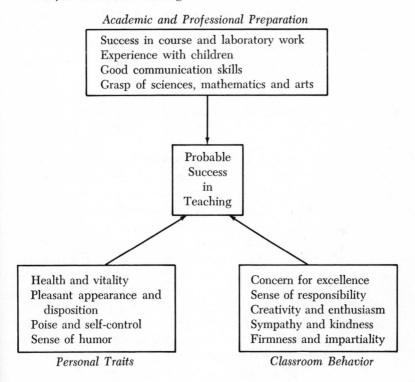

Academic and Professional Preparation

Success in course and laboratory work
Experience with children
Good communication skills
Grasp of sciences, mathematics and arts

Probable
Success
in
Teaching

Health and vitality
Pleasant appearance and
  disposition
Poise and self-control
Sense of humor

Personal Traits

Concern for excellence
Sense of responsibility
Creativity and enthusiasm
Sympathy and kindness
Firmness and impartiality

Classroom Behavior

FIGURE 14. SOME EVALUATIVE CRITERIA

---

[1] Italics added.
[2] Alleyne C. Haines, *Guiding the Student Teaching Process in Elementary Education* (Chicago: Rand McNally & Co., 1960), p. 225.

In discussing the problem of evaluative criteria—that is, what are we looking for in a student teacher?—one cooperating teacher has written:

"There are certain basic characteristics which are important in helping a student become a successful teacher. Physical fitness, vitality, a neat personal appearance, pleasant disposition, poise, self-control, sense of humor, imagination, initiative, and a genuinely friendly nature are some of these traits.

In the classroom the student should be concerned with excellence in achievement rather than with impressing the cooperating teacher. She should develop a feeling of responsibility and assist in the improvement of the class as if it were her own. The cooperating teacher has certain goals which must be attained, and the student should learn these goals and make it a part of her program to help achieve them. She should develop enthusiasm for each area of the curriculum. She must be creative and imaginative and make original contributions in helping to plan the teaching program. She should join with the supervising teacher to form a team in sharing the responsibility not only of the room but of all activities in which the supervising teacher is involved."

The student teacher should be sympathetic and courteous toward the pupils. Each child is an individual and needs special consideration of his temperament, abilities, interests, and capacities for learning. Children should be treated in the manner in which they are expected to treat others. They learn faster by example than by being told. The child, rather than the subject matter, should be placed at the center of the teaching effort. The student teacher must be kind, firm, and impartial in dealing with the children. Some children demand to be heard, whereas others will remain outside the group action if not solicited.

The alert student teacher approaches the teaching situations mentioned earlier as problems to be solved, and recognizes that teaching presents the challenge of discovering new and better ways of enriching children's learning. The cooperating teacher should demonstrate various methods which give insight into the teaching and learning process. The student teacher probably will not imitate these exactly; but, rather, the methods of the cooperating teacher should serve to stimulate the student teacher to try her own ways. "There is always a better way" should be a constant slogan.

A somewhat neglected area in student teaching is the relationship between the administration and the teaching staff. This, too, must be considered in establishing evaluative criteria. Many times student teaching represents the student's first opportunity to function as part of an adult environment and develop personal as well as professional relationships outside of college life. The utilization of this opportunity can be of great value in helping adjust to a teaching position and environment.

The hard-working student teacher, the "sweet" student teacher, the student teacher who is "kind" and "good" must possess, in addition to these commendable qualities, competence and effectiveness. It is essential that student teachers demonstrate the ability to guide children toward clearly established goals, that they can command the respect of children, parents, and other faculty members. The fact that teaching is not regarded as a profession by many elementary teachers is, in part, the fault of supervisors and cooperating teachers who have lacked the integrity and the strength to prevent the entrance into teaching of those who don't belong there. All sorts of excuses are used: "In another situation he might succeed." "My standards are probably unrealistically high." "It's too late to stop him now—the university has failed." Those who voice such rationalizations fail to give adequate consideration to the hundreds of children who will suffer under the inept leadership of the teacher who should have been guided into another career but wasn't.

It is not to be inferred from the preceding remarks that saying "No" is easy or that callous disregard for the feelings of a sensitive young person is recommended. Informing someone that in your very best judgment he should not, and, in fact, must not teach is one of the most difficult tasks the professional educator is ever called upon to perform; however, the supervisor and cooperating teacher were selected, in part at least, because of their competence and their ability to select, to appraise, and to evaluate. This process involves, inevitably, some changes in career plans and some serious damage to egos and self concepts. To take part in the protracted and distressing discussions which result in denying teaching certification to a prospective teacher is uncomfortable, and few people relish the authoritarian experience of telling someone he may not teach. Nevertheless, such decisions must be made, and there is little room for escapists or cowards. It is too late to say, "The college should have . . ." or "Why didn't someone . . . ?" It is fairly difficult to remove an incompetent teacher once he has a valid teaching certificate. The door, if it is to be closed, must be closed, and firmly, by those who have the greatest opportunity to judge a candidate's qualifications for teaching, his college supervisor and his cooperating teacher. The student teacher probably does not possess sufficient maturity or objectivity to see, without help and guidance, the qualities he lacks, his shortcomings, and the multiple reasons which cause those who are more experienced and knowledgeable to determine that he should not teach. Of course, he will have some capacity for self-evaluation and this will serve as the core of the serious and penetrating conferences and discussions about the student teacher's personal and professional qualifications for teaching. Nevertheless, the responsibility for making major decisions about a student teacher's professional future cannot be left entirely to the student teacher. The responsibility belongs to and must be accepted by his supervisor and the cooperating teacher. Fortunately, in only a few cases must these participants in the student teaching process say "No." For the most part, evaluation in student teaching consists of identifying and correcting areas of weakness and building upon demonstrated strengths and competencies.

There is a second important aspect of evaluation in student teaching, in addition to the assessment of one's observable performance. This involves making an educated guess about the student teacher's eventual competence as an experienced teacher, a prognosis of his success or failure. Here, too, the prediction will be a team effort; but the leaders of the team, the cooperating teacher and the college supervisor, should not hesitate to exercise their best and carefully considered professional judgment. Mistakes, in terms of overrating and underrating, are inevitable. The few errors made by the professional members of the student teaching team should not deter them from excluding from teaching those who show little or no promise of professional growth. It seems fairly clear that teaching will not acquire increased professional status as long as those who, by virtue of training and experience, should be able to predict with some accuracy the future performance of prospective teachers refuse to do so. This is not "playing God;" it is applying a tempered and well-seasoned professional yardstick and basing some judgments on the measurements secured. Speaking to the student teacher about such prediction of future competence, Burr, Harding, and Jacobs write:

As you approach the end of your student teaching elements of professional competence may be used as a basis for the evaluation of your growth—in your increasing competence in teaching. In that sense the appraisal will be of your past efforts and achievements, but, in an even more important sense, your self-analysis will point toward the future. Since no teacher ever "arrives," your growth will be relative to your past performance, present opportunities and potential resources, and relative as well to the competence of others. While you should complete your work competently to go out as a successful beginning teacher, you naturally should expect that your growth toward artistry in teaching will extend well beyond student teaching.[3]

It should be clear that the student teacher also has a part to play in this aspect of the evaluation process, as his maturity and his ability to be objective about himself dictate. Determining the level of the student teacher's involvement in the evaluation process is another of the responsibilities of the cooperating teacher and the college supervisor, and it should not be minimized or ignored. As a beginning teacher, one will almost certainly be expected to identify his strengths and weaknesses; and the student teacher will benefit a great deal from early and continuous involvement in evaluating his growth. It is no favor to the student teacher to protect him from assessing his work so his feelings will not be hurt, or because of his youth and his inexperience. It is no favor to the school administrator to lower standards so classrooms will be staffed. Quite recently, a superintendent stated that if state certification standards were properly applied and a poorly prepared young lady was not permitted to teach, "some first-graders would be without a teacher." This sounds plausible until it is also noted that as long as classrooms are staffed with teachers who are merely adequate or worse, there will be a level of education which is merely adequate or worse. Lowering standards will probably not solve the teacher shortage.

EVALUATING THE PREPARATION OF THE STUDENT TEACHER

Because this text is primarily concerned with student teaching, the aspect of the prospective teacher's education which precedes student

---

[3] James B. Burr, Lowry Harding, and Leland Jacobs, *Student Teaching in the Elementary School*, 2nd ed. (Copyright © 1950, 1958, Appleton-Century-Crofts, Inc.), p. 407.

teaching can receive only minimal attention here; however, successful performance in course work and laboratory experiences clearly forms the foundation upon which a successful student teaching experience rests.

As has been noted before, separation of student teaching from the rest of the process of preparing a teacher is somewhat artificial. Thus, it is inevitable that assessment of the student teacher's background, including his academic preparation and his work with children before student teaching will assume some significance in the total process of evaluating a student teaching performance. Two illustrative anecdotes may serve to underscore the importance of the student teacher's academic preparation and of his experiences with children before student teaching:

Nancy Jones began student teaching with the barest minimum of experience in working with children. A transfer to State University, she was not required to add to the ten hours of settlement house work which constituted the only laboratory experience she had obtained at the small liberal arts college she had attended as a freshman and sophomore. The first grade children in her student teaching group came from a suburban community that was upper middle class and competitively mobile socioeconomically. They were as different from the settlement house children as could be imagined. They were not grateful for but expected an extra amount of attention and many special services. Nancy now found not apathetic, disinterested parents but parents who stopped her on the street, at church, and in the supermarket to ask about their children's progress in reading or some other subject. Nancy's principal and cooperating teacher gave her adequate support and guidance, but her limited experiences with children severely handicapped her and almost led to her failure as a student teacher.

The children in John Edmunds' student teaching class constituted the brightest of three sixth grade classes. With the leadership of a teacher who was highly competent in math, these children had progressed far beyond the usual grade level expectations in mathematics. John felt that because he was a man he should have an upper-grade placement. Who ever heard of a male student teaching in the third grade? He knew also, however, that he had a serious weakness in mathematics. His high school demanded only a general math course and one year of algebra, and John's college advisor had "helped" him avoid math at the college level beyond the math methods course required of all elementary education majors. John might have succeeded with a less capable group, and even this group responded well to his guidance in literature and creative writing; however, his lack of competence and his insecurity in mathematics caused him to lose the respect of the cooperating teacher and the children. He failed in student teaching, largely because of an academic deficiency which could have and should have been corrected before student teaching.

John's deficiency might just as well have been in the area of science, or literature; Nancy's experience might have been limited to children of any other nearly unique group. The point is that these two people were seriously handicapped in student teaching because their preparation was weak in certain specific areas and the weaknesses were not corrected in time. In each of these situations the college supervisor failed to anticipate possible problems when the students were placed, but the issue of basic responsibility for the preparation of a teacher is also involved. The very term *general education* has supported a few "general" educators (professors of chemistry, English, and history) who wish to abdicate responsibility for the preparation of teachers—"Our task is *non*professional; what a student *does* with what we've helped him learn is none of our concern." The educationist has, too often, contributed to this concept by saying, in effect, "We *assume* breadth and depth of preparation; what happens in Professor Smith's economics class is none of our affair!" Of course, neither position represents the optimal contribution to the education of a teacher. A teacher's preparation must be based on a general and a professional education program which are complementary, not competitive, and by curriculum planning which recognizes the contribution which each part of a student's program should make if it is to produce a teacher who is an effective citizen, a literate human being whose communication skills are at *least* adequate for our modern world and are characteristic of a competent professional. When any part of a student teacher's preparation is weak, his teaching suffers, and so does the education of the children he teaches, in student teaching and thereafter. The precise pattern of an institution's teacher education program cannot and should not be prescribed, nor is this the focus of the evaluation process being discussed here. The alternative to the poor academic background of our elementary education teachers is not a national teacher education curriculum which is rigid. We are far from the time and place at which we can pinpoint and place with certain given aspects of a college curriculum and say this course or that sequence of courses is essential for the preparation of an elementary teacher, but this is not. The preparation of a prospective elementary teacher is, however, far too important to be the concern of professional educators alone. This should be a cooperative affair, and the failure of John Edmunds as a teacher of elementary school mathematics is no less the failure of the mathematics department at his college or university than the failure of those who supervised his professional preparation.

Evaluation of the performance of a student teacher will almost certainly include considerations which reflect upon the course work he has taken, both general and professional, and the quality and quantity of his experiences in leading, directing, and guiding groups of children. In assessing these aspects of a student teacher's training and preparation, the cooperating teacher, the college supervisor, and the student teacher should attempt to answer the following questions:

1. Are the student teacher's communication skills adequate for his work as a teacher and his role as a citizen in a democracy? Can he read, write, speak, and listen effectively?

2. Does the student teacher have an adequate grasp of those portions of the social sciences (geography, history, economics, anthropology, sociology, etc.) which will enable him to perform well both as a citizen in a democracy and as a transmitter of our democratic heritage to children and youth? When the responsibilities and commitments of our government are expanding at a very rapid rate, a good case can be made for insisting that skills, generalizations, and understandings relative to the social sciences must be expanded to include cultures and forms of societal organizations other than the familiar Caucasian-Western patterns; but this is a topic for another book, not this one.

3. In a world which is becoming increasingly scientific, or at least science-oriented, is the student teacher competent in his understanding of basic concepts and generalizations in both the natural and the physical sciences? More important, does the student teacher have an adequate grasp of the problem-solving process; does he understand the manner in which a scientist defines, attacks, and solves a particular problem?

4. Is the student teacher's knowledge of mathematics adequate?

Can he operate with confidence in the various branches of mathe-matics, at least at the level which can reasonably be expected of any well-educated person in today's computerized world?

5. Is the student teacher conversant with and comfortable in such creative fields as art, music, literature, and the dance? The pressures of modern society to the contrary, the creative person, the person who has the ability to say much about life with his hands and his heart, is to be highly valued; and the teacher who can inspire and cultivate creativity in children and youth is making a great contribu-tion indeed. Reference has been made to the cooperatively developed curriculum in teacher education. It is unfortunate indeed if the voice of the artist, the writer, and the musician is not heeded when such cooperative curriculum planning takes place.

6. Has the student teacher had experiences with children, before student teaching, which are adequate in depth and breadth? Does he know how children react and behave at various age levels? Does he recognize the influences of environment, as represented in various socioeconomic groups; and can he adjust to groups different from his own? Whether college credit is given for "laboratory experiences" with scout groups, settlement houses, and similar organizations en-rolling children in extra-school activities is far less important than that such experiences be provided at the level appropriate to meet each prospective teacher's needs. Flexibility is important in most aspects of a student teacher's preparation, but it is vital with reference to the extent of a student's work with children. It is unreasonable to expect a set formula, in hours, or weeks, or types of activities, to fit the needs of each of the vast number of students now preparing to teach.

When there are negative responses to any of these questions, the result will be a deficiency which will almost certainly affect student teaching negatively. The severity of the problem will help to deter-mine the corrective measures which will be taken. In most cases, some additional reading, and careful guidance by the supervisor and the cooperating teacher are all that will be necessary. In other cases, addi-tional course work may be recommended, perhaps to be taken during the summer before a student teacher's first year of teaching. Different types of experiences may be suggested—camp counselling, assisting with remedial classes in reading, etc. The program will be adjusted to fit the needs of the student concerned, but a student with academic weakness or one who lacks sufficient experience with groups of children should not be permitted to begin teaching without some attempt being made to correct such a weakness or deficiency. This is not an example of the public school's dictating the university's teacher education program. Rather, it is an example of the cooperative effort in teacher education which will result in increasingly better prepared teachers. The academic background of the student teacher and the experience he had with children prior to student teaching will be evaluated along with every other significant aspect of his work with children.

It may be added that the college supervisor plays a key role here; it is the college supervisor who is in the best position to note weaknesses and to work for improvement in programs on his campus. In the case of Nancy, measures could immediately be taken to prevent future transfers of experiences with children which are insufficient and inadequate. In John's case, advisors could be helped to see that it may be a disservice to students to advise them out of or away from courses which appear to be either difficult or distasteful, or both. Teacher education faculties are continuously evaluating their total programs, involving instructors in English, history, and other academic areas, as has been previously discussed. By virtue of his observations of the students in action, the college supervisor is in an ideal position to serve as a consultant to committees evaluating their teacher education programs.

Evaluating the Work of the College Supervisor and the Cooperating Teacher

It may be of some comfort to the student teacher to know that he is not the only one being scrutinized! Several situations have already been cited in which the cooperating teacher proved to be rigid, inflexible, lazy, or domineering. Some college supervisors have also provided inadequate help for student teachers. Mr. Young, busy preparing for his Ph.D. examinations, visits his student teachers only once, and then briefly. Dr. King is busy teaching classes, writing, and performing research; and he feels righteously indignant because he's the only senior staff member still required to supervise. Mrs. Johnson has a large and lovely home and a growing family; she took the job of supervisor largely because of the increased prestige it will give her. She had no idea she would have to drive so much, or that the jealousy from the teachers with whom she used to teach would be so obvious that it was almost tangible. The following guidelines are suggested for the college supervisor and the cooperating teacher attempting to assess the effectiveness with which they perform their vital functions.

The college supervisor:

1. Assigns to his job of supervisor as much time, effort, and preparation as is practical. Although his superiors cannot easily check on the number of student teaching visits he makes, or their duration, he does not put this last on his priority list, after teaching, writing, research, and committee work.

2. Uses all the tact and good humor at his command in his relations with public school personnel. Teachers and principals regard him with respect but not awe and treat him as a member of a team charged with the important responsibility of guiding a student teacher.

3. Accepts responsibility for informing curriculum committees and similar groups at his institution of areas of strength and weakness in the program, demonstrated as he watches numbers of student teachers.

4. Strives to know each of his student teachers well enough to perform the task of evaluating intelligently the student teachers assigned to him.

Ordinarily, the college supervisor assigns the student teaching grade,[4] and almost inevitably he writes a recommendation. Thus, he has the responsibility for doing this job carefully and with enough knowledge to do it intelligently. The following comments on the role of the college supervisor, from the 1964 Yearbook of the Association for Student Teaching, will serve well as a summary for this section on evaluation:

We are left with the question: Is the job of college supervisor redundant, repetitive of the role of the classroom supervising teacher? Could the classroom teacher incorporate its functions into this role? The answer is clearly "No" in the present time and situation.

As long as there are the two worlds[5] and there is good reason to

---

[4] Horace Nelson, "A Survey of Student Teaching Practices in Eight Southeastern States," *Journal of Teacher Education*, XIV (June, 1963), pp. 188–93.

[5] The college world and the public school world.

believe that they will persist for some time because of societal pressures, and as long as the college continues to vouch for individuals meeting certification standards, the college is obligated to stay in the field. The college supervisor is necessary as the agent of the college, but perhaps his role should be altered somewhat, given the dynamics of the present situation and the look ahead to "new horizons of professional unity."[6]

The cooperating teacher:

1. Accepts his student teacher where he is, with strengths and competencies to be built upon and expanded and with weaknesses to be corrected. He does not expect from the student teacher a level of performance which it has taken him several years of teaching to achieve.

2. Values the ideas and suggestions of the student teacher. He recognizes that the student teacher may emulate but should not imitate. A comment from the Association for Student Teaching Yearbook is pertinent here:

> Adopting many of the methods and habits of the supervising teacher may or may not be a good thing. Students are not always placed with teachers whose practices should be adopted. And even when the teacher is a very good teacher, a student should still be encouraged to develop ideas, methods and plans of his own. However, it is difficult for supervising teachers to encourage students to develop their own style of teaching. It is natural for supervising teachers to want their classroom procedures to be continued in the manner for which they have planned and to which they will return when the student has gone. Because of this, and because "real live children" are involved, the student teaching system is not one which encourages wide variation and experimentation. It is an essentially conservative system.[7]

3. Accepts the task of working with a student teacher as a professional obligation. Whether the tangible compensation is in the form of a cash payment, free tuition, or whatever, the real compensation is the knowledge that he has strengthened his profession by capably and conscientiously guiding the beginner who looks to him for help

---

[6] *The College Supervisor, Conflict and Challenge* (Forty-third Yearbook [Cedar Falls, Iowa: The Association for Student Teaching, 1964]), p. 169.

[7] *Ibid.*, p. 169.

and leadership. He does not complain about the additional work involved in being assigned a student teacher, and neither does he feel that this symbol of approbation, this "pat on the back," marks him as definitely superior to his colleagues.

4. Works with the college supervisor in a manner which is cooperative and beneficial to the student teacher. He avoids any attitude of subservience to, rivalry with, or conspiracy against the college supervisor.

5. Continues to work to improve his teaching techniques and methods, to learn to use the newest and best learning resources, and to add to his store of knowledge. His methods continue to be those which it will be well for the student teacher to observe and emulate.

EVALUATION PROCESSES AND TECHNIQUES USED BY THE SUPERVISOR AND THE COOPERATING TEACHER

As the cooperating teacher and the supervisor work with the student teacher in evaluating his work, the processes and techniques described in the following paragraphs should prove helpful and are, in fact, those which are now quite commonly employed.

Seminars and Meetings

At regularly scheduled times throughout student teaching a supervisor will meet with all of the student teachers assigned to him, or with those located in one school or school system. The agenda for such meetings or seminars may be highly structured and planned in advance, or the session may be problem-centered, built around the problems mentioned by the student teachers. A very effective technique used by some supervisors involves the establishment of an agenda committee made up of student teachers. This committee works with the supervisor in developing the agenda for each meeting. A few practical suggestions for seminars or meetings follow:

The student teachers' problems, treated generally, should form the core of each meeting. Problems which the supervisor feels should be discussed can be dealt with, but not unless and until those of immediate concern to the student teacher have been satisfactorily discussed and the student teacher's questions answered.

The individual and specific problems each student teacher presents might better be taken care of in a conference. If a specific problem is dealt with in a meeting, the identity of the student teacher concerned should be protected if at all possible. The supervisor may wish to illustrate a point by describing a classroom incident. Unless it is particularly complimentary to the student teacher concerned, it is less embarrassing if the student teacher is not specifically identified, especially during the first few sessions. If the atmosphere created during these sessions is as it should be and if the student teachers can focus on growth and increasing their effectiveness rather than as competing with one another, then student teachers may be willing to say, "This happened to me, and it would have been better if I'd. . . ." It is probably safer, though, in the beginning, to be protective of the student teachers' self concepts, and easily damaged egos.

Student teachers will profit from being directly involved in the meetings. There is little excuse for letting the meetings become simply a supervisor's review of student teachers' mistakes. The assignment of direct responsibility, in the nature of reports, discussion, leadership, recording and distributing notes or minutes, etc., will almost certainly pay rich dividends.

The meetings should be scheduled when they will interfere as little as possible with the student teachers' classroom activities. This is not to say that there is little or no value in the meetings but, rather, that the student teachers' primary responsibility is teaching and that the seminars, although designed to promote student teaching effectiveness, properly assume second place to classroom teaching.

Meetings should be scheduled far enough in advance so that the cooperating teacher and the student teacher can adjust their plans. If student teachers are excused from teaching responsibilities to return to campus for a meeting, some adjustments may need to be made which involve the cooperating teacher, and it isn't very helpful if the student teacher informs the critic at 8:00 A.M. that he's expected on campus that afternoon and that, of course, the cooperating teacher will be able to take over and teach.

The meetings are deserving of the supervisor's planning time and effort. Resource persons (a teacher of a methods class?), films, panel discussions, etc., can contribute a great deal to the growth of student teachers; but they must be arranged for in advance. The supervisor who overplans and leaves no room for problems of immediate concern to student teachers is making a mistake; but so is the supervisor who meets his student teachers with no advance planning at all, rationalizing that this is the nondirective approach.

If a balance is achieved between too much planning and not enough, if the student teachers are actually involved in the seminars, and if the supervisor can guide without dominating a great deal can be accomplished when groups of student teachers meet with their supervisor.

Conferences

Of at least equal importance with the meetings or the seminars are the conferences, involving the student teacher, his cooperating teacher and/or supervisor. Conferences differ from meetings in that the problems discussed relate more specifically to *one* student teacher, not a group of student teachers. The notes the student teacher has made will be used; so will the notes made by either or both of the other participants; but beyond this, the advance planning will not be as highly structured as it is for the meetings discussed in the preceding section. Suggesting that the student teacher take notes will help the cooperating teacher and the supervisor take notes with somewhat less anxiety about causing nervousness and upsetting the student teacher. If he's taking notes, too, he may be more easily convinced that all of this has as its purpose helping him become a more helpful and effective teacher. The most worthwhile conferences, those concerned with specific teaching methods or techniques at least, take place as soon after a lesson as possible.

These notes were made by a cooperating teacher as she watched a student teacher guide three different types of lessons. A brief description of the lesson taught precedes each set of notes.

The first lesson observed was a science lesson. Following a discussion of what seeds need in order to grow, the student teacher helped the children devise several "tests" or experiments. Some seeds were placed in soil, and the container was placed in a dark closet. (Will seeds grow without much light?) Other seeds from the same package were placed on a pad of wet paper towels, which was rolled up to retain moisture. (Will seeds grow without soil?) A third group of seeds was planted in a jar, in soil, with a lid sealed on with tape.

(Will seeds grow with very little air?) The children did most of the work, made most of the suggestions, and the problems they were trying to solve originated with them. The lesson, in a second grade, took about thirty-five minutes.

The cooperating teacher's notes:

> Tommy seemed a little bored; I think he knew exactly how these "tests" would come out—could one have suggested some other experiment for him or reading in science books, etc.?
>
> Although you kept things moving very well (even when Karen wanted to explore the 'seeds-in-the-dark' problem further) I wonder if 35 minutes wasn't too long? Could we have planned two lessons for this?
>
> The charts are pretty bad! I think your manuscript writing is not quite "up" to making charts before the children, notes on a pad to be transferred to a chart later would be better.
>
> Some of the children were having trouble hearing and seeing—this might have been better for a small group—one small group for each "experiment" maybe?

The next lesson observed was in spelling. Again, the entire class was involved in the lesson, which took about twenty minutes. The student teacher wanted to do something which would challenge the brighter children but not overwhelm those children who had difficulty with spelling. To the "basic" list of ten words (taken from a widely used spelling series) she helped the children add some words used in the charts relating to seed growth developed on the preceding afternoon. She began by reviewing the charts with the children and helping them select important words they would need as they reported on the progress of the seed "experiments." They selected *seeds*, *air*, *soil*, *sprout*, *grow*, and after much discussion *experiments* and *moisture*. A test was given to see how many of the basic list words the children knew, and one word from the new list was substituted for each basic list word spelled correctly. The children were responsive and seemed to enjoy the lesson a great deal.

The cooperating teacher's notes:

> How many children will be able to spell *moisture* and *experiments*? Were these wise choices? They certainly present challenges!
>
> What about Edward and George? They'll *never* get to these more interesting words will they? Perhaps the test should have been given first and the children who missed all or most of the words from the

basic list could have used the period for studying. Maybe, though, the "new" words, which are more interesting, will be learned more quickly, even by the "slow" learners.

You slipped back into your "dialogue" pattern—you and Pat carried on a conversation about *moisture* which completely excluded the rest of the class for several minutes. You need to be very careful about this; I'm surprised you didn't lose control of the group.

In the next lesson observed, a mathematics lesson, the student teacher's objective was to help children understand number sentences, a new term and concept which is introduced in the math series recently adopted for the school system. She began by writing on the board "Five and four are ten" and asking whether this sentence was true or false. The children responded eagerly and composed many sentences of their own; however, when Miss White, the student teacher, asked for a definition of a number sentence, she was greeted by silence. Then, she asked if "$3 + 3 = 6$" were a number sentence. Again, silence. After a quick review of the sentences the children had composed the student teacher dismissed the children for recess. She was bewildered and disappointed at the sad conclusion of a lesson which had begun in such a promising manner.

The cooperating teacher's notes:

Isn't it too much to try to teach both the number sentence idea and the idea of true and false sentences? Maybe not, for the bright ones especially, but I have a feeling some of the children were a bit "lost" trying to cope with both concepts.

Had you used numerals instead of "number words" in the beginning, the transition from five and four to 3 plus 3 might have been easier.

You called on Bob and Dick four times, and never Edmund and George. Why?

Leaving some unanswered questions about number sentences was a very good idea, I think. You have a good starting place tomorrow.

These notes could form the basis for three very productive conferences; teaching strengths and weaknesses alike are pointed out, and the notes, in many cases, are open-ended. The cooperating teacher does not assume that he knows all the answers but, rather, asks some questions he wants to discuss with the student teacher. Notes taken by the supervisor, also for the purposes of later conference discussion, would not differ markedly from the notes detailed here; and the supervisor would also attempt to build or strengthen and avoid giving the impression of knowing the solution to each problem. The conference which follows each lesson has great value; so has the conference which is held near the end of the student teaching period and which has as its purpose the evaluation of the student's growth over a longer period of time, rather than his effectiveness in teaching a specific lesson.

Many supervisors find that it is very helpful to keep a notebook in which notes of each visit are recorded. The notebook has several advantages over notes kept on cards or loose sheets of paper. First of all, it promotes better organization and makes it easier to assess growth over a period of time. A notebook is fairly easy to keep on file, and the supervisor will find it easier to write recommendations which are requested some time after a student has left campus. Supervisors who are responsible for twenty or twenty-five student teachers a quarter, three quarters a year, may find it difficult to write an intelligent commentary about a particular student teacher unless his records are fairly complete. A dated, carefully filed notebook may be part of the solution to this problem. The following comments are from the notebook of one college supervisor as he observed the growth of one student teacher through an eight-week period:

(first visit—second day of student teaching) Jan. 12, 19——

As I entered the room, I noticed that Gloria was helping a small group of children arrange a bulletin board. This was a board dealing with magnetism, and on one side Gloria and the children were arranging pictures of objects magnets would attract, and on the other side pictures of objects magnets would not attract. When there were disagreements the pictures were put aside and Gloria found the real objects, or something close to them for actual trial with a magnet. She seemed to be at ease with the children, and I was pleased to notice that the children were already accepting her as a teacher. At our conference after my observation, Gloria expressed enthusiasm for her work and especially for the freedom of atmosphere Mrs. Campbell provided so that Gloria could work with them in her own way.

Gloria's voice is shrill and quite unpleasant when she becomes tense (as she was while I was observing).

Although she had speech and hearing clearance, this evidently was not discovered and she told me I was the first one who had pointed this out to her. I'll continue to watch and listen, and she said she'd work on it—although it may have been a one-time occurrence.

Jan. 19, 19——

Gloria had a reading group today and it went pretty badly, I thought. She almost read from the manual when setting up her guide questions for silent reading and giving directions for the workbook. She didn't generate much enthusiasm for the story, but this was no more her fault than the story's—which was dull, in my opinion. She almost wept while we had our conference, and insisted that this reading group had never gone so badly before. We looked at the guide, and she agreed that she had relied upon it a bit too heavily—she could have rephrased the questions in a more interesting and challenging manner. I asked why she used this story, since it was rather dull. She said "skipping" a story had never occurred to her, and she'd check to see how Mrs. Campbell would react to the idea. She was upset over her performance and perhaps was seeking a scapegoat, but she suggested that Mrs. Campbell had given her little or no help in "setting up" her reading lessons other than observations of Mrs. Campbell's teaching and the discussions which had followed such observations.

Jan. 24, 19——

The math lesson I saw was rather traditional; of the every-child-on-the-same "problem" on-the-same-page variety. Gloria did have several activities to suggest for those who finished the assignment early, and she did not insist that the three or four slowest children finish the entire assignment. She seemed at ease, and her explanation of the assignment was clear and simple. This was not "new material" but I wondered if some brief review might have been helpful, especially for the slower children.

I talked with both Mrs. Campbell and Gloria after the children were dismissed for lunch. Mrs. Campbell commented that Gloria had resented her "sink-or-swim" approach at first, but claimed that Gloria's growth proved she was correct in insisting that Gloria solve her own problems in her own way. Mrs. Campbell had lunch room duty, so excused herself, after saying again that she was very very pleased with Gloria's growth and felt she had a great deal of potential. Gloria was quiet until Mrs. Campbell left, then she repeated her desire for more help, specifically, and when problems occurred. She said she felt lost not having known when she had been successful or when she had failed. I assured her that I thought I had noted average progress, and felt sure Mrs. Campbell had been sincere in complimenting her. Nevertheless, I left our conference feeling disturbed and feeling that somehow we were failing Gloria.

Feb. 1, 19——

Gloria's performance with the reading group was much better this time. The guidebook was nowhere in sight and her guidance of the discussion and the questions she asked were stimulating and challenging to this bright group of youngsters. She failed to notice the type of errors made by the children (or at least I did not *see* her use the pencil and notebook she had available). She admitted that she frequently forgot to do this, and said she was aware of the importance of keeping track of missed words and types of mistakes various children were making. I remained after the reading class to watch Gloria help finish the independent work period and help children evaluate their completed tasks. She was very directive "You *could* have finished that story, couldn't you?" But I suspect this was an imitation of Mrs. Campbell, who doesn't always use the "Carl Rogers approach," by any means! I think every child felt that his opinion was valued and respected, and most of the children exhibited marked ability to be objective about their work habits and their accomplishments.

Feb. 12, 19——

Mrs. Campbell was nowhere in sight and, in fact, was not even in the building—she had taken the day to visit another classroom. I arrived before school to see how Gloria handled beginning a day, planning, and helping children start on their independent work period. The children were a bit noisy before the bell rang, but settled down very quickly. I'm not sure, but I think my presence had a calming effect. Gloria was confident, relaxed and the children responded to her guidance easily and the routines were soon out of the way. Gloria asked for suggestions for independent work projects and listed any new ideas on the chalkboard. (Her manuscript writing leaves *much* to be desired. We must work on this!) The children quickly got the necessary materials and settled to their tasks while Gloria met the first reading group. I was very impressed. I'm not sure that Mrs. Campbell's non-directive approach can be given credit for this, but Gloria has certainly grown, matured, and is well on her way to becoming a very good teacher. No conference this time, I had to rush to another classroom.

Feb. 20, 19——

I visited during the afternoon this time, and watched Gloria develop a creative writing lesson. The snow was lush and thick, and falling fast, and she began by asking the children to look out the window and to think of some words to describe what they saw. These phrases were written on the board. (The manuscript writing has improved a great deal—I was sure it wouldn't take much practice!)

Then, the children were asked to write, for themselves, their feelings about the snow. Very few of the products were beautiful, but each one was original and, Gloria said, showed real improvement over their last writing, just before the holidays. No one was forced to read his poem aloud, but some children wanted to. The atmosphere Gloria helped establish was exactly right for creative writing, and an experienced teacher could hardly have produced better results or worked more effectively.

As these notes were reviewed in the final conference between the student teacher and his supervisor, the areas of strength and weakness became more clear, and the growth of the student teacher was obvious to both the student teacher and the supervisor. Using the notes also made it somewhat easier to be objective about areas of weakness and specific deficiencies. When a student teacher must be told that he cannot be recommended by his institution for a teaching certificate the notes provide invaluable support—support which may need to be marshalled in the event the student teacher disagrees with the judgment rendered and decides to take his case to a dean, a college president, or state certification officials. This is always unpleasant, but at least a supervisor with copious notes stands on firmer ground than the supervisor who can merely vaguely recall certain specific incidents which appear to indicate incompetence, but has nothing written or even especially well organized.

The Three-way Conference

Reference has been made several times to the importance of communication in the student teaching process. Conferences between the student teacher and each of the other participants, the supervisor and the "critic" are part of this process. Another part of the communication process is the three-way conference involving all of the participants. This type of conference is valuable if each participant approaches it with honesty, forthrightness and without absence of concern for making an impression or raising a grade.

The three-way conference is useful at any stage of the student teacher process. It may serve as a follow-up conference to a specific lesson or as a general summary conference near the end of student teaching.

Notes similar to those previously detailed are valuable components of a three-way conference. Differences in reaction to the same teaching incident are to be expected, and sometimes the differences are not slight. A supervisor observing the science lesson described earlier in the present chapter might have reacted very differently than the co-operating teacher to the number of tests or experiments performed. The reaction to the evident boredom of Tommy, and the poor chart work and the corrective procedures recommended might have been different as well. Discussing such differences openly and honestly with student teachers provides a basis for a rich learning experience— educational philosophy and educational psychology in action, full of life, as they seldom are in text books. As the student teacher partici-pates in a discussion about several approaches he might have taken to achieve a given objective or about whether or not his objectives were worthwhile and appropriate, he is forced to look at teaching, the disciplines involved, and the nature of the learning process criti-cally and objectively. His growth will undoubtedly be enhanced. A high degree of competence, of honesty, and of mutual respect for the personalities involved must be assumed if the results referred to are to be achieved; but these desirable qualities are present in the vast majority of student teaching situations.

Frequent student teaching conferences involving all three partici-pants have another advantage. In a very few cases, the student teacher feels caught between the supervisor and the cooperating teacher who apparently expect very different kinds of behavior from him. Occa-sionally, the student teacher explains away a poor teacher practice by claiming to the supervisor that this is the way his "critic" wants it done. Wherever problems result from poor communications, the best solution seems to be a face-to-face, honest discussion in which some decisions are made and some conclusions are reached. To some—a majority, perhaps—of the readers this seems obvious and the preced-ing discussion is unnecessary; however, in a surprising number of student teaching situations, messages, comments, and recommenda-tions are carried from one member of the team to another, and the result is confusion and misunderstanding. Some conference guide-lines follow:

The first essential is honesty. If any participant is less than honest in his remarks or recommendations, the student teacher will be left with a rather tarnished professional image, and the concrete and tan-gible results of the conference will be limited.

Another essential, and one which occasionally conflicts with the goal of honesty, is consideration for the other conference participants.

It is difficult for the student teacher to separate criticism of his teaching from criticism of him as a person. We teach as we are. The usual rules of courtesy, balancing compliments and criticism, and maintaining an attitude which is supportive and helpful are most important in each conference. Nevertheless, it is a mistake to be so kind, so polite, and so considerate, that weaknesses go unmentioned and therefore uncorrected. The conference should be held at a time when none of the participants is hurried, and in a place where interruptions can be kept to a minimum. A place other than the classroom is often recommended, and a Coke or a cup of coffee helps, especially if the conference is held at the end of a school day which has been long, difficult, and tiring. Some student teachers, cooperating teachers, and supervisors have found that a luncheon conference is productive and convenient. Notes or a checklist like that which follows can serve to focus a conference, to keep participants from missing the point or points which need to be discussed, and to give the conversation a professional rather than a social tone.

The following checklists have been developed to help the student teacher gauge his effectiveness in teaching a particular lesson. Either one or both could be used by the student as a device or devices for self-evaluation; or they may serve as the basis for conferences with the college supervisor or cooperating teacher.

There can be no specific number set as the ideal number of conferences. This will vary with the supervisor's student teaching load, the competence and experience of the cooperating teacher, and the type of help the student teacher needs most. Generally speaking, a conference should follow each visit, and two or three three-way conferences would seem to be minimal. Cooperating teachers are also classroom teachers. They must attend committee meetings, faculty meetings, and PTA meetings. They are responsible for parent conferences. College supervisors have many schools to visit and classes to teach, and they are also members of college committees, study groups, etc. There are increasing numbers of student teachers who are married and have homes and children to care for. All of these factors must be considered in determining the number of conferences. Professional obligations to student teaching should come first, but little will be accomplished in a conference in which one or more of the participants is primarily concerned about a delayed dinner, a missed parent conference or committee meeting, or some other immediate problem.

Evaluative Checklist No. 1

A. Planning   *5   4   3   2   1

    1. Were objectives clear, to teacher and children?

    2. Were appropriate materials selected, and were they ready for use?

    3. Were the plans made with due consideration for children's needs and interests?

B. The Lesson

    1. Was it appropriate for the age level (interest, length, etc.)?

    2. Was the topic important and significant?

    3. Did the children appear to be interested?

    4. Did the student teacher appear to be in charge at all times (discipline)?

    5. Were adjustments made for individual differences?

    6. Was the student teacher's knowledge of the topic at least adequate (hopefully for *more* than adequate)?

C. Evaluation and Follow-up

    1. Were activities planned which helped the student teacher and the pupils gauge how much had been learned?

    2. Were the evaluative devices chosen in terms of the objectives; were the objectives achieved?

    3. Were at least some of the children stimulated to pursue the topic independently? Did the lesson appear to be stimulating and encouraging to individual children who wished to learn more?

    4. Did this lesson assume a logical place in a sequence of learning experience?

---

* A decreasing scale—5 indicates that the quality is present to the fullest extent which can reasonably be expected in a beginner, 1 that the quality is not present or did not appear to be present during the observation period.

Evaluative Checklist No. 2[8]

Competencies	N.O.*	Below Aver.	Aver.	Above Aver.	Excellent
I. Personal					
A. Appearance					
B. Health and vitality					
C. Voice quality and use of English					
II. Attitudes					
A. Initiative					
B. Dependability					
C. Enthusiasm					
D. Poise—self control					
E. Adaptability					
F. Acceptance of suggestions					
G. Creativity					
H. Emphasizes clear and understandable English in every phase of learning.					
I. Uses legible handwriting, cursive and manuscript.					
J. Provides for summaries, reviews, or appropriate culminating activities at intervals.					
III. The Teacher Maintains an Atmosphere Conducive to Social and Emotional Growth					
A. Accepts each child as he is and attempts to understand him.					
B. Is at ease and natural with the children.					

* No opportunity to observe.

Competencies	N.O.°	Below Aver.	Aver.	Above Aver.	Excellent
C. Plans with children for appropriate behavior for different kinds of learning activities, e.g., times it is appropriate to talk quietly while others work.					
D. Maintains consistent and reasonable standards.					
E. Discipline used is readily seen by children to be a natural outcome of misbehavior.					
F. Reduces tensions which result from unfair competition—such as expecting a child to achieve beyond his capacity or development.					
G. Uses praise and encouragement to reward improvement in learning and behavior.					
H. Encourages individual creativity and provides time for expression of feelings.					
I. Promotes group feeling and sense of belonging.					
J. Plans time for relaxing moments and fun.					
IV. The Teacher Maintains a Physical Environment Conducive to Learning					
A. Arranges for physical comfort of children.					
Heating					
Ventilation					

° No opportunity to observe.

Competencies	N.O.[*]	Below Aver.	Aver.	Above Aver.	Excel-lent
Lighting					
Size of furniture					
Cares for special needs of handicapped children.					
Plans space for movement.					
B. Keeps room clean and materials in order.					
C. Arranges and distributes materials so that congestion and noise are kept at a minimum.					
D. Arranges furniture in best way possible for each learning situation.					
E. Uses imagination to create attractive room.					
V. The Teacher Evaluates Growth of Learners					
A. Uses cumulative records, test scores, and other data to describe the status of children's growth.					
B. Uses variety of techniques to evaluate growth.					
Standardized tests used as diagnostic instruments.					
Teacher-made tests					
Devises various types of tests.					
Attempts to construct tests which are valid.					

VI. Comments:

---

[*] No opportunity to observe.

Name_____Supervisor_____

Date_____Grade_____School_____

Cooperating Teacher_____

---

[8] Adapted from "Guideposts for Evaluation of Student Teaching," developed by the faculty in elementary education, Purdue University, 1964.

Written Evaluations of the Work of the Student Teacher

Because a letter grade is almost inevitably inadequate as an index of the student teacher's growth, his present competence, or his prospects for teaching success in the future, letters of recommendation are usually requested by placement offices, hiring officials, and even for registrars' files. Following are examples of two letters written by cooperating teachers regarding the progress and competence of the student teachers they guided. The first is a summary of judgment made by Mrs. Agnes Smith, supervising teacher, concerning the growth, accomplishments, and potentialities of Carolyn R. Jones, student teacher:

> Throughout our work together Mrs. Jones evidenced very real interest in children and showed definite growth in her understanding of them and of the meaning of the fundamental principles of education. The children liked and respected her, turned to her for help, and had confidence in her counsel. In her relations with the children she evidenced a quietly firm manner coupled with a good sense of humor. She also gained the respect of the principal and the other staff members.
>
> Mrs. Jones is a student of education. She prepared throughly, faced problems squarely, and made decisions based on good reasoning. She likes teaching and used all materials available to make her teaching a thing of which to be proud. She exemplified enthusiasm for her work and for the profession of teaching. It is my firm belief that she will begin her professional work with a desire and a great deal of ability to teach creatively.
>
> As her supervising teacher, I would recommend Mrs. Jones as an

able young teacher who should be a capable and cooperative member of any elementary school staff. There is every reason to believe that she will continue to grow both personally and professionally. In my opinion she possesses personal qualities and teaching abilities which are far superior to those of most beginning teachers.

The second is a report concerning the student teaching experience of Mrs. Janet Johnson:

Janet Johnson has an excellent beginning toward a teaching career. Of course, all teachers have problems, and some have more than others. The important thing is having the ability to recognize these problems and the determination to continually work toward improvement. Only in this way can we hope to approach excellence in our teaching. I feel Janet has this ability.

The lessons planned by Mrs. Johnson were superior. They were well thought out with definite objectives in mind. The well-planned lessons brought about a security in both the children and the teacher which was very desirable. Some areas, because of the teacher's interests, were better planned than others.

Mrs. Johnson accepted each child as he was and exhibited a sincere interest in each individual and his particular problems. Many of the children in the room showed much benefit because of this interest.

Another area of excellence was acceptance of criticism. A sincere desire to discuss problems and areas needing improvement was shown.

An area where improvement was needed was voice. Janet unfortunately does not have a voice which carries. However, this was recognized and much improvement was seen. It takes a certain amount of experience to develop a pleasant, audible voice quality. I feel that this problem will easily be overcome.

Discipline was a problem area. The problem centered on a lack of firmness. This class of fourth-graders is quite hard to handle, even for an experienced teacher. One reason for this could be that there are twelve girls and twenty-one boys. Also, an unusually large percentage of the children have problems, most of which have resulted from poor home conditions. This does not mean financially poor, however. Firmness along with a great amount of understanding are the keys to handling a group such as this.

In all other areas, Janet did a very acceptable job. There were a few minor problems which were not important enough to discuss. In general, a fine job was done.

Other staff members and parents were very complimentary. A friendly, professional attitude was shown at all times. Cooperation and sincerity were very apparent.

In summing up this report I would say that Janet Johnson will be a fine teacher with few problems.

> Miss Margaret Brown
> Supervising Teacher
> Fourth Grade

The following statements are those recorded by a college supervisor. The reader will note that there is included a supervisor's report about Janet Johnson. It might be interesting to compare the reports of the supervisor and the cooperating teacher. There are some striking differences in perception of the student's work and her attitude toward teaching.

> Student Teaching Summary: Jane Elson
> Supervising Teacher: Mrs. King, Grade 6

Jane had a very difficult and protracted beginning. Jane says Mrs. King refused to let her teach; Mrs. King says Jane did not *want* to get involved. Whatever the reason, Jane was the very last of the seven student teachers I supervised to get going.

Her manner was extremely calm and patient. She never raised her voice; in fact, I did not see much expression of anger, surprise or any other emotion throughout the student teaching experience.

Mrs. King expressed surprise at Jane's involvement toward the end of the six weeks, and at the depth of feeling the children had for Jane. She became, at last, part of the group, a teacher.

Jane's lessons tended to be rather traditional. I saw one "reading lesson" which was merely a discussion of a story in the reading text which most of the children had read silently. She spent much time giving individual attention to children.

Jane dresses attractively, has a soft, deep voice and smiles easily. She takes suggestions and criticisms well and has the ability to be quite objective about herself.

Jane seems to be a very intelligent young woman and indicated an awareness of her tendency to aloofness, coldness. Obviously, from the expressed feelings of the children at the conclusion of the student teaching experience, Jane managed to relate to them most successfully.

I think Jane might well be happier as a secondary school teacher, where there will be more content emphasis, but I am certain that she can be a successful elementary teacher.

> Ellen Ames
> College Supervisor
> State University

Student Teaching Summary: Janet Johnson
Supervising Teacher: Miss Brown, Grade 4

Janet had many "trials" during student teaching. She desired and failed to establish a close and friendly relationship with Miss Brown. Miss Brown had many personal problems and spent little time guiding or helping Janet.

Both Miss Brown and Miss Sonder, the building principal, felt that Janet had serious control problems, but on each of my visits, I found the children working, not "out of hand" in any sense, and responsive to Janet in a way which indicated both affection and respect.

Janet wanted to try grouping for arithmetic instruction, because she felt that many of the children failed to understand the processes they were using. Miss Brown did not feel this was a wise approach, and so Janet gave as much individual help as time permitted.

Janet's planning became consistently more effective as the student teaching period progressed. I doubt that she'll have any problems here at all.

Janet speaks her mind and is very concerned about children. Her staff relationships may suffer because of her tendency to say what she thinks. I'm sure this damaged her relationship with Miss Brown.

I'm afraid Janet may never teach, because student teaching was, for her, rather unrewarding. She'll need help, as most beginners do, but I feel the potential is there.

Ellen Ames
College Supervisor
State University

Student Teacher Self-evaluations

One of the most valuable experiences to which a student teacher can be exposed is that of evaluating his own growth and his probable effectiveness in his first year of teaching. Again, for purposes of comparison, Jane Elson's and Janet Johnson's self-evaluations are included.

Self-evaluation
by
Jane Elson

I'm afraid that many of my weaknesses are more glaringly apparent to me than my strengths, though I'm sure that I'm not even aware of many of my weaknesses.

My first difficulty was with discipline. No child was discourteous to me, there were times when the room was completely silent, and the children did do what I told them. However, many times the room was in a "dull roar" and I wasn't able to convince some of the lazier students to complete their work. There are, I believe, several reasons for this. To begin with I never stated set behavioral policies except when the need arose. I suppose I was at fault here but I didn't feel that I should disrupt Mrs. Tyson's classroom that completely. (I was also a "greenhorn" at this.) A second reason is that I am patient by nature and I could usually understand why they enjoyed behaving as they did. Only twice did I become angry, and they certainly quieted down then. Another problem is that I haven't developed the ability of talking to the class in such manner that they will all realize their mistakes and regret them. I suppose this will come with time and practice. My final reason for having a discipline problem was poor planning on my part.

My difficulties with planning I have mentioned several times in my journal.[9] One time I'll give an assignment that is too hard for the slow students and then turn around and give one that is too easy for the fast ones. I believe I improved on this as time went on. However, I still haven't come up with enough activities to keep the faster learners busy. (I have had them make bulletin boards, decorate the window, clean the room, arrange displays, do extra reports, set up experiments, do outside reading, and work some elementary algebraic problems.)

My handwriting is as atrocious as some of the children's English, and my vocabulary varies from slang to words that are beyond their comprehension.

I have yet to master (or come anywhere near mastering) the art of carrying on a discussion, for there are times when I have difficulty keeping everyone's attention, and I don't feel that I was always able to engender much enthusiasm in the subject being studied. Whether this is due to distractions which arose when some were not paying attention, my tone of voice and vocabulary, poor planning, or what— I'm not sure. However, I was quite fortunate in being able to have guests from India and Greece, slides from Hong Kong, and clothing from Japan and China. These things seemed to interest all of the children.

I've mentioned my patience and good humor as weaknesses, but I

---

[9] Jane's supervisor requested that each student teacher keep a log or journal n which he recorded what he did and his reactions to children and teaching.

also feel that they are strengths. I sincerely believe that the children have enjoyed having me as their student teacher, that I have shown interest in each student as an individual, and that I have given whatever attention possible, to the students who were having difficulties. I believe that my independent work sessions have worked out fairly well due partially to the above reasons, though I definitely need more practice. I like to think that I have approached each of the children objectively, though I know there were times when I didn't.

I don't feel that my appearance, reliability or interest need be questioned. I am looking forward to teaching next year, and although I definitely need improvement in all areas, I feel that I am off and running.

Self-evaluation
Janet Johnson

To evaluate oneself is very hard to do, for there is a tendency to be either too modest or too confident. In this short space, I will try to evaluate myself to the best of my ability.

First, I wish to say that I don't believe that I made any gross errors during my student teaching, however, this does not mean that I did not make many mistakes.

On the good side, I believe I was my strongest in areas of science, history and English. I planned several bulletin boards, had group experiments, showed filmstrips, brought in extra books and played games using facts already or recently learned. In spelling, I made up crossword puzzles, had spelling bees and made up scrambled word games to interest them in their spelling words. In history, I brought in other facets of the inventors or people they were studying about. For example, when they were studying the Wright Brothers, I showed a filmstrip, made up a bulletin board and told the story of the history of flights starting with the Greek myths.

In science, I lectured, drew pictures on the blackboard, had demonstrations and let them do the experiments on their own. In English, we made up poems in a large group, in small groups and individually. I also seated the children in small circles with approximately five persons in each group. This was their first experience with this and I felt that at the end it was fairly successful. My problems were in the areas of discipline, my need for lowering my vocabulary, my inability to anticipate certain behavior and plan for it, my inability to give long enough directions before placing the children on their own. I feel I still have a great deal to learn about this profession.

Assigning a Grade in Student Teaching

Because student teaching is a very complex process, and because assessment tends to be total, including many aspects of a student's personality as well as his subject matter competence and grasp of methodology, an increasing number of colleges and universities have moved away from the *A–F* scale and assign an *S* for students who are competent and should be certified and a *U* for those students who should not be certified. Any supervisor or cooperating teacher who has struggled with the problem of assigning *one* grade which reflects growth and achievement and is also a prognosis of future success realizes how difficult this task really is. What does an *A* mean? Excellence in achievement? Excellence in growth (what if the beginning was at such a high level that further growth could not reasonably be expected)? A prediction of excellence in teaching (without an unusual amount of help as a beginner)?

A letter grade probably represents an evaluation of all of these factors in a balance agreed upon by the group of supervisors who work directly with student teachers. After listing, in some detail, the objectives of student teaching—in behavioral terms, "The student teacher should be able to . . ."—the objectives can, to some extent at least, be arranged in order of relative importance. Such a list should prove to be very, very helpful to student teachers in assessing their own growth and to the supervisors who must assign grades. In a few institutions, the criteria by which a student teacher's effectiveness can be judged are developed cooperatively by supervisors, outstanding cooperation teachers, and students who have successfully completed student teaching. A group such as this might develop a set of criteria similar to these: The successful student teacher can effectively guide and control a group of children; has an adequate grasp of significant subject matter; studies children consistently and acts upon the knowledge he gains; plans adequately, locates materials, and is "ready" to teach; uses a variety of methods and material in an effort to meet children's needs.

The list above is merely suggestive and represents only a beginning. Each group of supervisors should feel responsible for developing, or at least re-examining, the list of objectives for the student teachers from their institution. The pattern of teacher education, especially the laboratory experiences, varies so from institution to institution that to include here a list which would fit even a small majority of student teacher situations would be an impossible task. It is enough to refer to the value of developing and constantly redefining the objectives which all of the participants in the student teaching process are working to achieve.

It should be stated again, that a student teacher should receive a grade which fairly and accurately represents his effort, his achievement, and his probable success as a beginning teacher.

Children Evaluate the Work of the Student Teacher

One of the best clues to the effectiveness with which a student teacher is working with children is the overt response of the children. Loretta Byers writes:

> If you have developed a sensitivity to pupil reactions, you will get indications every day of how children evaluate you as a teacher. You will observe their respect of you, or their lack of respect; their interest and participation—or their lack of interest; and the quality of work they produce under your guidance. You are evaluating your own progress through these overt manifestations.
>
> Occasional discussions with children can focus on evaluation of their learning experiences and give you some important clues as to their feelings about your teaching. Start the discussion with the focus on the learning activity rather than on you, the student teacher. At the conclusion of a reading lesson, you may say to your group, "How many like this story?" And then "How do you feel we are getting along in reading?" "Are you enjoying the reading period?" Sometimes the replies are surprising in that they reveal how much insight children have.[10]

Asking for comments from children after a lesson is one technique; with young children such discussion is more appropriate than asking for written comments. Another technique may be used. In response

---

[10] Loretta Byers and Elizabeth Irish, *Success in Student Teaching* (Boston: D. C. Heath & Company, 1961), p. 228.

to one student teacher's request for an evaluative statement from the children, a group of fourth-graders wrote the following comments:

> I think you will be a good teacher. You were hard but you were fair. At first, your assignments were too long, but you got better.

> I like you very much. I like the way you had us read in different books. Some of us didn't get to talk to you about our books very long, though. (This refers to the individualized reading program initiated by the student teacher and to the fact that the size of the group, and poor management of time, prevented holding individual conferences as often as is usually recommended.)

> At first I didn't know whether I'd like you. You talked too fast and you used big words. Later on, though, I got to know you better and now I think you're the best student teacher I ever had. You and Mrs. Browning like each other and you told us the same thing. You taught us almost like she taught us.

These children showed sensitivity about teachers and teaching; their reactions should receive some consideration when a grade is determined. In arriving at a student teaching grade, every aspect of the student teacher's performance should be considered, including the student teacher's evaluation of his success or lack of success and the children's reactions to his teaching.

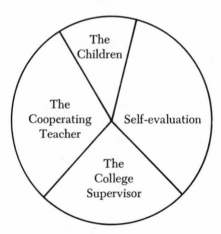

FIGURE 15.   TOTAL EVALUATION: WHO EVALUATES
THE STUDENT TEACHER

Summary

Each section in this chapter has dealt with one important aspect of the process of evaluation in student teaching. The following points have been emphasized:

1. Evaluation is a continuous process. In student teaching, the process begins when the student enters the teacher education program of his college or university.

2. The background of skills and knowledge and the student teacher's experiences with children cannot be avoided in the assessment of his work with children.

3. Several evaluative techniques have been used effectively by supervisors and cooperating teachers. These include note taking and completing checklists. The notes and checklists serve as the basis for conferences among the student teacher, his cooperating teacher, and/or his supervisor.

4. The seminar or meeting involving a college supervisor and all or a group of the student teachers assigned to him is another valuable method of helping student teachers examine their teaching techniques. Involvement of the student teachers in the planning and conduct of such meetings was strongly urged.

5. In assigning a grade for student teaching, the supervisor and cooperating teacher must consider the student's growth, his achievement, and his probable success as a teacher. It is essential that the welfare of future groups of children be considered in recommending certification. The student teacher who shows little promise of effectiveness in teaching should not be certified, regardless of the problems involved in denying certification. Minor and temporary unpleasantness is of secondary importance to the harm an ineffectual or incompetent teacher can inflict upon many children over a period of years.

Suggested Activities for the Student Teacher

1. Complete a copy of one of the evaluative checklists included in this chapter. Ask the cooperating teacher and the college supervisor to do this, as well. Use these three checklists as the basis for an evaluative conference.

To be of maximim benefit, this should not be postponed until the end of student teaching.

2. Ask for anonymous written evaluations from children (Grades 3–6). Discuss these with the cooperating teacher. It may be desirable to develop a brief checklist, to give the children some sense of direction in evaluating the work of the student teacher.

3. In one of the student teaching meetings, discuss the qualities you feel contribute most to effective teaching. In other words, develop your own list of criteria.

4. Write and discuss with your cooperating teacher a self-evaluative statement similar to those included here. It would be helpful to do this more than once during the student teaching period, although this may not be possible.

5. Try to obtain a list of criteria used by administrators and teachers in evaluating the work of beginning teachers. Discuss, in a student teaching meeting, the advantages and disadvantages of merit pay. If possible, ask an administrator who supports this principle and a teacher who opposes it to discuss their views before a meeting of student teachers.

SELECTED REFERENCES

Brown, Thomas J., and Bonich, Serafina Fiore. *Student Teaching in the Elementary School.* New York: Harper & Row, 1962, Chapter 10, "Learning to Plan Through Evaluation." *See also* Appendices *A*, *E*, and *F*.

Burr, James B.; Harding, Lowry W.; and Jacobs, Leland B. *Student Teaching in the Elementary School.* 2nd ed. New York: Appleton-Century-Crofts, 1958, Chapter 14, "Completing Your Work."

Byers, Loretta, and Irish, Elizabeth. *Success in Student Teaching.* Boston: D. C. Heath & Company, 1961, Chapter 12, "Evaluating Your Growth."

The College Supervisor: Conflict and Challenge. (Forty-third Yearbook) Cedar Falls, Iowa: The Association for Student Teaching, 1964, Part III, "The Challenge: New Approaches and Techniques."

Concern for the Individual in Student Teaching. (Forty-second Yearbook) Cedar Rapids, Iowa: The Association for Student Teaching, Chapter 10, "Individualizing Leadership."

Haines, Alleyne C. *Guiding the Student Teaching Process in Elementary Education.* Chicago: Rand McNally & Co., 1960, Chapter 12, "Making Recommendations About Student Teachers."

9

The Student Teacher and Evaluating Children

In the general discussion of evaluation which served as an introduction to Chapter 8, it was noted that part of the total evaluation process in student teaching is the assessment of children's growth. Michaelis refers to this part of the evaluation process in his definition of evaluation: "The process of determining the amount and quality of pupil growth and achievement, based on clearly defined purposes is called evaluation. Evaluation involves making judgments concerning the worth and adequacy of pupil achievement, adjustment or development."[1]

It hardly seems necessary to note that the successful student teacher will make every effort to judge the growth of the children in his classroom fairly and objectively and to guide the children effectively toward desirable goals. Learning has been defined as changing behavior; if this definition is accepted, then the student teacher who

---

[1] John V. Michaelis and Enoch Dumas, *Elementary School Student Teaching* (Englewood Cliffs, New Jersey: Prentice-Hall, Inc., 1962), p. 311.

produces little evident change, however this change is measured, can hardly be considered successful.

The reader is again reminded that evaluation is a continuous process, and it is hoped that the separation of this chapter from the preceding chapter dealing with evaluation of the over-all work of the student teacher will serve the purpose of better organization but will not work against seeing the total student teaching process as a whole and the role of evaluation throughout this process.

What techniques will the student teacher use in assessing children's growth? This is not a text dealing with tests and measurements, nor am I by any means an expert in this field. There is still another reason for the very general treatment this topic will receive here. There are nearly as many patterns of testing, of grading, and communicating children's progress to parents as there are student teaching situations. A detailed discussion of specific tests or other evaluative devices which the student teacher may never use is somewhat inappropriate in a text of this type. For a specific and authoritative analysis of various tests, the reader is referred to O. K. Buros' *Fifth Mental Measurements Yearbook*.[2] A review of a standard text dealing with evaluation in the elementary school[3] is also recommended.

It will be recalled that in the chapter dealing with planning, a thorough examination of each child's cumulative record folder was strongly urged. In the section dealing with getting started in student teaching it was suggested that the student teacher discuss the school's evaluation program with his cooperating teacher and the school principal. It is appropriate to repeat this advice here.

EVALUATIVE TECHNIQUES AND DEVICES

The following types of instruments or techniques are those very commonly used and are those with which a student teacher should be generally familiar:

---

[2] Highland Park, New Jersey: The Gryphon Press, 1959.

[3] For example, Harold Gray Shane and E. T. McSwain *Evaluation and the Elementary Curriculum* (New York: Holt, Rinehart and Winston, 1958).

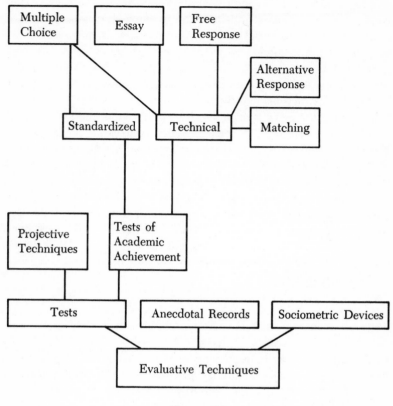

FIGURE 16

Tests of Academic Aptitude (Intelligence Tests)

These may be divided into two types, group and individual tests. The terms *group* and *individual* refer to the manner of administration. Tests such as the California Test of Mental Maturity are administered to groups of children. The Stanford-Binet is an example of a test in which the examiner and the subject work in a one-to-one relationship. Because the Wechsler Intelligence Scale for Children (another individual test) and the Stanford Binet are quite time-consuming and because a trained person should administer these tests, they are less commonly used than the group tests. Some school systems employ a trained psychometrist and attempt to give each pupil one Binet or W.I.S.C. while he is enrolled in elementary school.

Group aptitude or intelligence tests are more frequently used, perhaps being administered every third year. The student teacher may even be asked to administer such a test. If he is asked to do this, he will, of course, carefully read the manual accompanying the tests and follow the instructions precisely.

This is not the place to argue against overuse of or the overreliance upon the results of intelligence tests. They do help a teacher identify the limits within which a particular child is working. It seems obvious that a child's environment will influence test results and that a "poorly languaged" child will probably not perform well on intelligence tests, as they are presently designed. It is also true that most of the tests measure "intelligence" as society measures it, and verbal ability certainly plays a major role in, for example, an employer's assessment of an employee's competence. Some knowledge of a child's performance on a standardized intelligence test is a valuable asset to a teacher or a student teacher.

Tests of Academic Achievement

In most school systems, there exists a program of achievement testing. Usually such testing takes place once a year, and frequently this is in the spring. The purpose of such testing is to measure children's growth in specific academic areas. Achievement tests should always be selected in terms of the objectives developed by teachers in a given school system. Classroom teachers are occasionally heard to complain, "These tests *don't* test what I teach!" The administration of a test which doesn't measure what is taught indicates either that this teacher is pursuing his own objectives independent of other faculty members or that the wrong test has been selected. Some commonly used achievement tests are The Metropolitan Achievement Tests, The Stanford Achievement Tests, California Achievement Tests, and The Sequential Tests of Educational Progress.

The student teacher will probably find it wise and useful to notice the general pattern of test results; do the children, as a group, perform highest in reading? How do the math scores compare with the reading scores? Individual profiles are also significant. How much higher is John's math score than his language score? The student teacher will also want to note the scores on intelligence tests as they relate to achievement test scores. The terms *overachiever* and *underachiever* are now in some disrepute among certain educational psychologists, but it is still true that for some children there is a wide gap between capacity or aptitude, as measured, and achievement, as measured. Without undue concern for the terminology which can be properly applied to this gap, the student teacher can discuss such cases with the cooperating teacher; and discussions of this type will help the student teacher as he works with the children in his group.

If the student teacher is asked to administer standardized achievement tests, he should keep in mind that standardization implies the administration of the test to thousands of pupils all over the nation, under specifically controlled conditions. Time limits should be rigidly observed, and the student teacher should be very careful not to give any help with answers and should follow precisely the instructions for administration given in the test manual. It is easy to succumb to sympathy for a child or to desire to see the group perform well, and to give unwarranted suggestions or clues to answers. Hints, suggestions, and clues should be avoided; and the student teacher, during the administration of a standardized test, is not teaching but testing. The two roles should not be confused when a standardized test is being administered. Of course, all instructions should be clear, and these may be repeated or clarified whenever necessary.

The teacher, or the student teacher, is in control of the classroom atmosphere during a testing situation. He will largely determine whether the atmosphere is tense and highly charged or so relaxed and informal that children may be suspected of not really trying to do as well as possible on the "games." A middle position, somewhere between the two extremes described above, is desirable. Interruptions should be avoided; and, if necessary, a sign should be posted indicating that because of the testing, visitors are not welcome at this time. Routines (sharpening pencils, getting drinks, using the rest room, etc.) should be taken care of prior to the testing period. For young children testing periods should be brief, and appropriate activities for those who finish early should be clearly defined.

Scoring achievement tests is time-consuming labor. Even the most conscientious and dedicated teacher probably does not enjoy this task. For this reason, many standardized tests, from the fourth grade level upward, are machine scored. This often involves the use of a special pencil and always requires meticulous attention to making only the essential marks on a page and these only in the proper places. Machine scoring also requires that the completed test be packaged and sent away, not to be returned for several weeks.

One finds it difficult to weigh these alternative values and drawbacks to machine scoring; but, at any rate, the student teacher is seldom asked whether he prefers the objectivity and ease of machine scoring or teacher scoring with its diagnostic possibilities and more quickly available results. This is a problem he may have to help resolve in the future, however.

Teacher-made Tests

Student teachers frequently wish to devise their own tests to determine the effectiveness with which a particular lesson, or group of lessons, has been taught. The student teacher is probably familiar with the types of items included in such tests, but a brief review may be of some help.

ESSAY ITEMS

These merely ask for a comment or a discussion of a particular topic—"Discuss what you believe to be the major causes of the Civil War," "Why do you believe the United States Senate voted against our joining the League of Nations?" Items of this type give a child an opportunity to display organizational ability as well as knowledge of a particular topic. The highly verbal child performs well on tests containing items of this type, and the scoring or grading may be highly subjective. It is well to outline, before reading any answers, the points which should be included in a completely satisfactory answer and to use such an outline in determining each score.

ALTERNATIVE RESPONSE ITEMS

These include true-false, yes-no, and right-wrong response test items. Such items must be carefully worded and are often deceptively easy. Understanding of dates, names, amounts of money, and other factual and very specific types of information can be tested in this manner. For example: "The United States paid approximately seven cents an acre for Alaska"; "The Civil War began in 1861." If a child correctly interprets *approximately* and *if* one assumes that the Civil War began with Fort Sumter, these items are not unusually difficult. When true-false items are used, they should be based on excellent communication between teacher and child—and there should be little need for comments such as "But I thought you meant _____" in the discussion following a test.

COMPLETION ITEMS

These items ask for a "free response" completion of part of a sentence. "The depression was caused by _____" and "A noun is _____" are rather poor completion items because the nature of the desired response isn't clearly specified. Several responses are possible and may or may not be what the teacher wants. Economists disagree about the causes of the depression; what kind of respectable response can a fifth-grader make? If the part of the sentence supplied by the teacher clearly indicates the limits of the response expected, the completion item can yield valuable clues to a child's understanding of a topic.

MULTIPLE CHOICE ITEMS

Some testing experts consider this the only valid type of objective test item. It is similar to the completion item described above, except that the chance of misinterpreting the response that is wanted is minimized because the alternatives are specified. There is usually a fairly detailed "stem," followed by a number (four is usually considered best) of options, only one of which is correct. The following is an example of a multiple choice item:

Abraham Lincoln won the Presidential Election of 1860. The Major Candidates he defeated were:
- *a*) Stephen A. Douglas and Ulysses S. Grant
- *b*) Stephen Douglas and John C. Fremont
- *c*) Douglas, Fremont, and Breckenridge
- *d*) Douglas, Fremont, Grant, and Buchanan

MATCHING ITEMS

Another type of item very commonly used is the matching item. A name, amount of money, or date in one column is matched with the proper associated item in the second column, for example:

Connect the names of the states with the products for which each state
is best known.

a) Hawaii   1. potatoes
b) Idaho   2. pineapple
c) Florida   3. oranges
                    4. tobacco

Lines may be drawn connecting each pair of items, or the child may
write "$a = 2$, $b = 1$," etc. It is important that the child not be able
to solve the problem by the process of elimination, thus the addition
of an extra item in the second column.

A file of test items is a valuable teaching resource, and the student
teaching period is an appropriate time to begin collecting such a file.
Older children may profit a great deal from devising test items, and
this technique tells a teacher much about children's understanding
and skills.

Projective Techniques

Although such tests are usually administered by a school psychologist, and it is also a psychometrist or psychologist who interprets the
results, the student teacher should be familiar with devices such as
the Rorschach, the Thematic Apperception Test, and the Children's
Apperception Test. These tests can provide valuable insights into a
child's feelings about himself and his relationship to others. When
the interpretations of a projective device are included in a child's
cumulative record, it usually indicates that a problem or series of
problems have occurred and that the classroom teacher either felt
unqualified to deal with them or felt that his efforts to deal with the
problems had been unproductive. The child is referred to a trained
person who asks for and records his reactions to a series of pictures
or designs. The interpretation of the child's responses may be highly
subjective, and *should not* be attempted by an untrained person.

Anecdotal Records

There may be some objection to including anecdotal records in a
child's cumulative record. The basis for this objection is usually that
anecdotal records are highly subjective and often reflect a teacher's

intellectual bias. This is neither the time nor the place for a debate of the alternative positions. It is enough to say here that if anecdotal records have been kept, by either a child's previous teachers or his present teacher, they will add to the information a student teacher needs in order to work with children effectively. The student teacher is frequently asked to make anecdotal records, and the following are samples of anecdotal records kept by a student teacher during the observation phase of student teaching:

> John had a quarrel with Phillip on the playground over the interpretation of a basketball rule. John left the game when Phillip's position was supported by most of the other players.
>
> C. G.
9/24

> John refused to serve on a social studies committee after Phillip was elected chairman. John thought (and told everyone) he should be chairman because he had much first-hand information (newspaper clippings, magazine articles, etc.) about the committee's topic.
>
> C. G.

> John presented his report individually, and this supplemented the committee's report which preceded his. The report was brief, interesting, and very well organized. John's pleasure with the reception his report received was a joy to see.
>
> C. G.

There are a few well-established principles regarding anecdotal records; these need only the briefest review here.

1. They should record only and not purport to judge. In none of the records above did the student teacher attempt to explain, justify, or condemn John's behavior. It would be dangerous to attempt to make broad, sweeping generalizations on the basis of a few notes. A collection of such notes over a period of time can aid one in his efforts to help a child, however.

2. Anecdotal records should be dated and initialed. The time of day at which an incident occurred may or may not be significant. If it is significant, it should be recorded.

3. Anecdotal records may be kept in a notebook or in a card file. The notebook makes it easy to keep the notes in sequence but difficult to eliminate a note which it is no longer wise to include (concern-

ing a child who is suspected of stealing but is exonerated, for example). A card file presents filing problems; but because small stacks of cards can be placed in several convenient locations around the room, it is likely to be more comprehensive than the notebook, which is not always at hand when something significant occurs.

A problem which is often presented to those who work with student teachers is whether the student teacher should be asked to make a few anecdotal records about each child, or to select a few children for more thorough observation. It seems clear that the solution to this problem depends upon the student's previous experience with children. If the student has had a wide variety of experiences, then a "depth" study of fewer children (not only the deviant, the boisterous, or the very quiet) would appear to be more beneficial. If the student has had only limited experiences with children, a broader sampling might be better.

Sociometric Devices

The student teacher may wish to gather data about the status of various children in a group. A commonly used technique is asking for three responses to a question similar to the following: With whom would you like to work on the mural committee? With whom would you like to ride in a car on our trip to the post office on Thursday? If a question implies or suggests some action, then the action implied or suggested should occur. In this case, the child should work on a committee or ride with one of the three children he names.

Sociometric data should be confidential and may be withheld, especially from inquisitive and popularity-conscious parents. (The type of parent who says, "I'm more concerned that my child succeeds socially than academically. Being popular is so important," probably should be answered *most* cautiously, and the welfare of the child should be a first consideration.)

Most parents exhibit a balanced concern for their children's progress and achievement. The school obviously has a responsibility for effective communication with parents. The next section of this chapter deals with the student teacher's responsibilities in reporting to parents and the help the college supervisor and the cooperating teacher can provide in this important area.

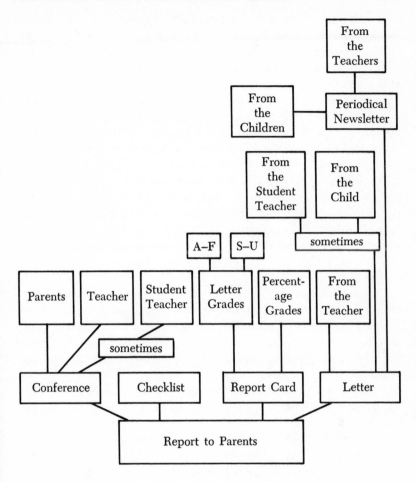

FIGURE 17. VARIETIES OF REPORTS TO PARENTS

REPORTING TO PARENTS

By far the most common method of reporting to parents is the report card, using a variety of symbols. *A* (Excellent)–*F* (Failure) and *S* (Satisfactory)–*U* (Unsatisfactory) are two systems which are frequently used. A few school systems still use percentages (85 per cent, etc.), and codes or keys at the bottom of report cards using the *A–F* system sometimes establish a numerical range for each grade (*C*— average—78–84 per cent).

The problems presented when such marking systems are used are well known and need only the briefest review here: First, an *A* does not mean the same thing to all teachers who assign this grade. Standards differ, and so does the interpretation of marks by different teachers. Then, the weight given to effort, rank in class, and progress differs from teacher to teacher and school to school. Also, a mark which serves as a stimulus for one child inhibits another. Some children stop working when it appears that a goal has been reached, and other children stop working when it becomes clear that a goal is unattainable. Even teachers who work "objectively" and try not to consider the effect a given mark will have on a pupil will admit that omitting such consideration is difficult if not impossible. Finally, a mark which has clear meaning to a teacher and perhaps to a child may fail entirely in communicating progress, effort, and/or achievement to a parent.

Grades continue to be assigned in spite of the problems presented. When a student teacher and his cooperating teacher confer about marks, it may be wise for each to keep in mind the following questions:

1. What are school policies regarding grades? What purposes are grades intended to serve?

2. To what extent do assigned grades take into account a child's effort, his rank in the group, his scores on standardized tests, and his growth since the previous report?

3. Are marks supplemented by notes or by conferences with parents? Do parents ordinarily do their part in the communication process; do they sign and promptly return report cards, write comments when these are requested, and keep appointments for conferences?

4. What is the cooperating teacher's "philosophy" of grading? Is he strict, a "hard grader"? Or is he fairly liberal with *A*'s? How does his feeling about grades compare with those of others on the staff? The school principal may be consulted about several of these questions or problems, since it is to be expected that the principal could be able to discuss reporting to parents on a school-wide or even a system-wide basis. It is very helpful to the student teacher if these problems or questions can be fully discussed. They can and should form the basis for conferences between the student teacher and the

cooperating teacher, and they can be focal points for student teaching meetings or seminars. The student teacher is entitled to some introduction to the vast number of conflicts and contradictions which occur whenever grades are given.

In some school systems, grades such as S (Satisfactory), N (Not entirely satisfactory), and U (Unsatisfactory) are given. A report card using such a marking system might look like this:

	Marking Period			
English	1	2	3	4
Writing				
Spelling				
Reading				
Language				

One more type of formal report card might be discussed. On cards of this type, one grade is assigned for a major curricular area, and the criteria for determining the grade are listed beneath the category.

Grading Code: *A*—Excellent   *R*—The child is doing below grade
 B—Good   level work, but making satisfac-
 C—Average   tory progress.
 D—Poor
 E—Failing

	Grading Period			
Arithmetic	1	2	3	4
Has a basic understanding of numbers				
Knows the number facts (at grade level)				
Can use the number facts				

Checklists

A few school systems use a checklist, in which certain qualities are listed—for example, "Child reads with understanding." Opposite such lists are columns headed with "almost always," "frequently," etc. The teacher places a check in an appropriate column. This is, perhaps, a bit more flexible than the letter grade system, but many of the same problems are still present. If this reporting system is used, it is beneficial if the student teacher can be helped to interpret "almost always" or "seldom," or whatever the column headings are, and can gain some understanding of the school's and the cooperating teacher's philosophy of grading. It is difficult enough for parents and children to interpret certain marking systems. They should not remain a mystery to the student teacher too! The following is an example of one section of the checklist type of report card used in some school systems:

Part I. A ✔ indicates satisfactory growth. Improvement is needed if any item is not checked.

Reading	Oct. 2	Dec. 1	Mar. 6	June 2
Understands what he reads	_____	_____	_____	_____
Reads aloud smoothly and naturally	_____	_____	_____	_____
Attacks unfamiliar words independently	_____	_____	_____	_____
Enjoys reading during spare time	_____	_____	_____	_____

Letters to Parents

Occasionally the student teacher may be asked to help compose a letter informing the parent of his child's progress in school. Such a letter usually (but not inevitably) communicates more effectively with parents than marks such as *A* and *U*. Terms such as *slow progress* or *remedial group* may lead to confusion or misinterpretation unless they are fully explained. If "pedagese" is avoided and if the teacher attempts to be honest, fair, and understanding (including comments about strengths and weaknesses), a clearly written letter does an effective job of informing parents about a child's progress and achievement. It is a very valuable experience for the student teacher to compose a parent letter and to evaluate this according to the following criteria:

1. Is the letter friendly in tone, but also professional—not too informal?

2. Are comments regarding weaknesses usually balanced with ap-

probation and compliments? Every child has a few strengths and competencies worthy of comment.

3. Does the letter suggest some specific measures parents may take to correct weaknesses and compensate for deficiencies? If the teacher plans some specific corrective measures, these may also be detailed, in order to inform the parents and to request their cooperation.

4. Is the letter clearly written, and is professional language, "pedagese," avoided? The direct opposite of this is *not* talking down to parents or using primer language which is insulting to parents' intelligence. Terms used should convey the writer's meaning very clearly and in an uncomplicated style and manner.

5. Does the letter employ correct grammar and spelling? If the letter must be handwritten rather than typed, such standards should be applied to the handwriting as well.

If the student teacher's letter meets the criteria established above, the cooperating teacher may wish to incorporate some of his ideas in letters which will actually be sent. Certainly, the student teacher's assessment of a child should be considered, if he has worked with the group long enough to make valid judgments. Finally, it might be noted that children profit by composing their own progress notes or completing checklists to be sent to parents with the more formal reports from the teacher.

Parent Conferences and Parent Meetings

It is generally agreed that parent conferences are the most effective means of informing parents about a child's progress. The same guidelines as those suggested for student teacher–cooperating teacher conferences might be reviewed here. The conference should be away from the teacher's desk, which is clearly an authority symbol. It should be held at a time when interruptions can be kept at a minimum and all the participants can feel relatively relaxed and free from pressure. Parent-teacher conferences should have a foundation of mutual respect, honesty, and concern for the child. Student teachers have been asked to participate in or at least to observe parent-teacher conferences, and they usually gain a great deal from this type of experience.

A cooperating teacher may also ask a student teacher to participate in meetings he holds with parents of children in his class. These meetings are usually held to inform parents about group projects or curricular changes; and if evaluation is dealt with, it is dealt with in general terms. Almost never is the achievement of a specific child discussed in meetings of this sort.

In addition to the parent meeting there are several other widely used techniques for communicating important information of a general nature to parents. A letter may be composed by the children, on a weekly or monthly basis, informing parents of school activities. The teacher may compose such a letter and have it mimeographed, and groups of teachers have composed such informative newsletters and pamphlets on a grade level or schoolwide basis. The student teacher will certainly want to acquaint himself with such newsletters or pamphlets, and his contributions to such projects may well be solicited.

The student teacher will surely profit from as many experiences with using and interpreting as many evaluation devices as possible. He will, of course, need careful guidance because of the sensitive and confidential nature of the area concerned. A student teaching experience which does not provide opportunities of the type described in this section is not as full, as rich, or as productive as could be hoped for.

THE COLLEGE SUPERVISOR'S ROLE

This participant in the student teaching process has been somewhat neglected in the discussion thus far, and it must be admitted that the college supervisor's role in the evaluation of children's progress and achievement is of less significance than that of the student teacher or the cooperating teacher. If, however, he feels some area of evaluation is being neglected—if, for example, the cumulative records have not been made available to the student teacher—he has an obvious responsibility to try to find out why this has happened and to make adjustments wherever possible. If a student teacher is not applying the best possible evaluative techniques, he may need the guidance of the college supervisor as well as that of the cooperating teacher.

The college supervisor also has the responsibility of informing the student teacher of certain evaluative procedures he may not have the opportunity to see in use in his particular student teaching situation. The student teacher can be asked to survey types of tests which are important and with which he's unfamiliar. He might be asked to construct test items or to compose a parent letter, if his cooperating teacher doesn't suggest this activity. If the student teachers, as a group, possess an inadequate store of knowledge regarding evaluation, it would be helpful to devote several student teaching meetings to this topic and to invite other qualified faculty members to serve as resource persons.

The cooperating teacher and the supervisor should confer about the evaluative procedures being observed and utilized by the student teacher. They can then plan for experiences which are not repetitive but will deepen and expand the student teacher's concept and understanding in this very important area.

Summary

Several techniques might be used by the student teacher in evaluating the progress of children. These include standardized intelligence tests and achievement tests. The student teacher must exercise the strictest care in administering such tests, observing time limits and following other instructions precisely. More subjective instruments or techniques were discussed in this chapter, including sociometric devices for determining a child's status in a group and projective tests for assessing a child's concept of himself and his relationships with others.

Anecdotal records are important additions to the evaluative technique a student teacher will probably use. The effective student teacher will try to gain as much information as possible about each child, and this will include teacher-made tests he carefully constructs to judge his effectiveness in teaching a unit or a particular lesson.

The student teacher probably has little opportunity to choose the types of tests used, but he has a definite responsibility to familiarize himself with the instruments used. He also has some responsibility to participate, as his competence permits, in the process of communicating children's progress to parents. He can help the assignment of grades and in the composition of parent report letters. He may also observe or participate in parent conferences and parent meetings. Any information confided to the student teacher to help him in working with children will be treated confidentially, and he can begin the process of becoming truly professional at this early period in his preparation. His supervisor and his cooperating teacher can be of tremendous assistance as he gains acquaintance with many different types of instruments and evaluative techniques. The student teacher who does not participate in evaluating children's growth and progress is very limited and even handicapped when he is expected to assume full teaching responsibility.

Suggested Activities for the Student Teacher

1. Discuss the school's grading policy with the principal and the cooperating teacher. Discuss this policy or philosophy, in a positive manner, in your student teaching seminar.

2. Write a parent report letter regarding the child of whom you did a case study, or another child whom you feel you know fairly well. Discuss this with the cooperating teacher.

3. Begin an anecdotal record file soon after student teaching begins. Discuss these at a student teaching meeting, with the purpose of improving them and developing a system for collecting data of this type about children.

4. With the consent of the principal and the cooperating teacher administer and plot the results of a sociogram.

5. Arrange for evaluative conferences with the children in one reading group, or take a random sampling. Ask those who don't participate in conferences with you to write brief report letters, for example:

I do my best work in _____.

I wish I knew _____.

_____ is very hard for me; I need lots of help.

6. Survey each child's cumulative record. You should be able to answer the following questions:

a) What is the range of scores on the intelligence tests?

b) What is the mean score? The median (on intelligence tests)?

c) What is the range of scores on an academic achievement test in:
   1. Reading?
   2. Mathematics?

d) How many children have scores which are below grade level? How many have scores above grade level?

7. At the conclusion of a unit of instruction, develop a test which you

can administer. Discuss the test, and the results, with the cooperating teacher.

SELECTED REFERENCES

Brown, Thomas J., and Bonich, Serafina Fiore. *Student Teaching in the Elementary School.* New York: Harper & Row, 1962, Chapter 10, "Learning to Plan Through Evaluation."

Burns, Paul C., and Brown, Daniel. *The Student Teacher Evaluates Pupil Progress.* Cedar Falls, Iowa: The Association for Student Teaching, 1962.

Buros, O. K. *Fifth Mental Measurements Yearbook.* Highland Park, New Jersey: The Gryphon Press, 1959.

Burr, James B., Harding, Lowry W., and Jacobs, Leland B. *Student Teaching in the Elementary School,* Chapter 10, "Evaluating the Progress of Children."

Byers, Loretta, and Irish, Elizabeth. *Success in Student Teaching,* Chapter 9, "Evaluating Pupil Growth."

Haines, Alleyne C. *Guiding the Student Teaching Process in Elementary Education,* Chapter 10, "Increasing Competence in Evaluation."

Michaelis, John U., and Dumas, Enoch. *The Student Teacher in the Elementary School.* Englewood Cliffs, New Jersey: Prentice-Hall, Inc., 1960, Chapter 11, "Evaluation of Children's Learning."

Wingo, G. Max, and Schorling, Raleigh. *Elementary School Student Teacher.* New York: McGraw-Hill Book Co., Inc., 1960, Chapter 13, "Guidance of Children"; Chapter 14, "The Broader Concept of Appraisal."

10

Finding a Teaching Position

Student teaching is not considered an end in itself. It marks a point at which those who guide the education of a prospective teacher evaluate their program and its products. It is also a transitional period during which competent and promising young people cease being college or university students and become professional novices. The education of a teacher does not stop with the successful conclusion of student teaching, or even with the completion of requirements for a master's degree, which in some states becomes the last hurdle to be surmounted in securing a professional certificate. A major thesis of this book has been, in fact, that working with a student teacher is in itself a valuable component of the education of a teacher, since it forces one to scrutinize and evaluate his teaching practices much as he did when he himself was a student teacher. For these reasons, the final chapter of a student teaching book is most helpful if it causes readers to look ahead, not backward, and to view student teaching as a beginning, not a conclusion.

To restate, very briefly, the ingredients of a successful student teaching experience, it might be said that the following constitute a foundation from which a prospective teacher can look ahead to a reward-ing series of experiences as a beginning teacher:

Successful student teaching is built upon adequate academic prep-aration and a wide variety of experiences with groups of children.

Prior to student teaching, the three major participants in the student teaching experience make concerted efforts to become ac-quainted with each other and with the setting in which student teach-ing will take place.

During student teaching, the student teacher participates in a wide variety of teaching experiences, working with individuals and with groups of many types and sizes. He becomes actively involved in working with children as quickly as his abilities and self-confidence permit.

The student teacher is involved in planning with and for children. Planning is of several types, including day-to-day planning, long-range planning, and pupil-teacher planning. The student teacher is not expected to copy the plans of the cooperating teacher or to plan in exactly the same way as the cooperating teacher plans.

The student teacher has become acquainted with learning re-sources of many kinds—texts, films, tapes, etc.—and he has used these resources effectively.

The student teacher has been involved, at appropriate levels, in the process of evaluating the work of children. This has included guiding children in self-evaluation and has led, naturally and easily, to the student's evaluation of every aspect of his performance as a teacher.

Those charged with the responsibility of guiding the student teacher, the college supervisor, and the cooperating teacher have ac-cepted the student teacher as he is and where he is. When major deficiencies exist, in experiences with children or in academic prepa-ration, corrective and remedial measures are taken.

The supervision and guidance of a student teacher does not em-phasize the imitation of an example, no matter how excellent, or the following of a prescribed pattern. The student teacher should be helped to develop methods and techniques which are appropriate for him as a unique individual and to increase his own professional strengths and competencies, which may differ from those of his co-operating teacher and his college supervisor.

The supervisor and the cooperating teacher work together through meetings, seminars, and conferences to provide help and guidance for the student teacher. They neither overwhelm the student teacher with suggestions and ideas for changes nor do they abandon the student teacher in the mistaken notion that this is the proper alternative to too much supervision.

Assuming adequate knowledge of the student teacher's performance and a sincere effort at making a prognosis of his future teaching effectiveness, the supervisor and the cooperating teacher will communicate to hiring officials their most honest professional judgment; and they will make every effort to deny certification to those who are clearly unfit to guide children and youths.

Placement Procedures

Assuming a foundation of the strength described, the prospective teacher is ready to seek a teaching position; the purpose of this chapter is to provide some help in this important area. Occasionally, a student teacher who could be expected to be quite a successful beginning teacher does not succeed in his first position; in a few cases, the student teacher for whom the prognosis is not good *does* succeed. Clearly, one's first teaching position can promote or inhibit growth; and the college supervisor and cooperating teacher can be very helpful in assisting the student teacher in finding the right position.

Finding the right teaching position usually involves completing certain papers and one or more interviews with hiring officials.

Placement Papers

Ordinarily, student teachers are asked to complete a set, or several sets, of papers which are similar in nature to most questionnaires. The information requested usually relates to the student's academic grades and his participation in campus activities. A transcript of grades is requested in some cases, and most hiring officials (supervisors, principals, superintendents, or personnel directors) place more than minor emphasis upon this list of courses and grades. It is probably unrealistic to expect college freshmen to be concerned about the record they will be accumulating and how this will appear to a hiring official in three and a half years. For this reason, freshman grades are, perhaps, less important than the *trend* of a student's grades. This trend will be, one hopes, upward. One's professional courses are frequently of more interest, and motivation is somewhat higher. For both of these reasons, it is justifiable to expect better grades at the junior or senior levels. A number of hiring officials have commented that the grade in which they place the last credence is the student teaching grade! They say that student teaching has become a two-grade course, the superior students receiving an *A* and the average students a *B*. Much more reliance is placed upon the written recommendations of the supervisor and the cooperating teacher; thus the emphasis upon the need for objectivity, fairness, and honesty in writing such recommendations.

Why are students asked to list their campus activities, especially those in which they've accepted leadership roles? Such information is probably requested because administrators have found that success in working with people in college, especially in a leadership capacity, indicates probable success in working with groups as a teacher. Teachers not only work with groups of children, but they volunteer for or are placed on textbook-selection committees and committees responsible for revising a report card or developing a curriculum guide, and they work with parent groups of many types. A person who belonged to no groups, curricular or extracurricular, while he was in college is unlikely to respond positively to requests for service from his professional associations, local, state, or national. Of course, some students are occupied, while in college, with jobs which they must hold in order to pay fees, room and board, etc. Increasingly, women with family responsibilities are enrolling in professional courses, and such women have little time for sororities or even campus service groups or honoraries.

There are, in short, good reasons for being *inactive* on campus, but placement questionnaires usually provide an opportunity for listing such reasons. Most hiring officials are favorably impressed with a small, selective list of campus organizations to which a student belonged, especially if the student was chairman or president of one or two of these.

An autobiography is sometimes requested, and the emphasis here should probably be on those experiences which caused the student to decide upon teaching as a career. Important travelling experiences should be included, particularly if such travels took one out of the United States. Extensive travel, either within the United States or in Europe, Africa, or Asia, can be of tremendous value to a teacher as he attempts to help children understand others' ways of life; and the personal values of travel need not be recounted here. Teachers tend to come, largely, from middle class segments of our society, and middle class persons can perhaps profit most from exposure to members of different socioeconomic groups.

A detailed list of experiences with children is usually requested. The following checklist may help the student in recalling such experiences:

1. College-centered laboratory experiences, such as observation in the campus laboratory school or work with groups of children in connection with a children's literature course or a music methods course.
2. Work in community service agencies—settlement house work, YWCA, YMCA, Girl Scouts, Boy Scouts, Campfire Girls, etc.
3. Work with religious agencies—teaching Sunday school classes, working with youth groups, and Bible school teaching.
4. Camp counseling—work with camp groups in sports, arts and crafts, storytelling, dramatics, etc. Work in church camps and day camps is included in this category.
5. Work with children in recreation centers—playground supervision, teaching swimming at public or private pools.
6. Baby-sitting, if such work included supervision of group play or planning activities for more than one or two children.

The list included here is merely suggestive. The student teacher may include any experience with groups of children for which he has accepted leadership responsibility.

The data referred to in the section dealing with student teacher placement is usually requested for job placement papers as well: information concerning marital status, age, parents' occupation(s) and educational level(s), and the previous school experiences of the student teacher. Photographs may be requested, but as with statements indicating race and religious preference, laws in several states prohibit requiring these. It would seem unwise for a school administrator to hire a beginning teacher whose race or religious preference would cause him to be rejected by people in the community with whom it is very important that he work effectively. An experienced teacher might be able to overcome this obstacle; it is perhaps too much to expect a beginner to do so.

Basic information regarding age, marital status, etc., *is* required for the student's application for a teaching certificate, issued by the state department of education; and both the placement papers and the application for a certificate usually require some evidence of reasonably good health. The application for a teaching certificate often requires a physician's signature, and this signature is supposed to follow a relatively thorough physical examination. As has already been noted, teaching is a demanding profession, emotionally and physically; and it is a profession which those who cannot meet its demands should not enter. Placement forms vary, of course, but the information discussed here is requested on the great majority of such forms.

The temptation to exaggerate, even to falsify, if certain information is detrimental to the student's job opportunities, should be firmly resisted. Falsifying information about experiences one hasn't really had (travel, books recently read, etc.) or about one's age or marital status will accomplish very little, and much harm will result if the prevarication is discovered. There are enough problems in the first year of teaching without attempting to live up to or conceal the truth about some information written on the forms. In completing personnel forms of any type, honesty is the best policy.

Interviews

Papers, even when honestly and objectively completed, are rather cold and impersonal. Although when a student takes a teaching position several hundred miles from his home, the placement papers and some correspondence may constitute the only communication between the prospective teacher and the hiring personnel, the great majority of hiring officials prefer to interview a candidate for a teaching position. The candidate is probably more secure, as well, if he feels he can begin his teaching career in a situation where at least one face is familiar and he has found answers to some of the questions he would hesitate to ask in a letter. The value of an interview is underscored by the miles and miles travelled by personnel directors for the larger school systems. Many hiring officials make long and tiring trips, early in the spring, visiting the larger institutions and setting up interview headquarters at large metropolitan hotels—all for the purpose of personally meeting and talking with candidates and letting them meet someone who can give direct answers to questions about teaching in the school system he represents.

What should a student teacher expect from an interview? Perhaps the following dialogue will give some concept of the content of a typical interview.

SECRETARY IN PLACEMENT OFFICE: Mr. Smith will see you now, Miss Moore. Through that door to Room *C*, please.

JANE: I'm Jane Moore, Mr. Smith. I'm very happy to meet you.

MR. S.: Delighted to meet you, Miss Moore. Won't you be seated? I've surveyed your placement file rather carefully. Your supervisor is quite enthusiastic about your capabilities; and Dr. Johnson doesn't write such recommendations for all his student teachers, believe me! How do you explain Miss Hughes's less enthusiastic recommendation, Miss Moore?

JANE: I can only say I worked hard, very hard, and that nothing I did ever seemed quite right. She was very critical of my work, and I'm sure she wouldn't have approved of the *A* Dr. Johnson gave me! It wasn't a very happy time, Mr. Smith, I can assure you. I hope I'm not as bad as Miss Hughes thinks I am, but I suspect Dr. Johnson has overrated me. I do know I want to teach, and to be a very, very good teacher. I'll work hard, and . . .

MR. S.: Jane, if we had any doubts about your competence, we wouldn't have wasted our time or yours with this interview! We know you'll work hard and we feel you'll do well. What grade level are you most interested in?

JANE: Primary, I think, but probably not first grade, my very first year of teaching at least.

MR. S.: I notice you play the piano and that art and music are both strong interests. This is good. We have a second grade opening and a third. The second grade opening is in a poor, culturally deprived section of our city—how does this appeal to you?

JANE: My student teaching was in a community like that. I didn't react negatively to the poor language, and the body odors; and I don't think I became too upset when children came to school without breakfast or poorly clothed. I rather enjoy working with these children, in fact.

The interview could be further detailed—undoubtedly Jane's marital status or her willingness to start out on her own, away from her parents, would be discussed. So would living conditions in the community; typical class size; and salaries and fringe benefits, such as hospitalization insurance. In an interview such as the one repeated here, ideas and aspirations are shared, and each participant takes the measure of the other. If properly handled, an interview need not be threatening. Mr. Smith very skillfully put Jane at ease, and at least the portion of the interview quoted here could be considered mutually beneficial.

The personal appearance of the candidate is very important. The major reason for an interview is to enable the hiring official to make a face-to-face assessment of the candidate. The candidate will, of course, be appropriately dressed: gloves, low heels, stockings, if a woman; a jacket, shirt, and tie, if a man. Care in grooming and cleanliness are assumed. Poise is often underemphasized in discussions of interviews. The candidate who twists a handkerchief, tugs at his ear, pulls on a strand of hair, etc., makes a very poor impression. It is too much to expect the candidate to be completely relaxed and at ease, but the outward evidences of nervousness—a giggle, a foot constantly in motion—should be avoided if at all possible. An experienced interviewer listens to what the candidate says, judges the quality of the questions the candidate asks, and watches the way the candidate listens. What the candidate *is* is betrayed by what he says as well as by the way he looks and behaves. Neglect of any of these aspects may result in the candidate's *not* getting the job. A brief warning may be in order here. A few interviewers use "shock" tactics in order to ascertain a candidate's poise and his ability to react quickly and positively to an unexpected question; the interviewer may ask a very personal question or request an explanation for one poor letter of recommendation. The major purpose of such questions is to test the candidate's poise, and the interviewee should keep this in mind.

Letters of Recommendation

Recommendation statements were reproduced in Chapter 8, so it will be enough here to restate the importance of fairness, objectivity, and honesty in such letters and to remind the writers of such letters that readers expect recommendations to be based upon adequate knowledge of the student's work and on some prognosis of future teaching success.

Whether an interview, placement papers, a letter of recommendation or some combination of these is instrumental in bringing together a hiring official and a candidate, there are certain questions which should receive satisfactory answers if the teaching position is to be mutually rewarding to the teacher, school administrators, and the children who will be taught.

THE STUDENT TEACHER DECIDES UPON THE KIND OF POSITION HE IS PREPARED TO ACCEPT

Certification laws vary from state to state, but the prospective teacher needs to inquire, before accepting a job, whether he is prepared for and will be certified to teach in a self-contained classroom or in a departmentalized school; if in a departmentalized school, what subjects is he certified to teach? There appears to be an increasing trend toward departmentalized elementary schools, but most teacher education institutions continue to prepare teachers for self-contained classrooms—in which one teacher supervises the work of one group of children in all subjects. There is a special problem for teachers interested in teaching in a junior high school. Some junior high schools are completely departmentalized, whereas others are organized around a core of subjects, one teacher teaching both math and science, or both language arts and social studies. If the junior high school is departmentalized, secondary school certification requirements rather than elementary ones may be applied. Occasionally, if a student plans ahead, the additional hours needed in academic subjects may be taken instead of other electives, but two separate student teaching experiences may be required.

Another question which relates to this general field is that of grade level. In some states, a primary certificate is issued, certifying the teacher to teach in the first three grades, with perhaps the addition of kindergarten. Such a certificate usually signifies more work in art, music, creative dramatics, and particularly in the language arts field, with emphasis on beginning reading.

Checking certification requirements for the state in which the student wants to teach is essential, for the student who considers himself well qualified almost surely does not want to accept a position for which the state considers him inadequately prepared. After four years of study and work in the field of general and professional education, a teacher is entitled to more than "temporary" or "emergency" certification. In a few states, specific course requirements in a course in state history or audio-visual education, for example—must be taken before even provisional certification will be granted. This is inevitable, and a beginning teacher who takes a job in a state with rather unusual requirements does so with the understanding that additional courses must be taken. This is rather different from finding that one's kindergarten-primary certificate does not entitle him to teach in a fourth grade, or that he is teaching fifth and sixth grade math and science with a certificate which clearly states he is certified to teach in a self-contained classroom.[1] These situations can result in one's being classed as a temporarily certified teacher, even after successfully completing four years of a teacher education program. The type of certificate to which one is entitled should be checked, and so should the requirements for a job one is considering. It is also important to check the reciprocity agreements between the state in which one has prepared and the one in which one intends to teach. Such agreements usually apply to provisional or tentative licensing only, and not to permanent or "life" licenses.

There are new organizational patterns in education which may influence licensing in the near future; but, thus far, they have had little or no effect on legislative requirements for teaching certificates. *Team teaching*, as usually defined, refers to a semi-departmentalized type of organization. One teacher, variously called a senior teacher, coordinator, or master teacher, works as a chairman of a team of teachers, and children occasionally work in a group of ninety or a hundred. When they are organized in large groups, it is for the purpose of hearing a lecture, seeing a demonstration or film, or participating in some other activity appropriate for groups of this size. More frequently, however, children work with aides, junior teachers, or other members of the team, in small groups. Teachers are usually chosen

---

[1] For a brief but enlightening discussion of trends in elementary teacher certification, the reader is directed to James B. Conant's *The Education of American Teachers* (New York: McGraw-Hill Book Co., Inc., 1963), Chapter 7.

to work in various subject areas, according to their competencies, interests and preferences; thus the reference to departmentalization. The senior teacher or chairman of the team is more often chosen because of demonstrated teaching competence in *many* subject areas, not one, which represents something of a contradiction, unless administrative ability is the primary criterion in the selection of such a person.[2]

Another educational innovation receiving a good bit of attention at the present time is the nongraded elementary school, or at least the primary division of the elementary school. Again, it should be noted that no state certification requirements govern the selection of a teacher for an ungraded class. In fact, the concept underlying the ungraded school would work toward the elimination of the "primary" and "intermediate" certificates, since progress through the elementary school is considered unitary and is judged or evaluated on an individual basis. That is, a child may require two, three, or four years to progress through the "primary" block, but no particular distinction is accorded the child who is judged ready for the work of the intermediate grades in two years, nor is any shame or stigma attached to remaining in the primary unit for four years. This at least is the claim of Goodlad,[3] and other proponents of this concept of school organization; and the number of school systems adapting this pattern lends support to their claims.

There appears to be a growing tendency to support experimental organizational patterns, sometimes before such patterns have received adequate trial. At least, it can be said that teachers graduating and in possession of valid certificates today may need to prove their flexibility, their ingenuity, and their ability to attack educational problems creatively. The answer to the student teacher's question, "What kind of position am I prepared to accept?" can be only tentative, and his security must rest in his ability to grow and develop. He will, of course, check certification requirements in the state in which his teacher education institution is located, as well as the requirements of the state in which he accepts a position.

---

[2] J. T. Shaplin and H. F. Olds, *Team Teaching* (New York: Harper & Row, 1964).

[3] John Goodlad, *The Nongraded Elementary School* (Rev. ed.; New York: Harcourt, Brace & World, Inc., 1963).

Types of Questions Asked in the Interview

The brief dialogue between the hiring official and the candidate included in the introductory section of this chapter suggested some areas of discussion. More detailed questions or topics will be outlined here; for example, the candidate may ask:

1. In what type of community is the school in which I would be teaching located? (Far too many beginners are placed in positions in school communities which have been vacated by more experienced teachers. If the beginning teacher feels qualified and ready to teach in a culturally deprived community, well and good; but most beginners do not desire such positions and are, in fact, ill-prepared for them.) What living conditions may I expect to find? Are rents high? Is housing plentiful?

2. Are the parents of the children in the school system typically cooperative and supportive, or is there antagonism and a poor working relationship between the school and the parents?

3. What is the "failure" or "retention" policy? How is a child's growth and progress reported to parents?

4. What committee responsibilities do elementary teachers in this system have? Do teachers in this school system participate *actively* in professional organizations, local, state, and national? Are teachers encouraged to attend national conferences?

5. What opportunities for in-service growth are provided? Are workshops, seminars, etc., sponsored by the school system? Is financial assistance provided in order to encourage graduate work or course work in areas of special interest to a teacher?

6. Is there a salary schedule? How does one advance on the salary schedule? Is "merit" pay a board policy? If so, how is it administered?

7. What policies govern sick and maternity leaves? Are funds contributed by the board for hospital insurance and major medical insurance? These last two items are indeed mundane, and including them here is not intended to suggest that a prospective teacher would refuse a position in a system which had few or no sick leave provisions or other so-called fringe benefits. Matters of salary, insurance, and promotion or advancement policies are important, however; and it is naive to deny their significance. Hiring officials are aware of their

significance and also realize that a candidate may be reluctant to discuss them, so they will probably refer to them openly and without embarrassment.

8.   What sort of supervisory help is provided? Is there a consultant or supervisor in music? In art? In physical education? Is there a special education class? Is there a reading specialist? What is the role of the classroom teacher in referral to specialists, and what are his responsibilities when a consultant is teaching?

9.   What equipment is ordinarily provided? How are materials ordered? Are texts and workbooks ordered for teachers, or may teachers decide which ones they wish to order? Are there adopted texts? If so, must they be used as prescribed in the teachers' guides? Is there a curriculum guide for the school system?

10.   What is typical class size? What is the school day—when does it begin, and when does it end? What duties do teachers ordinarily perform before school, at recesses, at lunch time, and after school?

Obviously, the typical thirty-minute interview does not permit discussion of even a majority of these questions. It is unrealistic to suggest that the prospective teacher may possess all of the information implied by these questions before he accepts a teaching position. The hiring official controls the interview, but he will probably be favorably impressed by the prospective teacher who has at least a few important questions to ask; and having a few questions to ask will probably contribute to the candidate's security during the interview. It hardly seems necessary to note that an interview which takes place in or is supplemented by a visit to the community and the school is infinitely more helpful to both participants as each makes an important decision about a teaching position.

Although this book is not written to be of special assistance to principals, supervisors, and other hiring officials, it may be of some help to the candidate to know what the hiring official is looking for.

Reliance on College Course Grades

The *pattern* of grades is probably more significant than grades in a given semester or in a certain series of courses. Freshmen are often troubled by problems related to the transition from high school to

college, and grades often improve after adjustment problems have
been solved. Those students who do not solve their adjustment problems usually leave school, and their grades are not normally of concern to a prospective employer. Many highly motivated students,
anxious to teach, perform at a much higher level after they can see
some application of course work to their professional goal. To say
this is wrong, that academic courses are just as important (perhaps
more so) to teaching success as professional courses, does little good.
At any rate, a prospective teacher's grades usually show an upward
trend after the freshman year, and grades in professional courses are
frequently somewhat higher than they are in the academic or general education courses. A hiring official may pay particular attention
to averages, point averages, indexes, or some other indication of
average scholastic achievement and to the trend of grades throughout the student's four-year college program.

How Much Reliance Can be Placed on Written Recommendations?

The problems involved in assigning grades in student teaching
have already been discussed and need not be reviewed here. A written recommendation is almost sure to communicate more effectively
any combination of strengths and weaknesses possessed by the student teacher; and there is no other practical way of letting a principal
or supervisor know precisely what types of help a candidate may need
as a beginning teacher. Some college instructors use a very brief
checklist, from which a secretary assembles a "letter of recommendation." Such a letter hardly seems worth writing! An instructor who
does not recall a student well enough to compose a letter of recommendation which says something should either request a brief
interview to refresh his memory or politely decline to write the letter.
"I know of no reason to expect less or more than an average performance from Jane Doe" is not a very helpful comment for Jane's prospective employer. If a letter is carefully and honestly written, by
someone who has adequate knowledge of a student's achievement
and progress, a principal or supervisor can be guided in assessing
strengths, weaknesses, and types of help the beginner may need.

JUDGING THE QUALIFICATIONS OF A CANDIDATE ON THE BASIS OF AN INTERVIEW

Helpful as a placement interview is, it does represent just one face-to-face contact between interviewer and interviewee. Can one decide whether or not to hire a candidate on such limited evidence? The interview, of course, is not intended to provide the sole evidence; added to the placement data and the letters of recommendation, it can give a fairly accurate picture of a candidate. Application of the criteria previously mentioned, observing or noting the candidate's poise, appearance, voice quality, evidence of motivation for teaching excellence, and interest in children will help the principal, superintendent, or hiring official make his final judgment in an interview. Of course, the interview may be supplemented by conferences with the candidate's supervisor or college instructors who are well acquainted with the student. This leads rather directly to the next area of concern.

THE RESPONSIBILITIES OF THE SUPERVISOR AND THE COOPERATING TEACHER IN HELPING A STUDENT TEACHER SECURE A POSITION

There is, at most teacher education institutions, a placement officer or perhaps a staff of placement officials and clerks. With their help available, why should the supervisor be concerned about a student's first teaching experience? The work of personnel in a placement office is generally confined to the filing and transmission of papers and the arranging and scheduling of interviews. Matching a prospective teacher with the best teaching position for that teacher requires more of a personal touch than most placement offices possess. There are exceptions, of course; and if a placement director knows each and every candidate well enough to screen the job opportunities and assist in the matching process just described then, indeed, the supervisor need not be concerned. In most cases, however, the supervisor and the cooperating teacher know the student, as a teacher, better than anyone else; and it seems reasonable that they should assist the student in finding a position, if their help is requested. This help may be through conferences which supplement the interview, personal letters which provide specific information requested by a hiring official, or by helping a student weigh the alternative merits of two positions. Help of this type is not interference, and although there is the risk of underestimating or overestimating a student's potential as a teacher, if the recommendations and advice are based on reasonably adequate evidence and given honestly and sincerely, it is unlikely that the supervisor will regret giving it. A supervisor who fails to warn a prospective employer of weaknesses which could result in a teacher's failure is not doing the candidate a favor, and he certainly is not contributing to better education for children.

Techniques for Helping the Student Prepare for Beginning Teaching

In addition to the conferences and personal recommendations already discussed that are designed to help a student teacher find a position for which he is well equipped, there are techniques which a supervisor can use to help a student teacher prepare for his first teaching experiences.

Plans for the First Week of School

Many supervisors find that it is helpful to devote at least one student teaching meeting to a discussion of beginning the school year. Some ask that student teachers complete a set of plans, written and in detail, for the first week of classes. If student teachers have adequate knowledge of their teaching positions and know the learning resources which will be available to them, this may be an appropriate activity. Otherwise such plans may be as artificial as those made in connection with methods courses in reading or mathematics.

Review of Learning Resources

The cooperating teacher and the supervisor may work together in helping a student focus on the types of learning resources he used and may help him explore further materials and aids which he used inadequately. This same technique could also be used in reviewing tests or evaluative devices of several kinds. The goal here is not so much remedial as it is to help the student become better prepared for the day when he will have complete responsibility for a classroom. It is important that the supervisor and the cooperating teacher work together in providing these summarizing or wrap-up types of activities, to avoid needless repetition.

The Cooperating Teacher

In addition to the activities suggested above, which can be initiated by the cooperating teacher as well as the supervisor, there are certain types of assistance which the cooperating teacher is in the best position to supply. His discussion of a teacher's responsibility to professional organization will be both practical and realistic, which will make such discussions particularly significant to the prospective teacher. These same qualities will mark his discussion of problems the student teacher may anticipate in his first year. Practicality and realism are not synonymous with cynicism, however; and it is hoped that in discussions with the student teacher, bitterness, cynicism, and sarcasm will play little or no part.

Personal recommendations to a school administrator present special problems to the cooperating teacher; the following request is typical, as well as possibly embarrassing, to the cooperating teacher:

BARBARA: Miss Jacobs, Don, my husband, has decided to work on his master's next year and I'd like a teaching position here at Madison School. I've liked *all* the teachers, and I wonder if you'd say something to the principal or the superintendent for me. It would be such a help!

This is all well and good *if* Barbara has done a good job during student teaching and if she can be recommended without undue reservation. *If*, however, Barbara's performance and potential are only average or somewhat below average, or if Miss Jacobs knows of good reasons for feeling Barbara might succeed elsewhere, but not at Madison School, then Miss Jacobs is in an uncomfortable position indeed! It will not surprise the reader to find that honesty is the first recommendation here—well ahead of consideration for Barbara's feelings. If Miss Jacobs can recommend Barbara as a conscientious young woman who will need lots of help her first year, and if Barbara is hired with this understanding, Miss Jacobs has a clear conscience. If, however, in order to be "nice" to Barbara, Miss Jacobs overplays Barbara's strengths and leaves her weaknesses unmentioned, Miss Jacobs' reputation is bound to suffer, and so will the children in Barbara's classroom.

Whether the student teacher accepts a position in the school system in which he did student teaching or in another school system, the advice of the cooperating teacher will almost certainly be solicited regarding the final choice. The cooperating teacher has a definite responsibility to provide the student teacher with an honest assessment of his strengths and weaknesses, as these relate to a particular position. For example, if Barbara's success at Madison School during student teaching had been due, in large measure, to her ability to relate to children of lower socio-economic levels, then success in a similar teaching position probably could be assumed. If the problems presented by lower-class children all but overwhelmed her, then she should be warned against taking a teaching position where she would face such problems alone. The student teacher with a deficiency in mathematics should, of course, work to remedy this deficiency but meanwhile should avoid a teaching position in which children might know more than he does about mathematics! Throughout the evaluation process, these points have been covered by effective supervisors and critics. It is enough, here, to say that the prospective teacher is entitled to a warning about any problem areas of which he may be unaware.

A unique problem, for the cooperating teacher, is presented when a student teacher becomes a professional colleague. The relationship must change slightly, at least; for, one hopes, the student teacher has been hired on his own merits, not because he effectively imitated his cooperating teacher. It also seems certain that there will be a tendency for the new teacher to turn to his former cooperating teacher for help and advice. There may be times when this is flattering, but it may also become a burden. It is less likely to become a burden if self-reliance and independence were primary values and objectives during student teaching. It is less flattering and is a cause for concern if the beginner rejects all the techniques he saw used so effectively during student teaching. This may be characterized as latent adolescent rebellion; but, whatever its cause, the cooperating teacher should maintain a sense of humor and make himself available for such help as is requested.

A cooperating teacher whose student teacher succeeds as a beginning teacher can feel a real sense of pride. Being close enough to
observe the beginner's growth at first hand is very, very rewarding.

Follow-up Techniques

Faculty members in elementary education frequently wish to
evaluate their programs by contacting graduates. Conferences with
beginning teachers involving recent graduates and faculty members
have proved to be very effective. Newsletters have been helpful; but
these provide, essentially, only one-way communication. Checklists
and questionnaires, completed by beginning teachers and returned
to campus, yield valuable information about a program's strengths
and weaknesses.

Each of these techniques or devices yields the added dividend of
helping the beginner with problems which are immediate and real.
Comments from graduates are frequently humbling to faculty members, but they need to keep in mind that the experiences of the first
year of teaching can be and usually are overwhelming and that the
teacher is engaging in some self-criticism as well as criticism of his
program of preparation for teaching. "Why didn't you . . . ?" is frequently answered, "We *did*, but you didn't avail yourself of this
opportunity!" Of course, justified criticism should be heeded and
needed changes instituted; but accusations of beginning teachers may
well have an emotional basis, and faculty members should be objective in evaluating highly critical comments from former students as
well as comments which are overly effusive in their praise. Because
the responsibility for success during one's first year of teaching is
essentially his own, it is to the student teacher who will very soon
assume the role of beginning teacher that the remainder of this chapter is directed.

IN-SERVICE GROWTH

An entire book could be devoted to the thesis that an effective
teacher never stops growing. This point has been made throughout
this book, and it now seems appropriate to suggest means by which

such growth can be fostered and encouraged. Partly because Conant's proposal for a probationary period has received a great deal of attention, and partly because I believe that too many beginning teachers are abandoned and receive inadequate help, his suggestions will be noted first:

> During the initial probationary period,[4] local school boards should take specific steps to provide the new teacher with every possible help in the form of: (a) limited teaching responsibility; (b) aid in gathering instructional materials; (c) advice of experenced teachers whose own load is reduced so that they can work with the new teacher in his own classroom; (d) shifting to more experienced teachers those pupils beyond the ability of the novice to handle effectively, and (e) specialized instruction concerning the characteristics of the community, the neighborhood, and the students he is likely to encounter.[5]

It can be argued that few teachers, in this era, remain in a position three years—in at least one school system 75 per cent of the staff is new every year. It can also be argued that the three-year specification is too inflexible; some teachers will require longer, others (most, it is to be hoped) less time. These arguments beg the issue, however. Beginning teachers *do* need the help of older, more experienced teachers; and the "master teachers" deserve released time in which to provide needed help and guidance for beginners. In a few schools a "buddy" system or a "big brother" system has been tried—a senior staff member being assigned to each new teacher. This is certainly a step in the right direction.

The experienced principal knows beginning teachers will have many questions, and he meets with them separately and more frequently than he meets with the total staff. His attitude suggests a willingness to answer questions and to help in the solution of problems which may seem trivial (By what time should the attendance slip be sent to the office? Should the lunch money be totaled?) but are of real concern to one without teaching experience. Frequent classroom visits are very important if the principal is to provide help and assistance when and where it is needed.

---

[4] By *probationary period*, Conant means a period of three years, during which time a beginning teacher would receive the types of help he suggests here from senior staff members.

[5] Conant, *The Education of American Teachers*, p. 212.

Some of the larger school systems employ one or more supervisors whose job it is to visit the classrooms of first-year teachers, help them with organizational problems, the location of learning resources, etc. Wherever supervisors are employed, they almost inevitably find that much of their time is spent with beginning teachers. Unfortunately, principals have a building to administer, and supervisors have so many jobs to do they usually wish they were twins. The beginning teacher, too often, does not receive the consistent, unhurried guidance he needs. Thus, the assignment of an experienced, successful classroom teacher to help each beginner would seem to be one solution to the problem of too many beginners dividing too little administrative and supervisory time.

Beginning teachers profit a great deal when they are freed from teaching responsibilities to visit other classrooms. Perhaps the principal can teach for the beginner or perhaps such visits can be arranged to take place while children are working with a specialist. Many school systems provide a visiting day, and at least one principal has been known to suggest that teachers who wish to use a day for visiting telephone the administrator's office and report that they are ill! Such subterfuge shouldn't be necessary, but this principal obviously believes in the value of teachers visiting classrooms to see other methods and materials.

Portions or sections of pre-school conferences can well be devoted to problems of concern to beginning teachers. Teachers associations (and it is hoped the first-year teacher will join one or more of the professional groups organized to help him) frequently include topics and plan meetings which are of special interest to first-year teachers.

In addition to attending meetings, workshops, clinics, and conferences, planned to meet his special needs and interests, actively participating in the same in-service activities as other members of the staff can help the beginning teacher learn a great deal. A heavy load? Yes. It is to be hoped that the beginner did not expect an easy, relaxed first year! He has much to learn; and many of his learning tasks must be completed quickly, for the benefit of the children for whom he's responsible. The growth which must take place during the first few weeks of teaching can be aided, fostered, and encouraged; and several techniques for doing just this have already been suggested. The major burden must be borne by the beginning teacher, however. No one can accomplish the task of growing, of increasing his competence, for him. Part of the reward of teaching lies in its challenge, and most beginning teachers will tell you that *challenging* is an apt word for describing their first year!

Summary

Student teachers begin student teaching accepting, for the most part, the challenge of a large task. Too often, at the end of student teaching, the task is viewed as completed, when in reality the creation of a teacher has only begun.

In this chapter, some detailed suggestions have been given for helping the student secure his first teaching position, and the role of each of the participants in the student teaching process has been discussed. Letters of recommendation, interviews, and placement papers have been dealt with as they applied to making the transition from student teacher to teacher.

The college or university staff has several opportunities to provide help to the beginning teacher and, in so doing, to gather data by which its own program might be evaluated.

The administrators of a school system also bear much responsibility for aiding a beginning teacher, responsibility which is often shirked because of limitations of staff and time. It was suggested that one possible solution to this problem is the assignment of an experienced teacher whose task it is to help a beginning teacher, to answer questions, and settle problems.

The real task, finally and inevitably, belongs to the teacher. He must show the interest, the concern, the desire, to grow; and he must indicate his willingness to work as hard as is necessary to provide the best possible education for the children for whom he is responsible. Student teaching is behind him, and he now embarks upon the never finished task of becoming a teacher who is creative and sensitive and for whom personal and professional growth is as natural as breathing.

Suggested Activities for the Student Teacher

1. Invite a group of first-year teachers to discuss with your group "What I Wish I'd Asked in My Interview."

2. Review your evaluative material; discuss with your supervisor and cooperating teacher which strengths are most significant for obtaining a position and which weaknesses are most in need of correcting. That is, change the focus of one of your final conferences from determining a grade to qualifications for a specific teaching position or several positions you may be offered.

3. During a student teachers' meeting, act out an interview with a hiring official. Ask for comments and involve as many student teachers as time will permit.

4. Invite a hiring official to address your group of student teachers— he may wish to discuss the criteria he uses in deciding which teachers to hire, behavior of a candidate during an interview, etc.

5. Write a statement detailing "My Ideal Job." Be relatively specific about:

   a) Grade level
   b) Type of community
   c) Size of community
   d) Facilities

After listing the components of an ideal job, reread your paper and underscore those things which are *really* important. This should help you phrase questions which will obtain the information which is really important to you in deciding on a teaching position.

SELECTED REFERENCES

Brembeck, Cole S. *The Discovery of Teaching*. Englewood Cliffs, New Jersey: Prentice-Hall, Inc., 1962.

Burr, James B.; Harding, Lowry W.; and Jacobs, Leland B. *Student Teaching in the Elementary School*. New York: Appleton-Century-Crofts, 1958, Chapter 15, "Looking Beyond Student Teaching."

Byers, Loretta, and Irish, Elizabeth. *Success in Student Teaching*. Boston: D. C. Heath & Company, 1961, Chapter 13, "Preparing for the First Year."

Conant, James B. *The Education of American Teachers*. New York: McGraw-Hill Book Co., Inc., 1963.

Goodlad, John. *The Nongraded Elementary School*. Rev. ed. New York: Harcourt, Brace & World, Inc., 1963.

Michaelis, John U., and Dumas, Enoch. *The Student Teacher in the Elementary School*. Englewood Cliffs, New Jersey: Prentice-Hall, Inc., 1960, Chapter 12, "Your First Position."

National Commission on Teacher Education and Professional Standards. *The Development of the Career Teacher: Professional Responsibility for Continuing Education.* Washington, D. C.: The National Educational Association, 1964.

Shaplin, J. T., and Olds, H. F. *Team Teaching.* New York: Harper & Row, 1964.

Wingo, G. Max, and Schorling, Raleigh. *Elementary School Student Teaching.* 3rd ed. New York: McGraw-Hill Book Co., Inc., 1960, Chapter 16, "Beyond Student Teaching."

SAMPLE
APPLICATION FOR STUDENT TEACHING

STATE UNIVERSITY COLLEGE OF EDUCATION

Miss
Mrs._____   Date_____
Mr.   (Last name)   (First)   (Initial)

Campus Address:_____   Campus Telephone_____
              (Street)   (City)

Home Address:_____   Home Telephone_____

Parents' or Guardians' Name and Address:_____

Prerequisites for Student Teaching

Place an OK beside each prerequisite which you believe you have completed. If you have deficiencies at this time, indicate when and how you plan to remove each one.

_____1.   Senior Standing._____
_____2.   Residence._____
_____3.   Provisional Acceptance for Teaching._____
          (Speech and Hearing Clearance, Health Check, Grade Average
          or Cumulative Index.)

_____4.   Field Experience Prerequisite for Student Teaching._____

Indicate the grade level at which you prefer to teach   _____ 1st choice

                                                         _____2nd choice

                                                         _____3rd choice

A.   Indicate in which of the following geographical areas you prefer to do your student teaching. Show first, second, and third choices by marking 1, 2, 3.

_____University Town (Local)   _____Central City (Urban)
_____Campus Laboratory School   _____Ridgeview (Suburban)
_____Rockmount (Rural-consolidated)

B.   Briefly outline your reasons for your first choice:

C.   I prefer to do my senior year student teaching during the:

1st semester_____   2nd semester_____
              (state year)   (state year)

Please Place an
application
photograph in this
space

                              _____
                              (Last)   (First)   (Middle)   (Date)

                              Present Address_____
                                              (Street) (City) (Telephone)

                              Home Address_____
                                              (Street)   (City)   (State)

Age_____ Birthplace_____

Marital status when student teaching:

single_____ married_____ children's ages_____

I will_____will not_____have an automobile to use while student teaching.

When did you first decide to teach?_____

When did you enroll in a teacher education program?_____

When do you want to do your student teaching?_____

List your hobbies and check the appropriate phrase:

	actively pursue	occasionally pursue	pursued when younger
1.			
2.			
3.			
4.			
5.			

Check skills which will help you in teaching:

play piano_____   operate film projector_____

singing_____   typewrite_____

dramatics_____   run mimeograph_____

rhythms and dance_____   list others: _____

games_____   _____

science club_____   _____

storytelling_____   _____

List places where you have travelled and indicate when you were there:

Military service:

In your opinion, which of your personal characteristics will contribute most to your teaching success?

In your opinion, do you have any traits which may have a negative affect upon your teaching?

Describe any physical disabilities which might affect your teaching.

High School experiences:

    Name and location of high school._____

    Approximate number in graduating class._____

    Extra-curricular activities in high school._____

    _____

High school honors and awards:

College experiences:

    Other colleges attended:

    College degree completed at_____ Date_____

College honors and awards:

Extra-curricular activities:

Work experiences:

type of work   location   date

Community Service activities: Give the nature and extent of your participation and responsibility in church, camp, recreation, youth organizations and other forms of service to others. Indicate those from which you received the most satisfaction and benefit, giving reasons for your choices.

Experiences with children or young people:
nature of experience   age group   location   length of experience   year

Write a brief autobiographical sketch. Describe factors which have influenced you to want to become a teacher. Describe aspects of parental, home, and community influence which may bear upon your teaching success. (Use the back of this page if necessary.)

List courses you have completed in each of the following areas by subject area, number, course title, and credits (e.g.,) Ed. 301—Teaching the Language Arts in the Elementary School—4. Also list courses you plan to complete prior to, or during, student teaching.

Professional Education

Ed. No.   *Course Title*   *Credit*

Second Major (if applicable)

Subject Area   *No.*   *Course Title*   *Credit*

Courses to be completed before, or during, professional semester.

Subject Area   *No.*   *Course Title*   *Credit*

Grade Average or
Cumulative Index_____   Name of your adviser_____

INDEX

THE
STUDENT TEACHING
PROCESS
IN
ELEMENTARY SCHOOLS

The author says:

"Student teaching provides one of the most significant experiences encountered by a student preparing to teach. The quality of the experiences he has and the level of guidance and help he receives will do much to influence the kind of teacher he will become. This book maintains that this important task, or process, involves at least three major participants and that each of these must perform his task honestly, sincerely, and with a high level of competence if we are to prepare the kinds of teachers our elementary schools need so desperately. It is hoped that this text will aid and enhance the work of these three major participants in the student teaching process—the student teacher, the college supervisor, and the cooperating teacher.

THE STUDENT TEACHING PROCESS IN ELEMENTARY SCHOOLS has an important message for each participant in the student teaching process. It generates the kind of understanding that helps bypass pitfalls and makes difficult situations much easier to handle. With each participant in the student teaching process able to see and understand each other's viewpoint, growth and progress are the rich and natural rewards.